Across the South of Asia

Professor Robert L. Brown
Los Angeles County Museum of Art, 2013, Los Angeles, California
(Photograph by Leah Trujillo, Photo © Museum Associates/LACMA)

Across the South of Asia

A Volume in Honor of Professor Robert L. Brown

Edited by
Robert DeCaroli
Paul A. Lavy

Foreword by
Tushara Bindu Gude

DK
PRINTWORLD
Publishers of Indian Traditions

Cataloging in Publication Data — DK
Courtesy: D.K. Agencies (P) Ltd. <docinfo@dkagencies.com>

Across the South of Asia : a volume in honor of Professor Robert L. Brown / edited by Robert DeCaroli, Paul A. Lavy ; foreword by Tushara Bindu Gude.
pages cm
Contributed articles.
Includes bibliographical references and index.
ISBN 9788124610053

1. Buddhist art — South Asia. 2. Buddhist art — Southeast Asia. 3. Hindu art — South Asia. 4. Hindu art — Southeast Asia. 5. Material culture — South Asia. 6. Material culture — Southeast Asia. 7. Art, South Asian. 8. Art, Southeast Asian. I. Brown, Robert L., 1944- honouree. II. DeCaroli, Robert, 1970- editor. III. Lavy, Paul A., 1971- editor.

LCC N7300.A27 2019 | DDC 709.5 23

ISBN: 978-81-246-1005-3
First published in India in 2020

Printed and published by:
D.K. Printworld (P) Ltd.
Regd. Office: Vedaśrī, F-395, Sudarshan Park
(Metro Station: E.S.I. Hospital), New Delhi - 110015
Phones: (011) 2545 3975, 2546 6019
e-mail: indology@dkprintworld.com
Website: www.dkprintworld.com

In loving memory of

Roxanna Brown

and

Julie Romain

Foreword

IT is fortuitous that this volume of essays dedicated to Robert L. Brown — Bob, as he is affectionately known — is being published at a particularly significant moment in his career. As I write the foreword, Bob is completing his final year as a full-time professor in the Department of Art History at the University of California, Los Angeles (UCLA), where he has taught for the last thirty-three years. This year also marks Bob's last year as a curator in the Department of South and Southeast Asian Art at the Los Angeles County Museum of Art (LACMA), where he has held a special appointment, concurrent with his UCLA professorship, since 2001. Few may be aware that Bob's professional career actually began at LACMA, in 1981, shortly after he received his PhD from UCLA. Although Bob worked at LACMA for just a few years before returning to UCLA, in 1986, as a faculty member, the museum has figured prominently throughout his teaching and professional life. Though some may still view the university and the art museum as antipathetic, Bob's erudite scholarship — which has often drawn tremendous insights from a centering of vision upon the object — is instructive of the ways in which these two worlds can successfully be bridged. Bob's embrace of both the gallery and the classroom as spaces for the cultivation of eye and intellect is among the many things that made him a compelling and effective teacher. The wide range of his research interests, his facility with cultural traditions and materials drawn from across broad geographical and temporal boundaries, and the very nature of much of his writing reflect the mind of a consummate scholar-curator.

How Bob arrived at his career as an art historian is a tale that can be told only in its broad sketches; despite his warm personality and generous nature, Bob has always been a private man. He was born in Colorado and raised largely in South Dakota and upstate New York. His family settled in New Mexico, where Bob completed high school and later received his undergraduate degree in English from the University of New Mexico. He joined the US Peace Corps in 1966, serving for two years as an English instructor at the Ubol Teachers College in northeastern Thailand. Thus began Bob's earliest sustained exposure to the country in which an important portion of his work would later be based. This episode in his life also brought him into the broader South Asian ambit; it was on his way home from Thailand that Bob made his first visit to India.

US military forces were still heavily engaged in Vietnam in 1968, and Bob was conscripted into the army as soon as he returned stateside. Fortunately, he was posted to the island of O'ahu, Hawai'i. His primary duties involved running the massive military computers at Schofield Barracks. It was on O'ahu that Bob received his first formal training in art history through a course on Indian art taught by Prithwish Neogy at the University of Hawai'i, Mānoa. Neogy had been one of Stella Kramrisch's students at the University of Calcutta. Bob recalls that Neogy, on the first day of class, expressed strong doubts that a non-Indian could ever truly know Indian art, but the two became good friends. In 1971, with this single course under his belt, Bob decided to enter the doctoral program at UCLA under the tutelage of J. Leroy Davidson.

At that time, Davidson was a figure well-known across various scholarly circles and art fields. Although he was a specialist in Chinese art, during the 1940s, as an assistant director and curator at the Walker Art Center and Visual Arts Specialist for the US State Department, he became something of an expert on contemporary art as well. Davidson's interests came to embrace India and Southeast Asia in the early 1950s. He brought to his work in the region the same attentiveness to object and context that is evident in his work on China, which included his seminal 1954 study on the *Lotus Sūtra* in Chinese art. Bob has reflected:

> I was Davidson's last student and thus had perhaps the advantage of working with him when his art historical ideas were the most synthesized and defined. What he taught was a methodology, by example as much as pronouncement; what he did not teach was dogma.

Bob's ability to find alternative approaches to even seemingly exhausted subject matter — Sārnāth Buddha images, for instance — reflects this inheritance. The rigor of his intellect, the clarity of his writing, the perceptiveness of his questions, and his open mind made him an exemplary role model and teacher to his own students.

Bob entered UCLA just a few years after Davidson had organized the exhibit *Art of the Indian Subcontinent from Los Angeles Collections,* which was held at the campus art gallery in 1968. The exhibition gave expression to the growing west coast interest in South Asian art, and the emergence of southern California as a center of collecting and knowledge. At this same moment, across town, LACMA was negotiating the acquisition of the acclaimed Heeramaneck collection, with which Bob would later work. Davidson passed away in 1980 and Bob subsequently studied under Deborah Klimberg-Salter and Joanna Williams, completing his dissertation under the latter. Bob had come to know Williams during the periods he spent at UC Berkeley taking Thai language courses. He also traveled for several months in India with Williams as she was researching her book *The Art of Gupta India: Empire and Province* (1982).

It is perhaps not surprising then, given this background, that Bob's interests would frequently turn to Gupta art, and also to the nature of the relationships between India and Southeast Asia, where adoption of Indian artistic styles is attested in the visual record from about the sixth century. Bob's dissertation on the monumental stone *dharmacakra*s of Dvāravatī culture also grappled with issues of visual and iconographic sources for formative Southeast Asian sculptural traditions (*The Dvāravatī Dharmacakras: A Study in the Transfer of Form and Meaning*, UCLA, 1981). Opportunities to further delve into these subjects presented themselves during Bob's post-graduate employment at LACMA, when he worked on the landmark 1984 exhibition *Light of Asia: Buddha Sakyamuni in Asian Art*. Bob's essay for the exhibition catalog, along with his object entries, covered a broad geographic area, and in them one finds mention of subjects he would later take up in his academic research — distinct iconographies, such as the walking Buddha image, for instance, or the stylistic innovations of and internal consistencies between Southeast Asian Buddhist imagery. Bob's innovative and insightful scholarship on these subjects arose from his perceptive discernment of the complex cultural and ritual operations — often inextricable from one another — that shaped Indian and Southeast Asian visual forms.

The bibliography that follows will indicate, perhaps better than a descriptive essay, the tremendous breadth of Bob's scholarship, which has addressed the visual traditions of first century BCE Central Asia to twentieth-century colonial historiography. Much of his work has focused on the Buddhist and Hindu artistic traditions that flourished during key historical periods in what are now present-day Pakistan, India, Myanmar, Thailand, Cambodia, and Indonesia. His particular concern with the nature of artistic influence has contributed greatly to present understandings of artistic and cultural adaptation and exchange across these areas. His various essays present important perspectives on pilgrimage, narrative, sacred space, ritual, divinity, relics, miracles, and aesthetics, among other topics. While he has always remained object-focused, Bob also engages with relevant theoretical perspectives; some of his important recent essays, addressing the gendered body and materiality, for instance, are models for others working with pre-modern traditions.

In the last several years we have seen the retirement of several esteemed senior scholars, many of whom — like Bob — belong to a generation that shaped the field of South and Southeast Asian art history. We can expect much from the various students they have trained. That is certain. It is not without some sadness, however, that we note the quiet withdrawals of such giants from our professional environments. I speak on behalf of all Bob's former students when I acknowledge the tremendous impact he has had on our lives, not only through his scholarly guidance, but also through the precious gifts of his time, patience, humor, and kindness.

Los Angeles, June 2019 **Tushara Bindu Gude**

Preface

All too often, modern scholarship limits its scope according to the boundaries of contemporary nations and current geopolitical borders. Academic expertise frequently ties itself artificially to these pre-defined spaces and in so doing often does a disservice to the past. It is no great revelation to point out that people of the past defined the limits of their political and cultural reach in ways that are very different from those found on modern maps. Ancient rulers, merchants, and priests understood the reach of their influence and defined foreignness in ways that would be deeply unfamiliar to those only knowledgeable of the modern world. Yet, despite the well-recognized truth in these observations, it is still relatively rare for scholars to research in ways that transcend modern boundaries.

This collection of essays invites readers to take a broad view of Southern Asian art and culture by providing both a wide geographic and chronological scope. The articles are united only by their focus on art historical and archaeological concerns and their concentration on Southern Asia, reaching from the borders of ancient Persia to the island kingdoms of Indonesia. Each essay on its own constitutes a solid, well-grounded academic study, but taken collectively they provide a wide and inclusive view of issues of art and material culture that span the region and invite comparison.

With this ambitious scope in mind, contributors to the volume were free to explore topics that impacted any aspect of the region. Naturally many opted to concentrate on a single issue or regional topic but others decided to take on topics that explicitly examined trans-regional or transnational ideas. Even those essays which seem more narrowly focused hold implications for wider issues that impact the ways we understand far-reaching processes and innovations.

By taking this approach, this volume is a tribute to Prof. Robert L. Brown whose lifetime of teaching has always emphasized connections as well as differences. His own scholarly publications reach from Afghanistan to Indonesia, with special emphasis on the early history of India and the Dvāravatī tradition of Thailand. Over his professional career, he has trained a large cohort of students (many of whom are contributors to this volume) whose expertise truly does reach across the south of Asia.

This publication was made possible, in part, through funding provided by the Los Angeles County Museum of Art's Southern Asian Art Council. We wish also to thank Kay Talwar and Helene Cooper — both former chairpersons of the council — for their generous support.

Contents

Part I
South Asia before 1400 CE

Part II
South Asia after 1400 CE

Part III
Southeast Asia

Works of Prof. Robert L. Brown

Books

1996, *The Dvāravatī Wheels of the Law and the Indianization of South East Asia*, Leiden: E.J. Brill.

2014, *Carrying Buddhism: The Role of Metal Icons in the Spread and Development of Buddhism*, Amsterdam: J Gonda Fund Foundation of the KNAW.

Edited Books

1991, *Ganesh: Studies of an Asian God*, Albany: SUNY Press; Delhi: Sri Satguru Publications.

1997, *Living a Life in Accord with Dhamma: Papers in Honor of Professor Jean Boisselier*, Bangkok: Silpakorn University (with Natasha Eilenberg and M.C. Subhadradis Diskul).

1999, *Art from Thailand*, Bombay: Marg.

2002, *The Roots of Tantra*, Albany: SUNY Press (with Katherine Anne Harper).

2005, *Encyclopedia of India*, 4 vols., Farmington Hills, MI: Thomson Gale (with Stanley Wolpert as editor-in-chief).

Translated Book

2008, *Studies on the Art of Ancient Cambodia: Ten Articles by Jean Boisselier*, Phnom Penh: Reyum, 2008 (tr. and ed. with Natasha Eilenberg).

Exhibition Catalogs

1984, *Light of Asia: Buddha Sakyamuni in Asian Art*, Los Angeles: Los Angeles County Museum of Art, 1984 (with Pratapaditya Pal et al.). (Essay on Southeast Asian art and all Southeast Asian Catalog entries.)

2014, "Dvāravatī Sculpture," in *Lost Kingdoms: Hindu-Buddhist Sculpture of*

Early Southeast Asia 5th-8th Century, ed. John Guy, New York: Metropolitan Museum of Art, pp. 189-91.

2015, "The Buddha's Smile: Art of the First Millennium," in *Buddhist Art of Myanmar*, ed. Sylvia Fraser-Lu and Donald M. Stadtner, pp. 45-54, New Haven: Yale University Press.

2019, *The Jeweled Isle: Art from Sri Lanka*, Los Angeles: LACMA (with Bindu Gude, Donald Stadtner, Lakshika Gamage).

Online Scholarly Catalog

Catalog of the Southeast Asian Collection at LACMA, launched November 2013 (seasian.catalog.lacma.org)

Research Articles

1978, "The Four Stone Façades of Monastery I at Ratnagiri," *Artibus Asiae*, 40(1): 5-28.

1978, "Stone Buddha Images on Stelae from Ratnagiri," *Journal of Asian Culture*, 2: 103-13.

1984, "Indra's Heaven: A Dharmacakrastambha Socle in the Bangkok National Museum," *Ars Orientalis*, 14: 115-30.

1984, "The Śrāvastī Miracles in the Art of India and Dvāravatī," *Archives of Asian Art*, 37: 79-95.

1984, "Light of Asia: Buddha Sakyamuni in Asian Art," *Arts of Asia*, 14(1): 69-80.

1985, "The Art of Southeast Asia: Collection of the Los Angeles County Museum of Art," *Arts of Asia*, 15(6): 114-25.

1986, "Recent Stupa Literature: A Review Article," *Journal of Asian History*, 20(2): 215-32.

1987, "Note on the Recently Discovered Gaṇeśa Image from Palembang, Sumatra," *Indonesia*, 43: 95-100.

1987, "Female Imagery in Ancient Khmer Sculpture," in *Apsara: The Feminine in Khmer Art*, ed. Amy Catlin, pp. 7-10, Los Angeles: The Women's Building.

1987, "John D. Rockefeller 3rd," in *American Collectors of Asian Art*, ed. P. Pal, pp. 53-72, Bombay: Marg.

1988, "Bodhgaya and Southeast Asia," in *Bodhgaya: The Site of Enlightenment*, ed. Janice Leoshko, pp. 101-24, Bombay: Marg.

1989, "The Pong Tuk Lamp: A Reconsideration," *Journal of the Siam Society*, 77(2): 9-20 (with Anna M. Macdonnell).

1990, "God on Earth: The Walking Buddha in the Art of South and Southeast Asia," *Artibus Asiae*, 50(1-2): 73-107.

1990, "A Lajja Gauri in a Buddhist Context at Aurangabad," *The Journal of the International Association of Buddhist Studies*, 13(2): 1-16.

1991, "Gaṇeśa in Southeast Asian Art: Indian Connections and Indigenous Developments," in *Ganesh: Studies of an Asian God*, ed. Robert L. Brown, pp. 171-234, Albany: SUNY Press.

1992, "Indian Art Transformed: The Earliest Sculptural Styles of Southeast Asia," in *Panels of the VIIth World Sanskrit Conference*, pp. 40-53, Leiden: Brill.

1994, "Rules for Change in the Transfer of Indian Art to Southeast Asia," in *Ancient Indonesian Sculpture*, ed. Marijke J. Klokke and Pauline Lunsingh Scheurleer, pp. 10-32, Leiden: KITLV Press.

1995, "Images of Ganesha from Southeast Asia," in *Ganesh: The Benevolent*, ed. Pratapaditya Pal, pp. 95-114, Bombay: Marg.

1995, "Three Southeast Asian Sculptures in the Pacific Asia Museum Collection," in *Studies and Reflections on Asian Art History and Archaeology: Essays in Honour of H.S.H. Professor Subhadradis Diskul*, pp. 335-42, Bangkok: Silpakorn University.

1997, "The Emaciated Gandharan Buddha Images: Asceticism, Health, and the Body," in *Living a Life in Accord with Dhamma: Papers in Honor of Professor Jean Boisselier*, ed. Natasha Eilenberg, Subhadradis Diskul, and Robert L. Brown, pp. 105-15, Bangkok: Silpakorn University.

1997, "Narrative as Icon: The Jātaka Stories in Ancient Indian and Southeast Asian Architecture," in *Sacred Biography in the Buddhist Traditions of South and Southeast Asia*, ed. Juliane Schober, pp. 64-109, Honolulu: University of Hawaiʻi Press.

1998, "Expected Miracles: The Unsurprisingly Miraculous Nature of Images and Relics," in *Images, Miracles, and Authority in Asian Religious Traditions*, ed. Richard Davis, pp. 23-35, Boulder: Westview Press.

1998, "The Miraculous Buddha Images: Portrait, God, or Object?," in *Images, Miracles, and Authority in Asian Religious Traditions*, ed. Richard Davis, pp. 37-54, Boulder: Westview Press.

1998, "Dvaravati Sculpture of Thailand," *TAASA Review: The Journal of the Asian Arts Society of Australia*, 7(4): 9-11.

1999, "Some Remarkable Cham Sculptures in American Museums," *Lettre de la Société des Amis du Champa Ancien*, 6: 3-11 (with Natasha Eilenberg).

2000, "The Walking Tilya Tepe Buddha: A Lost Prototype," *Bulletin of the Asia Institute*, 14: 77-87.

2001, "Pyu Art: Looking East and West," *Orientations*, 32(4): 35-41.

2002, "The Feminization of the Sarnath Gupta-Period Buddha Images," *Bulletin of the Asia Institute*, N.S. 16: 165-79.

2003, "Place in the Sacred Biography at Borobudur," in *Pilgrims, Patrons, and Place: Localizing Sanctity in Asian Religions*, ed. Phyllis Granoff and Koichi Shinohara, pp. 249-63, Vancouver: UBC Press.

2003, "A Magic Pill: The Protection of Cambodia by the Recitation of the Vīṇāśīkhatantra in AD 802," *Udaya: Journal of Khmer Studies*, 4: 1-6.

2004, "Ritual and Image at Angkor Wat," in *Images in Asian Religions: Text and Contexts*, ed. Phyllis Granoff and Koichi Shinohara, pp. 346-66, Vancouver: UCB Press.

2005, "Vākāṭaka-Period Hindu Sculpture," in *The Vākāṭaka Heritage*, ed. H.T. Bakker, pp. 59-65, Groningen: Egbert Forsten.

2006, "Vijayanagara: The End or the Beginning?," in *Sangama: A Confluence of Art and Culture During the Vijayanagara Period*, ed. Nalini Rao, pp. 1-6, Delhi: Originals.

2006, "The Nature and Use of the Body Relics of the Buddha in Gandhara," in *Gandharan Buddhism: Archaeology, Art, Texts*, ed. Pia Brancaccio and Kurt Behrendt, pp. 183-209, Vancouver: UBC Press.

2008, "The Act of Naming Avalokiteśvara in Ancient Southeast Asia," in *Interpreting Southeast Asia's Past*, ed. Elisabeth Bacus, et al., pp. 263-72, Singapore: National University of Singapore.

2008, "Selections from the Southeast Asian Art Collection of the Los Angeles County Museum of Art," *Arts of Asia*, 38(3): 75-87.

2009, "Nature as Utopian Space in the Early Stupas of India," in *Buddhist Stupas in South-Asia*, ed. Akira Shimada and Jason Hawkes, pp. 63-80, New Delhi: Oxford University Press.

2010, "A Khmer Sculpture of Rahu in the Los Angeles County Museum of Art," in *Abhinandanamālā: Nandana Chutiwongs Felicitation Volume*, ed. Leelananda Prematilleke, pp. 331-35, Bangkok: SPAFA Regional Centre of Archaeology and Fine Arts.

2011, "The Importance of Gupta-period Sculpture in Southeast Asian Art History," in *Early Interactions between South and Southeast Asia: Reflections on Cross-Cultural Exchange*, ed. Pierre-Yves Manguin, A. Mani, and Geoff Wade, pp. 317-31, Singapore: Institute of Southeast Asian Studies.

2011, "A Khmer Viṣṇu Image in the Los Angeles County Museum of Art," in *From Beyond the Eastern Horizon: Essays in Honour of Professor Lokesh Chandra*, ed. Manju Shree, pp. 183-90, New Delhi: Aditya Prakashan.

2011, "A Sky-Lecture by the Buddha," *Bulletin of the Indo-Pacific Prehistory Association*, 31: 17-24.

2011, "An Aesthetic Encounter: Khmer Art from Thailand, Cambodia, and Vietnam," *Orientations*, 42(3): 50-56.

2013, "Telling the Story in Art of the Monkey's Gift of Honey to the Buddha," *Bulletin of the Asia Institute*, 23: 41-50.

2013, "Three Wood Buddha Sculptures from Myanmar (Burma) in the Los Angeles County Museum of Art," *Artibus Asiae*, 73(1): 219-29.

2017, "The Trouble with Convergence," in *India and Southeast Asia: Cultural Discourse*, ed., A.L. Dallapiccola and A. Verghese, pp. 37-50, Mumbai: The K.R. Cama Oriental Institute.

Forthcoming, "Gupta Art as Classical: A Possible Paradigm for Indian Art History," in *Indology's Pulse: Arts in Context; Essays Presented to Doris Meth Srinivasan in Admiration of Her Scholarly Research*, ed. Gerd Mevissen and Corinna Wessels-Mevissen, Delhi: Aryan Books International.

List of Figures

bronze inlaid with copper, silver, Los Angeles County Museum of Art, M.84.32.1a-d

3.3. Standing Crowned and Jewelled Buddha (perhaps the Buddha Amoghasiddhi), Kurkihār, Bihar, India, Pāla period, *circa* early eleventh century CE, bronze with silver and copper inlay, Metropolitan Museum of Art, New York, 1987.142.319

3.4. Vairocana Buddha in *bodhiyaṅgī-mudrā*, Nālandā, Bihar, India, Pāla period, *circa* eleventh century CE, gilt bronze, National Museum, New Delhi (Photograph by John C. Huntington, Courtesy of the John C. and Susan L. Huntington Photographic Archive of Buddhist and Asian Art, scan no. 27304)

4.1. The Buddha reaching enlightenment at Bodh-Gayā surrounded by the additional seven Great Pilgrimage sites associated with the life of Śākyamuni, *circa* tenth-eleventh centuries CE, stone, H. approx. 3.7 m. Currently in a temple outside of the village of Jagdishpur, two miles south of Nālandā (Photograph by Kurt Behrendt)

5.1. *Mahākapi Jātaka*, Vedikā roundel, Bharhut Mahāstūpa, Bharhut, Madhya Pradesh, India, Śuṅga period, 100-80 BCE, sandstone, Indian Museum, Kolkata (Photograph courtesy of Michael Gunther, Wikimedia Commons, licensed under the Creative Commons Attribution-Share Alike 4.0 International, accessed on 23 August 2018 from https://commons.wikimedia.org/wiki/File:Mahakapi_Jataka_in_Bharhut.jpg)

5.2. Durgā battling Mahiṣāsura, north wall, Mahiṣāsuramardinī Cave Temple, Māmallapuram (Mahābalipuram), Tamil Nadu, India, Pallava period, *circa* seventh century CE, granite (*in situ*) (Photograph courtesy of Richard Mortel, Wikimedia Commons, licensed under the Creative Commons Attribution 2.0 Generic, accessed on 23 August 2018 from https://commons.wikimedia.org/wiki/File:Mahishasuramardini_Mandapam,_Pallave_period,_7th_century,_Mahabalipuram_(34)_(37426040256).jpg)

8.3. Kṛṣṇa's Ball, India, Gujarat, Kachchh (Kutch), Māṇḍvī, *c.*1875–1900, *repoussé* gold, height: 2⅛ in. (5.4 cm); diameter: 2 in. (5.08 cm), Los Angeles County Museum of Art, South and Southeast Asian Acquisition Fund, M.2002.37a-b

8.4. Portal with Tympanum (detail), India, Gujarat, Kachchh (Kutch), dated 1871, wood with copper and iron fittings, 68 × 30⅛ × 7 in. (172.72 × 76.52 × 17.78 cm), Los Angeles County Museum of Art, Gift of Mr. and Mrs. Freeman Gates, M.72.51.1a

8.5. Ceremonial Cloth and Heirloom Textile with Row of Female Musicians, India, Gujarat; traded to Sulawesi, eastern Indonesia, seventeenth century, mordant and wax resist (*batik*) block printing and painting on plain-weave cotton, 42 × 200 in. (106.68 × 508 cm), Los Angeles County Museum of Art, Costume Council Fund, M.2005.10

9.1. "Fort, Ram-nagar," from *Views of Benares Presented by the Maharaja of Benares, circa 1883–1907*; Albumen print, 21.5 × 29 cm, Los Angeles County Museum of Art, Gift of Gloria Katz and Willard Huyck, M.2012.149.1 (Photo 1)

9.2. "Golden Temple and Aurangzeb's Mosque," from *Views of Benares Presented by the Maharaja of Benares, circa 1883–1907*; Albumen print, 21.5 × 29 cm, Los Angeles County Museum of Art, Gift of Gloria Katz and Willard Huyck, M.2012.149.1 (Photo 28)

9.3. "Bhadaini Water-works" and "Rani Sursar Ghat," from *Views of Benares Presented by the Maharaja of Benares, circa 1905-1907*; Albumen print, 21.5 × 29 cm, Los Angeles County Museum of Art, Gift of Gloria Katz and Willard Huyck, M.2012.149.1 (Photo 3)

9.4. "Rana-mahal Ghat," from *Views of Benares Presented by the Maharaja of Benares, circa 1883–1907*; Albumen print, 21.5 × 29 cm, Los Angeles County Museum of Art, Gift of Gloria Katz and Willard Huyck, M.2012.149.1 (Photo 9)

11.5. Viṣṇu, first observed in Ayutthaya, Thailand, but believed to have come from Wiang Sa district, Surat Thani Province, Thailand, *circa* late sixth–early seventh century CE, stone, H. 1.31 m, Bangkok National Museum, inv. no. KKH 13 (Photograph by Paul Lavy)

11.6. Mahendrapottrāḍhirājan and queens, south wall, Ādivarāha Cave Temple, Māmallapuram (Mahābalipuram), Tamil Nadu, India, Pallava period, seventh century CE, granite (*in situ*) (Photograph courtesy of the American Institute of Indian Studies, accession no. 21519, negative number A21.70)

11.7. Viṣṇu, found at Wat Tho, Ratchaburi Province, Thailand, *circa* seventh century CE, stone, H. 1.52 m, Bangkok National Museum, inv. no. KKH 7 (Photograph by Paul Lavy)

11.8. Gajalakṣmī with attendants, east wall, Ādivarāha Cave Temple, Māmallapuram (Mahābalipuram), Tamil Nadu, India, Pallava period, seventh century CE, granite (*in situ*) (Photograph courtesy of the American Institute of Indian Studies, accession no. 21514, negative number A21.74)

11.9. Goddess, Si Thep, Phetchabun Province, Thailand, *circa* seventh-eighth century CE, greenish ferruginous sandstone, H. 1.35 cm, Linden-Museum Stuttgart, acc. no. SA 34 180L (Photograph by Donald Stadtner)

12.1. View of Arjuna Group, Dieng Plateau (Photograph by Bokyung Kim, 2002)

12.2. Śiva riding Nandī, *circa* eighth century, volcanic stone, Kailasa Museum, Dieng Plateau (Photograph by Bokyung Kim, 2011)

12.3. Viṣṇu riding Garuḍa, *circa* eighth century, volcanic stone, Kailasa Museum, Dieng Plateau (Photograph by Bokyung Kim, 2011)

12.4. Brahmā riding a Haṁsa, *circa* eighth century, volcanic stone, Kailasa Museum, Dieng Plateau (Photograph by Bokyung Kim, 2011)

Part I
South Asia before 1400 CE

1

Heat and Hunger

The Emaciated Buddha and the Significance of Fasting

Robert DeCaroli

As described in both Yoga manuals and in the late Vedic literary tradition, *tapas* (heat) is the byproduct of intense physical and mental austerities.[1] This concept refers to both a reserve of potent, purifying spiritual energy and to literal heat that is often, but not exclusively, produced through intense ascetic practices, self-discipline, and self-mortification. One of the most frequently encountered techniques for producing *tapas*, and the purification it engenders, involves undertaking periods of fasting. In the *Ṛgveda* (I.105.8) the concepts of heat and hunger are already associated and in the *Śatapatha Brāhmaṇa* (9.5.1.2-4, 4.5.1.6-9, 3.1.2.1) it is stated quite directly that "the whole practice of *tapas*, it is when one abstains from food" (Kaelber 1976: 359).

Such descriptions call to mind a well-known, albeit rare, form of the Buddha (or future-Buddha) in which he appears emaciated.[2]

---

1 As in the *Kaṭha Upaniṣad* (*circa* the third century BCE) and the *Yogasūtra* (*circa* the second century CE).

2 It is likely that not all emaciated images of Śākyamuni were intended to depict the same moment in his life. Some examples appear to portray events prior to his attainment of Buddhahood. It is, therefore, inappropriate to refer to all these images as Buddhas. See for example the eighth-century Kashmiri ivory in the Cleveland Museum of Art (Leonard C. Hanna Jr. Fund 1986: 70) that almost certainly depicts events prior to the enlightenment (*fig.* 1.2).

The earliest known examples of this subject were created in the ancient region of Gandhāra, which now encompasses parts of northern Pakistan and eastern Afghanistan, and include images like the famous examples from Takht-i-Bahi (*fig.* 1.1) and Sikri (Spooner 1911: 140).[3] It is primarily this earliest corpus of examples, dating from the first to the fourth centuries CE, that concerns us here.

References to the importance of fasting and its connection to the production of *tapas* can shed light on the significance that emaciated images of Śākyamuni held for audiences in the early centuries of the Common Era. Textual sources that pre-date the sculptural images describe individuals who undertook extended periods of fasting as becoming purified through their ordeal, which was understood as burning off mortal imperfections. Visual representations of Śākyamuni demonstrating this form of exceptional self-discipline might, therefore, be read as intentionally associating the *tathāgata* with these very specific states of elevated purity. Before considering why some members of the early Buddhist community chose to represent Śākyamuni in such a state of privation, it is helpful to recall that Buddhism was still establishing itself during these centuries, and these fasting images were produced alongside some of the earliest Buddhist images in the region. In other words, they were created before any expectations of traditional or canonical Buddhist artistic forms had been firmly established.

As recorded in the *Nidānakathā* (183-205), *Lalitavistara* (372-97, 442–591), *Buddhacarita* (182-87) and other narrative texts which relate portions of the Buddha's biography, there are two possible moments of fasting with which we might associate these images. Most scholars have followed Alfred Foucher in connecting the emaciated Buddha statues to a six-year period of fasting that took place prior to Siddhārtha's achievement of Buddhahood (Foucher 1905: 381-83). This event occurred when, after abandoning his

[3] The Takht-i-Bahi image is sometimes identified as being from Sahri-Bahlol.

decadent existence at court, Prince Siddhārtha adopted the life of an ascetic and undertook a period of intense self-mortification alongside a group of like-minded hermits. During this time, he surpassed them all in his rigor and self-discipline, taking the traditional practices to self-punishing extremes. For example, the *Buddhacarita* describes him as having, "wasted away, so that only skin and bone remained, with fat, flesh, and blood all gone" (Johnston 1995 [1936]: 183). The *Mahāsaccaka Sutta* of the *Majjhima Nikāya* is more visceral in its descriptions, stating that:

> The bones of my spine when bent and straightened were like a row of spindles through the little food. As the beams of an old shed stick out, so did my ribs stick out through the little food.
>
> — Horner 1954: 300

Given these descriptions, it is understandable why so many scholars have linked this period of Śākyamuni's life to the emaciated images, however, more recent scholarship has suggested a second possibility that takes place shortly after he ends this first period of fasting (Brown 1997: 105-15).

After enduring six years of privation, Śākyamuni ultimately concludes that this path of intense self-punishment is not conducive to his goals and resolves to break his fast. He does so by accepting a meal of milk-rice offered by a woman, who is named Sujātā in many of the textual sources (Bays 1983: 2.399-408; Johnston 1995: 185; Rhys Davids 1937: 186).[4] Immediately after doing so, Śākyamuni heads to Bodh-Gayā where he ultimately achieves enlightenment and attains Buddhahood. What follows is a second period of fasting that lasts forty-nine days. Over this period, a number of miraculous events occur as the Buddha reflects on his recent enlightenment, but, throughout these extraordinary circumstances, the meal fed to him by Sujātā remains his only food.

Robert L. Brown has argued that it is this second period of fasting, after Śākyamuni's attainment of Buddhahood, which is

---

[4] In the *Buddhacarita* her name is Nandabālā.

being represented in the early images (Brown 1997: 110-11). Brown uses the Takht-i-Bahi image to support this attribution by noting the secondary decoration on the pedestal depicts events that directly precede the moment the Buddha broke this second fast (*fig.* 1.1). Specifically, two wealthy merchants, Trapuṣa and Bhallika, pass near to the Buddha's location when a local goddess traps the wheels of their carts. When they investigate the cause of their hindrance, the well-meaning deity tells them that the Buddha is nearby and encourages them to offer him donations. Excited by this news, they immediately set out to present him with gifts of food, thereby becoming the first lay donors (Bays 1983: 2.581-89). The pedestal of the Takht-i-Bahi image faithfully depicts the trapped cart and the offering of food, which, Brown concludes, makes this narrative the more likely interpretation for the main image as well (Brown 1997: 110-11).[5]

Noting the contrast between the plump form of the Buddha on the base and the skeletal main Takht-i-Bahi figure, Anna Maria Quagliotti offers a third interpretation of this sculpture (2008: 68-69). She argues that the Buddha's *abhaya-mudrā* and the gifts in the hands of the merchants situate this scene at the moment the merchants first meet the Buddha and, therefore, before his meal. From this observation, she concludes the image represents two distinct narrative moments. The main image, she argues, depicts the Śākyamuni at the end of his six-year fast; whereas, the base shows events after the Buddha's enlightenment (ibid.: 65-68).

Complicating matters further, in the *Nidānakathā* version of the Buddha's life, the author asserts that the Buddha lost his *lakṣaṇa* (the physical marks) that identified him as a great man, during his six-year fast and that they only returned after he ate Sujātā's

[5] Brown raises some questions about an example in the British Museum which shows Vajrapāṇi, two male donors and a female donor that Foucher has identified as Sujātā. I wonder if this female figure is not the local goddess who alerted the merchants to the Buddha's presence. In some versions, she is identified as the merchants' reincarnated mother.

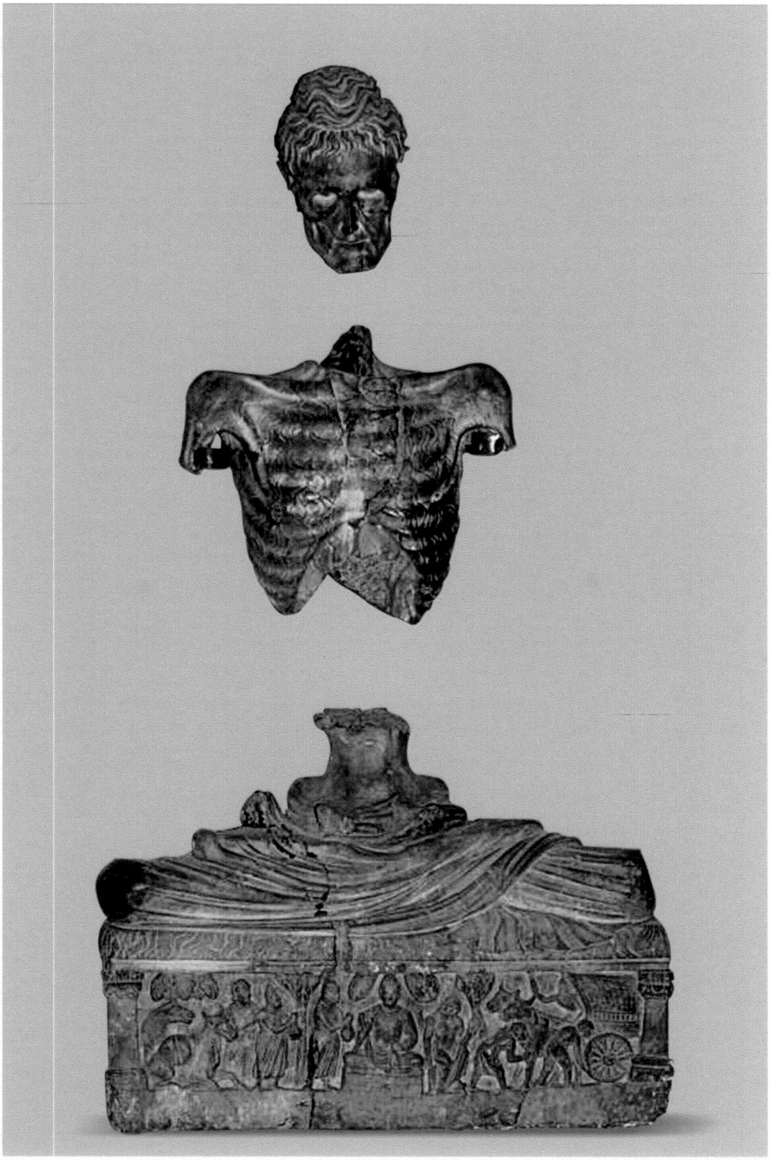

fig. 1.1: Emaciated Buddha, Takht-i-Bahi, Pakistan, fourth-sixth century CE, stone

fig. 1.2: Fasting Buddha, Kashmir, India, eighth century CE, ivory

fig. 1.3: Seated Śākyamuni, Ahicchattra (Mathurā Region), India, second century CE, red sandstone

meal. Therefore, the presence of distinguishing features, like the *ūrṇā* (the mark between the eyes), halo, and *uṣṇīśa* (the cranial protuberance), would seem to corroborate that it is the forty-nine-day fast being presented in these images and not the longer fast that preceded Sujātā's offering. Yet, some caution is called for because the *Nidānakathā* postdates the images from Gandhāra and it is not clear how widely this version of events was accepted. For example, later examples which do depict Sujātā's offering of food, still clearly represent Śākyamuni's *lakṣaṇa* (Rhys Davids 1937: 183) (*fig*. 1.2).

The limited number of examples and the inconsistency of the details make it difficult to identify emaciated images with a single event from Śākyamuni's life. Such narrative complications make it prudent to interpret each image separately and make it plausible that at least two different events might be represented by such images. By setting aside the question of narrative, however, perhaps we can approach these images in a different way. It is worth asking what significance fasting held and why some Buddhists living in the first few centuries CE elected to depict Śākyamuni in this seemingly weakened state.

Understanding the significance of this sort of self-discipline requires asking what practitioners traditionally hoped to achieve by undertaking such hardships. As stated previously, the production of *tapas* was an immediate consequence of these austerities, but if the early literature is any indication, rarely was this an end in itself. Rather, the goal seems to have frequently been purification through the removal of both spiritual and physical imperfections.

The earliest literary references to *tapas* appear in the *Ṛgveda,* in which the gods are beseeched to provide fiery heat capable of driving off evil spirits (*rākṣasas*). By the time of the *Atharvaveda,* however, *tapas* is generated by the ritual expert himself and is used to expel unwanted and unclean external influences (Kaelber 1979: 193-96). The authors of the Brāhmaṇas subsequently elaborated this process and developed the notion of *tapas* as a ritually generated means of purification. In this literature, the details of a consecration process known as *dīkṣā* are explained and its success was, in part, contingent on generating *tapas* through fasting. This undertaking requires that the sacrificer readies himself for his role in officiating a ritual by undergoing an elaborate set of preparations aimed at purifying his body, his ritual implements, and his environs (Kaelber 1979: 200-05). In this system, the ritual purity of the sacrifice is assured by the consuming heat of actual fire which burns off or drives away that which is not pure. This association between heat and purity also provides the logic that underpins the concept of self-purification through fasting. In this case, it is the "heat" generated through fasting that consumes the body and leaves behind only that which has been purified by the ordeal (Kaelber 1976: 358-59). The fires of hunger, stoked by steadfast mental effort, provide the crucible that purify and transform the practitioner. Typically, these fasts, as described in the Brāhmaṇas and later sources, lasted for a set amount of time, ranging from a few days to a month, during which time only specially prepared milk was drunk. The conditions of specific fasts varied from case to case. For example, in one version of the month-long fast the amount of nourishment consumed is contingent on the phases of the moon (Kaelber 1979: 209-10).

An association between flame and asceticism is narrativized dramatically in the third book of the *Mahābhārata* (207-10). In this tale, the god of fire (Agni) grows vexed at the radiance produced by the austerities of Sage Aṅgīras. When Agni withdraws from the world, Aṅgīras is able to heat and light creation in his absence. Ultimately, Agni is compelled to admit that the sage's splendor is the premier fire in the world, which acknowledges the potency of the internalized sacrificial fire that Aṅgīras generated by his austerities (Buitenen 1975: 640).

No matter the specific conditions, however, the textual tradition invariably draws a parallel between the consuming heat of fire and the consuming heat of the body's hunger, both of which were believed to only leave behind that which had been purified and freed of pollution. In the case of the practitioners themselves, this pollution was associated with their own mortality. The *Śatapatha Brāhmaṇa* asserts that this process of burning off human impurities is of vital importance because "what is human is inauspicious to the sacrifice" (Eggeling 1988: 1.4.1.35, 1.7.2.9, 1.8, 1.29; Kaelber 1979: 201). The success of the ritual is, therefore, contingent on the practitioner attaining a state free of those mortal qualities that might hinder interaction with the divine. The *Śatapatha Brāhmaṇa* goes on to clarify this requirement by stating that, "He who is consecrated . . . becomes one of the deities" (Eggeling 1988: 3.1.1.8-9; Kaelber 1979: 201-02). In short, the successful completion of this process allows the practitioner to achieve something akin to a divine state. The nature of this apotheosis is hinted at by another passage in this text. It stipulates:

> After the completion (of the sacrifice) he divests himself (of the vow), with the text 'Now I am he who I really am.' For, in entering upon the vow, he becomes, as it were, nonhuman; and as it would not be becoming for him to say, 'I enter from truth into untruth;' and as, in fact, he now again becomes man, let him therefore divest himself (of the vow), with the text: 'Now I am he who I really am.'
>
> – Eggeling 1988: 1.1.1.6; Kaelber 1979: 201-02

The passage describes a moment at the end of the ritual when the practitioner is releasing the elevated state he had attained and is once again returning to his status as a mere human. The phrasing makes it clear that for the duration of the vow, while the practitioner is fasting, he had become a "non-human" (*amānuṣa*). This claim might be confusing, but a look at other sources reveals the term's meaning in this context. Frequent references to "non-humans" appear in litanies of demigods wherein the word is used as a broad and inclusive designation for divinities and spirits (Bhat 1998: 395; Misra 1979: 2 n. 3; Rhys Davids, Foley and Woodward 1917-1930: 271). The word is not easily translated but refers to a class of divine beings that are above humans and, therefore, has connotations suggesting the supernatural and superhuman. For the writers of *Śatapatha Brāhmaṇa*, it would seem that purification in the hunger-stoked fires of *tapas* elevated the practitioner into a state that transcended his humanity and made him akin to the gods with whom he was expected to interact in the performance of his ritual duties.

A variation on this sentiment is suggested by passages found in Patañjali's *Yogasūtra* which state that from austerity rises the destruction of impurity and the perfection of the body and senses. The text goes on to clarify that when coupled with self-study, austerities provide unity "with the desired deity" (*iṣṭa devatā*) (Chapple and Viraj 1990: ii, 43-44). The implication is that the practitioner is preparing himself by removing those things which make him unworthy of self-identification with the divine focus of his devotions. Certainly, there are differences between the *Yogasūtra* and Brāhmaṇas, and they are significant, but in both cases, fasting and the production of *tapas* are identified as conducive to cultivating one's divine nature and as being effective in removing the impediment of impurity.

If the prevalence of these sentiments, which link fasting to divinity, is any indication of widespread views at the time, it is worth reassessing the significance of Śākyamuni's emaciated state in early Gandhāran sculpture. In discussing a second or third century emaciated Śākyamuni image from Lahore, Giovanni Verardi suggests a link between the *tapas*-generating practices of Śākyamuni and what he believes to be a ceremony involving a fire altar depicted on the base of the image (1994: 38-39). While there are reasons to question some of his conclusions, Verardi is one of the few authors to move past the novelty of Śākyamuni's skeletal appearance and recognize the significance of his self-mortifying actions.[6] The sculptural works

[6] What Verardi identifies as a fire altar may be a censer. He relies primarily on the sixth century (or later) *Vairocanābhisambodhi Tantra* to explain the ritual being performed by monks on the image's base. Anna Maria Quagliotti builds from Verardi's work, but associates the emaciated form with Buddhist cemetery-based mediation practices rather than *homa* rituals (2008: 74-75).

of Gandhāra, due to their stylistic and cultural links to the Greco-Roman world, have frequently been described as emphasizing the Buddha's humanity or as being more representative of a human-centered and naturalistic world view when compared with works of the same period created in other parts of South Asia (Dehejia 2000; Fisher 1993: 44-47; La Plant 1992: 27). By contrast, the early Buddhist images from Mathurā have often been characterized as invoking visual associations with gods because their wide eyes, broad shoulders, and frontal stance are closely linked to the sculptural forms of *yakṣas* and other local deities found in many parts of the subcontinent (*fig.* 1.3) (Coomaraswamy 1927: 298, 301-05). Even the pronounced bellies and broad chests characteristic of Mathuran sculptural forms have repeatedly been described as being indicative of Yogic practice and breath control. Because of these visual ties to depictions of deities and academic assumptions regarding the bodily shapes of *yogins*, early Mathuran works were often regarded as being more spiritual, introspective, or contemplative than their counterparts from the north-west (Dehejia 1996: 178-79; Fisher 1993: 44-47; Marshall 1960: 3).

The resulting characterizations of early Buddhist imagery, therefore, have tended to reinforce and perpetuate simplistic tropes of the West as worldly and the East as mystical. These descriptions are particularly salient to the current discussion because the exposed anatomies of the emaciated images have been hailed as the quintessential example of the Gandhāran fixation with physical forms at the expense of deeper spiritual truths (Karetzky 1989: 163-68). In light of the textual material previously discussed, it seems advisable to rethink that characterization. Although naturalistic in style, the subject matter of the emaciated images is intensely spiritual and is tied to Yogic concepts as deeply, and perhaps even more explicitly, than their Mathuran contemporaries.

There is a shared logic in the way sculptors from both regions sought to visually represent the spiritual power of Śākyamuni. Artists working in each style drew from pre-existing traditions to emphasize the purity and puissance of Śākyamuni. In so doing they produced vastly different visual forms, but, nevertheless, highlighted Śākyamuni's superhuman traits. The gaunt, emaciated images of Gandhāra and the plump, bold Mathuran types may seem to have nothing in common, but just as the Mathuran artists forged visual ties between Śākyamuni and images of deities, so too the Gandhāran sculptors represented him in the exalted state of an ascetic sanctified by self-mortification. The emaciated images not only provided viewers visual evidence of Śākyamuni's exceptional self-discipline and conviction, they also evoked his attainment of the divine states mentioned in the literature and identified him as surpassing human imperfection. The artists in Gandhāra, just like their counterparts in Mathurā, drew upon recognizable visual forms associated with divinity and spiritual might and, in so doing, present a figure worthy of veneration and respect.

It is something of an irony that scholarship on the relationship between Gandhāra and Mathurā, which were so intensely cosmopolitan and interconnected, has been dominated for so long by discussions of their stylistic differences. The links and exchanges between the two regions have been long acknowledged, but too frequently ignored (Lohuizen de Leeuw 1979: 377-400). Both regions' cultural remains include coinage and edicts that display multiple languages, present depictions of various ethnic modes of dress, and exhibit inscriptional and archaeological evidence of trans-regional travel and trade (Coomaraswamy 1927: 316; Mitterwallner 1986: 152, 190-203; Vogel 1971: 25, 33). Perhaps most significantly, during the centuries bracketing the cusp of the Common Era large portions of both regions fell under the political control of the same dynasties ruled by the Śaka and Kuṣāṇa kings.

These connections suggest that there are good reasons to look for similarities in the motivations for artistic production and that such inquiries may reveal concerns which transcend regional differences. By looking beyond the surfaces of the bold Mathuran and emaciated Gāndhāra images, we can identify similarities in the choices made by the artists and donors responsible for their production. Both sculptural forms emerge very early in the history of Buddhist figural art and are counted among some of the first representations of Śākyamuni ever produced. And, in both cases, the choices made by the creators of the images reveal an interest in displaying the divine qualities attributed to Śākyamuni. As the Buddhist community spread into new regions, such visual assurances of Śākyamuni's spiritual achievements must have been compelling to devotees and non-believers alike. Rather than showing the Teacher in a moment of weakness or emphasizing his human frailty, the sculptors of the Gandhāran emaciated images were drawing upon the visual language of asceticism to reveal Śākyamuni in the midst of a spiritually charged ordeal that captured him at his most pure, perfected, and divine.

This is not to say, however, that such sculptural forms were popular with all Buddhists. The limited number and regional specificity of the emaciated images would strongly suggest otherwise. In an insightful recent article, Juhyung Rhi explores the possible textual sources for the Gandhāran emaciated sculptures and, in so doing, identifies a small corpus of early Buddhist texts that are not critical of Śākyamuni's practice of asceticism. This acceptance is in contrast to the prevalent tendency toward overtly denouncing Śākyamuni's privations as misguided and ineffective in attaining enlightenment. Rhi suggests these manuscripts constitute a separate tradition, exemplified by texts like the fourth-century *Karuṇāpuṇḍarīkasūtra* and a second-century CE Chinese translation of the *Lalitavistara*, which do not treat the Buddha's asceticism as inherently negative (2008: 125-34). Quite to the contrary, the *Karuṇāpuṇḍarīka* looks upon Śākyamuni's exertions favorably, and goes so far as to enumerate the many positive benefits for devotees who see the Buddha in the midst of his austerities (ibid.: 141-42). Such passages reveal that at least some Buddhists in the early centuries CE were not averse to seeing the Buddha expressing, or even gaining, his spiritual success through ascetic practices similar to those described in the Brāhmaṇas and the *Yogasūtra* literature. Naturally, it would be unwise to assume that these texts constitute the full range of associations connected to fasting, but the vigorous way most Buddhist sources reject Śākyamuni's asceticism suggests they viewed such self-mortification as being linked to rival modes of spirituality.

Given the history of competition between Buddhism and Brāhmanic forms of devotion, it is not surprising that sympathetic views on the value of Śākyamuni's asceticism are, to my knowledge, absent from South Asian sources postdating the fourth century. Buddhism was certainly well-established by then and had developed its own ways of expressing and visualizing the Buddha's spiritual attainments without recourse to images of fasting. Yet, images of the emaciated Śākyamuni did not disappear entirely.

At the end of his analysis of the emaciated Buddhas, Brown (1997: 115) demonstrates the persistence of these images in Bodh-Gayā where, by the seventh century, they had become associated with health and healing. This interpretation may represent a new, or alternative, way of understanding the starving images. The narrative scene depicted in some later images may reflect this shift in meaning. It is interesting to note that while the Takht-i-Bahi image depicts a narrative context that takes place after the Buddha was enlightened, an eighth-century ivory from Kashmir, now in the Cleveland Museum of Art, depicts events that suggest the period of asceticism that precedes the enlightenment (compare *figs.* 1.1 and 1.2). On the left-hand portion of this small image, the sculptor depicted Śākyamuni's decision to accept a food offering from a woman, possibly Sujātā. These events almost certainly depict the end of the six-year fast, and, therefore, take place prior to his attainment of Buddhahood. Is it possible that this change in narrative context reveals a shift in priorities, one that sought to emphasize more effectively the image's association with suffering and recovery?

This earlier event from the Buddha's life highlights the dramatic shift in Śākyamuni's physical state during and after his ascetic ordeal. This shift can be seen in the carving as the emaciated central form is flanked by a post-meal image of Śākyamuni, fully restored to health. Additionally, these events provide one of the very few moments in the Buddhist narrative tradition in which Śākyamuni actually discusses his own bodily well-being. Although the eighth century is a long time after the earliest images were produced and Bodh-Gayā is a long way from Gandhāra, I wonder if these later images may also have worked on a second level that complemented the narratives of Śākyamuni's physical recovery. Is it possible that the persistence of ideas about purification allowed the image of a *tapas*-filled sage to retain significance as a particularly potent icon for those seeking to purge impurities from their own bodies and seeking an end to their own health-related ordeals? If so, then the emaciated Buddhas may have been seen paradoxically as both a co-sufferer and as a purified being with the potency and compassion necessary to provide delivery from that pain.

References

Bays, Gwendolyn (tr.), 1983, *The Lalitavistara Sūtra: The Voice of the Buddha, The Beauty of Compassion*, 2 vols., Berkeley: Dharma Publishing.

Bhat, M.S., 1998, *Vedic Tantrism: Rgvidhana of Saunaka with Text and Translation*, Delhi: Motilal Banarsidass.

Brown, Robert L., 1997, "The Emaciated Gandharan Buddha Images: Asceticism, Health, and the Body," in *Living a Life in Accord with Dhamma: Papers in Honor of Professor Jean Boisselier*, ed. N. Eilenberg, S. Diskul and R. Brown, pp. 105-15, Bangkok: Silpakorn University.

Buddhacarita, see Johnston 1995.

Buitenen, J.A.B. van (tr.), 1975, *The Mahābhārata: Book 3 The Book of the Forest*, Chicago: University of Chicago Press.

Chapple, Christopher and Yogi Ananda Viraj (tr.), 1990, *The Yogasutras of Patanjali: Analysis of the Sanskrit with Accompanying English Translation*, New Delhi: Sri Satguru Publications.

Coomaraswamy, Ananda K., 1927, "The Origin of the Buddha Image," *The Art*

Bulletin, 9(4): 287-329.

Dehejia, Harsha V., 1996, *The Advaita of Art*, Delhi: Motilal Banarsidass.

Dehejia, Vidya, 2000, "Buddhism and Buddhist Art," in *Heilbrunn Timeline of Art History*, New York: The Metropolitan Museum of Art. http://www.metmuseum.org/toah/hd/budd/hd_budd.htm

Eggeling, Julius (tr.), 1988 [first published 1882], *Śatapatha Brāhmaṇa According to the Text of the Madhyandina School*, Sacred Books of the East, 5 vols., Delhi: Motilal Banarsidass.

Fisher, Robert E., 1993, *Buddhist Art and Architecture*, World of Art Series, New York: Thames and Hudson.

Foucher, Alfred, 1905, *L'ArtGréco-Bouddique du Gandhāra: étude sur les origines de l'influenceclassique dans l'artbouddhique de l'Inde et de l'Extrême-Orient*, Paris: E. Leroux.

Horner, I.B. (tr.), 1954, *The Collection of Middle Length Sayings* (*Majjhima Nikāya*), vol. 1, Oxford: Pali Text Society.

Jamison, Stephanie W. and Joel P. Brereton (tr.), 2014, *The Rigveda: 3-Volume Set*, South Asia Research, Oxford: Oxford University Press.

Johnston, E.H. (tr.), 1995 [first published 1936], *Aśvaghoṣa's Buddhacarita or Acts of the Buddha*, Delhi: Motilal Banarsidass.

Kaelber, Walter O., 1976, "Tapas, Birth, and Spiritual Rebirth in the Veda," *History of Religions*, 15(4): 343-86.

——, 1979, "Tapas and Purification in Early Hinduism," *Numen*, 26: 192-214.

Karetzky, Patricia, 1989, "Hellenistic Influences on the Formation of a Biographical Cycle Based on the Life of the Buddha," *Oriental Art*, 25: 163-68.

Lalitavistara Sūtra, see Bays 1983.

La Plant, John D., 1992, *Asian Art*, New York: McGraw-Hill.

Lohuizen de Leeuw, J.E. van, 1979, "New Evidence with Regard to the Origin of the Buddha Image," in *South Asian Archaeology*, ed. H. Hartel, pp. 377-400, Berlin: Dietrich Reimer Verlag.

Mahābhārata, see Buitenen 1975.

Majjhima Nikāya, see Horner 1954.

Marshall, John H., 1960, *A Guide to Taxila*, Cambridge: Cambridge University Press.

Misra, Ram Nath, 1979, *The Yaksha Cult and Iconography*, New Delhi: Munshiram Manoharlal.

Mitterwallner, Gritli von, 1986, *Kuṣāṇa Coins and Kuṣāṇa Sculpture from Mathurā*, Mathura: The Government Museum.

Nidānakathā, see Rhys Davids 1937.

Quagliotti, Anna Maria, 2008, "New Considerations on Some Gandhāran Fasting Buddhas," in *Miscellanies about the Buddha Image*, ed. C. Bautze-Picron, pp. 65-75, South Asian Archaeology Special Sessions 1, Oxford: BAR Publishing.

Ṛg Veda, see Jamison and Brereton 2014.

Rhi, Juhyung, 2008, "Some Textual Parallels for Gandhāran Art: Fasting Buddhas, Lalitavistara and Karuṇāpuṇḍarīka," *Journal of the International Association of Buddhist Studies*, 29(1): 125-34.

Rhys Davids, Caroline Augusta Foley, and Frank Lee Woodward (tr.), 1917-1930, *The Book of the Kindred Sayings*, 5 vols., Bristol: Pali Text Society.

Rhys Davids, T.W. (tr.), 1937, *Buddhist Birth Stories (Jātaka Tales) and the Commentarial Introduction Entitled: Nidānakathā The Story of the Lineage*, London: Routledge and Sons.

Śatapatha Brāhmaṇa, see Eggeling 1882.

Spooner, David Brainerd, 1911, *Excavations at Takht-i-Bahi, Archaeological Survey of India Report 1907-08*, Calcutta: Superintendent of Government Printing.

Verardi, Giovanni, 1994, *Homa and Other Fire Rituals in Gandhāra*, Supplement 79(54), Naples: Istituto Universitario Orientale.

Vogel, Jean Philippe, 1971 [first published 1910], *Archaeological Museum at Mathura*, Delhi: Indological Book House.

Yogasutras of Patanjali, see Chapple and Viraj 1990.

2

An Unrecognized Sculpture of the Haṁsa Jātaka
From Nālandā Site No. 2

Nicolas Morrissey

It is probably fair to say that amongst the extensive architectural remains discovered at the Buddhist monastic complex of Nālandā, the structure found at Site no. 2 — rather awkwardly situated on the margins of the main monastic residential area and just east of *vihāra*s numbered 7 and 8 — has persisted as the most enigmatic.[1] Virtually every aspect of this structure, its date, source(s) of patronage, original architectural form, and even its religious affiliation, lingers either contested or wholly unresolved. In part, this is a consequence of the lacunary nature of the archaeological record from this particular area of the site. Following clearance operations undertaken there by D.B. Spooner (1915-16: 36-38; 1916-17: 47), only the remnants of a roughly square dressed stone plinth measuring approximately 100 ft by 120 ft (30 x 36 m) survived intact, rendering the architectonic features of the overall structure inaccessible.[2]

---

1 For a concise summary and description of the excavated remains at Nālandā, including a site plan, see most recently Asher 2015: 42-69.

2 The reports of Spooner provide a useful description of what little remained of this structure following initial clearance at Site no. 2. Already at this early period, though, it was noted that some of the stone sculptures of the plinth appeared incomplete and others had been haphazardly placed, which, along with the inconclusive orientation of substantial

Significantly, however, this extant plinth supports an elaborate stone frieze comprised of 220 well-preserved sculpted panels embedded in fairly diminutive (one-foot square; 30 x 30 cm) niches separated by a series of decoratively carved pilasters (*fig*. 2.1). This rich corpus of sculpture, which has been very tentatively dated on the basis of style to the seventh century CE, includes a wide array of representations: dancing figures, different varieties of birds, geometric patterns, celestial musicians, amorous couples (*maithunas*), *makaras*, flying *gandharvas* and *vidyādharas*, *kīrtimukhas*, *guhyakas*, and *vināyakas*, as well as, intriguingly, a significant number of figures that have been identified as Brāhmanical deities, such as Agni, Sūrya, Śiva, Skanda/Kumāra, Durgā, and Lakṣmī (Asher 1980: 49, 2015: 81-86 and figs. 4.19-24; Deva and Agrawala 1950: 202-12).[3] A small, indeterminate number of panels within this corpus have also been identified as narrative illustrations of themes drawn from both Epic and Purāṇic sources (Asher 1980: 49; 2015: 82; Deva and Agrawala 1950: 202-12), in addition to one representation of the well-known story of the "loquacious tortoise," attested in numerous literary sources including the *Pañcatantra*, *Hitopadeśa*, *Kathāsaritsāgara* as well as the Pāli *jātaka* collection (Deva

stone and brick debris found at the site, has raised questions in regard to whether or not the surviving plinth was the result of renovation — or even the erection of a new structure on top of a pre-existing building — utilizing materials salvaged from a different source, an issue that remains unresolved; see further discussion in Asher 1980: 48; Deva and Agrawala 1950: 198-99; Huntington 1984: 24; Page 1923: 1-22; Sastri 1942: 24-26.

[3] For further observations on the date and style of these sculptures, generally noted to possess characteristics indicating a post-Gupta date, but only anticipating those of the Pāla period, see Asher 1980: 49 and Huntington 1984: 24. This chronological attribution might find support, albeit marginal, from a small number of short, mostly unintelligible inscriptions found on stone slabs of the plinth, rather optimistically described as "pilgrim records," which "cannot be later than the 6th or 7th century A.D." (Deva and Agrawala 1950: 198; Majumdar 1969: 122; Sastri 1942: 24).

and Agrawala 1950: 205 no. 61, fig. 3; Yuyama 1991).[4]

Predictably, perhaps, the anomalous location of the structure at Site no. 2, its uncertain architectural attributes, and the decidedly heterogeneous nature of its corpus of sculpture have prompted divergent interpretations in regard to the cultic context that instigated its initial construction and ensuing ritual use(s). Almost seventy years ago, for example, Krishna Deva and V.S. Agrawala argued on the basis of the seemingly non-Buddhist elements evident in the plinth sculptures that the structure must have been a Hindu temple, "probably dedicated to Śiva" which thereby provided "valuable documentation of the eclectic religious phase of Brāhmanical Hinduism in the early medieval period" (1950: 198-99).[5] Alternatively, the presence of so-called "Hindu" or "non-Buddhist" elements in this sculptural corpus has certainly not deterred suggestions that the structure discovered at Nālandā Site no. 2 was Buddhist (Asher 1975: 111; Gail 1999: 131-39; Hermann-Pfandt 2008: 62; Huntington 1984: 24). Such suggestions, however, have invariably relied on the rather liberal invocation of Tāntric Buddhist textual sources containing descriptions of *maṇḍalas* that incorporate a host of Brāhmanical deities (Asher 2015: 86; Gail 1999; Huntington 1984: 24). Sources that describe *maṇḍalas* of this type would include, of course, an undeniably wide range of texts, but those cited most commonly have been the *Sarvatathāgatatattvasaṁgraha*, *Mahāvairocana*

[4] Although both Asher, and Deva and Agrawala include references to sculptures depicting scenes from both the *Rāmāyaṇa* and *Mahābhārata*, as well as the Kr̥ṣṇa cycle of myths, these have been little studied and such identifications should be regarded as tentative, if not tenuous.

[5] More recent studies have increasingly focused on the perceptible interactions between Buddhist and Brāhmanical cults made evident by the extant art historical and epigraphic records of the medieval period from Buddhist sites throughout Bihar, including Nālandā. However, the nature of these interactions remains far from clear and a matter of considerable theoretical debate; see, for example Amar 2012; Prasad 2013; Verardi 2003; and though slightly farther afield, Linrothe 1990.

Tantra, *Mañjuśrīyamūlakalpa*, and late compendiums such as the *Niṣpannayogāvalī*, each of which does indeed include delineations of *maṇḍala*s in which Brāhmanical deities appear, typically in a subsidiary role, as *laukika* (mundane) or guardian figures relegated to the margins — or even exterior — of the complex and highly specified groupings of deities positioned in concentric circles around a central, primary transcendent (*lokottara*) Buddha or other Buddhist cult figure (Bautze-Picron 1996: 114-15; Hermann-Pfandt 2008; Mallman 1964).[6] Accordingly, the structure at Nālandā Site no. 2 has been envisioned by some as an architectural instantiation of a Buddhist *maṇḍala* conforming to this model, wherein the lowest portion of the foundation with the sculpted frieze corresponds to the *laukika* realm or outermost of the series of concentric circles of deities (Asher 2015: 86; Gail 1999: 139; Hermann-Pfandt 2008: 62; Huntington 1984: 24).[7]

Undoubtedly, much more extensive research will be required in order to adjudicate between these disparate — and, as they currently stand, arguably unconvincing — characterizations of the structure at Nālandā Site no. 2. In order to accomplish this, however, it would seem necessary to substantially broaden the scope of inquiry, that is to say, to look beyond the relatively small proportion of sculpted imagery preserved at the site that has been

---

[6] The *laukika*/*lokottara* distinction within various Buddhist sources has been extensively studied, most recently in Seyfort-Ruegg 2008. The role of Brāhmanical deities as *laukika* beings in Buddhist *maṇḍalas* was already noted in Tucci 1949: 217. See also Dalton 2011: 64-66 for an analogous discussion of the Indian precedents of similar developments in Tibetan Buddhist contexts.

[7] Compare Huntington and Chandrasekhar (2000: 64-65), for example, who have even explicitly coined the term "*maṇḍala* hall" in reference to the structure at Nālandā Site no. 2. Implicit in some aspects of these discussions is the notion that the structure at Nālandā might be viewed as a prototype for the later — and far more elaborate — cruciform-type temples at monastic complexes such as Pahāṛpur, Antichak, and Mainamatī, though note that reservations in regard to this hypothesis have been expressed by Lefèvre (2012: 241-43; 2014: 132).

fig. 2.1: Excavated Stone Plinth with embedded sculptures, Nālandā Site no. 2, Bihar, India, *circa* seventh century CE

fig. 2.2: *Haṁsa Jātaka* Sculpture, Northern Face of Stone Plinth, Nālandā Site no. 2, Bihar, India, *circa* seventh century CE

fig. 2.3: *Kacchapa Jātaka*(?) Sculpture, Northern Face of Stone Plinth, Nālandā Site no. 2, Bihar, India, *circa* seventh century CE

isolated as specifically "Hindu" or "Brāhmanical" and, therefore, consequently "non-Buddhist."[8] As one small step in this direction, this paper takes as its focus a little-noticed sculpted panel within the extant corpus from Nālandā Site no. 2, in order to suggest that it may be an as yet unrecognized depiction of a specifically Buddhist narrative, the *Haṁsa Jātaka* (*fig.* 2.2). If this identification is tenable, then this sculpture would at least be of interest as a remarkably rare instance of a *jātaka* representation dating to the later period of Indian Buddhist art.[9] Additionally, however, this identification may also be of considerable interest in the present context as it might recommend a serious reconsideration of the longstanding presumption that no overtly Buddhist themes are discernible within the extant sculptures from the structure at Nālandā Site no. 2 (Asher 1980: 48-49). Indeed, in light of the distinct possibility that the narrative of the *Haṁsa Jātaka* evident in this sculpture appears to be, to my knowledge, without a parallel outside of Buddhist literature and — with only one possible exception — all known art historical representations of this *jātaka* in Indian sculpture and painting can be traced to Buddhist sites, this would seem to be especially the case.

Iterations of the *Haṁsa Jātaka* appear across a fairly broad range of Indic Buddhist literary sources.[10] In addition to three related,

---

[8] According to Asher (1980: 49; 2015: 82), this type of imagery may in fact only comprise as little as 10 percent of the overall corpus of sculpture from Site no. 2.

[9] There are only a handful of known *jātaka* representations that can be dated later than the Gupta–Vākāṭaka period. For an interesting group of *jātakas* found on a lintel within the Buddhist temple at Aihoḷe, see Melzer 2010. Two other unprovenienced sculptures, though likely from Pāla period Bihar, depict isolated examples of the *Haṁsa Jātaka* and the "Peacock" *Jātaka* (Bautze-Picron 1987, 1998; Leoshko 1989; Pal 2007).

[10] As is well known, there are numerous examples outside of Buddhist literature in which characters similar to the *Haṁsa Jātaka* appear, perhaps most notably in the *Pañcatantra* and the *Kathāsaritsāgara*, but these narratives bear little resemblance in terms of structure and content to the versions of the *Haṁsa Jātaka* in Buddhist sources, and cannot, therefore,

though variously titled, versions preserved in the Pāli *Jātaka-aṭṭhavaṇṇanā* (Cowell 1901: vol. 4, no. 502 *Haṁsa Jātaka*; Cowell 1905: vol. 5, no. 533 *Cullahaṁsa Jātaka*; no. 534 *Mahāhaṁsa Jātaka*), Sanskrit versions figure prominently in Āryaśūra's *Jātakamālā* (Meiland 2009: 27-80) and, in a much abridged form, in the *Dhanapālāvadāna* of Kṣemendra's *Avadānakalpalatā* (Vaidya 1959: 203).[11] A considerably different narrative, although still clearly identifiable as a version of this *jātaka*, is also preserved in Sanskrit in the *Saṅghabhedavastu* of the *Mūlasarvāstivāda-vinaya* (Gnoli 1978, pt. II: 192-94).[12] With the latter instance as the only notable exception, these Pāli and Sanskrit versions remain quite consistent in terms of narrative development with only small variations in terms of minor details.

The fullest treatment of the narrative occurs in the *Jātakamālā* of Āryaśūra, which recounts in the florid style characteristic of this collection, the machinations conceived of by King Brahmadatta of Varanasi to capture a pair of geese — the *bodhisattva* and Ānanda in former births as the goose-king, Dhṛtarāṣṭra, and his general, Sumukha, respectively — whose virtuous qualities and physical beauty had been effusively described to him by the ministers and brāhmaṇa elders of his court. In order to secure their capture, King Brahmadatta constructs a beautiful lake on the outskirts of the city and falsely promises immunity to all creatures who visit it. Despite the admonition of Sumukha to be wary, Dhṛtarāṣṭra, along with his flock, descend at the lake, and subsequently he becomes trapped in a

be accurately viewed as parallels. See, as one example, the story of two geese befriended by a king in the *Kathāsaritsāgara* (Mallinson 2007: 69).

11 The *Haṁsa Jātaka* also appears in the Khotanese *Jātakastava* and is also referred to in a recently published anthology of *avadānas* found in Turkmenistan (Dresden 1955: 437-38; Karashima and Vorobyova-Desyatovskaya 2015: 155).

12 Comprehensive citations of the various parallels of this version in Tibetan, Chinese and Japanese can be found in Karashima and Vorobyova-Desyatovskaya 2015: 155-57 n. 3; see also Panglung 1981: 207-29, esp. 208-09, 211, 214, 217, 219, 221, 223-24, 228.

snare set by a fowler dispatched by the king. At Dhṛtarāṣṭra's urging, the entire flock flees to safety, except for Sumukha who refuses to leave and remains with the goose-king, proclaiming his loyalty and determination to share his fate. When the fowler finds the birds, he is naturally astonished that only one was ensnared, and inquires of Sumukha why he too did not flee. Sumukha reiterates to the fowler his complete loyalty and friendship to his king and implores the fowler to release Dhṛtarāṣṭra. Greatly affected by the words and actions of Sumukha, the fowler agrees and releases Dhṛtarāṣṭra from the snare. In turn, Sumukha requests that the fowler take both he and Dhṛtarāṣṭra to be presented to King Brahmadatta. The fowler accedes to the request and brings them before the king, to whom he recounts the astounding events of their capture and release. King Brahmadatta, duly amazed, then honors the geese by offering Dhṛtarāṣṭra a throne suitable for a king and Sumukha a cane seat appropriate for a chief minister. The *bodhisattva* then counsels Brahmadatta on the virtues of just kingship, and Sumukha too converses with the king about the value of friendship and proper etiquette. Having generously rewarded the fowler, the king then sets both of the geese free, and they fly away together to rejoin their flock. Interestingly, the epilogue appended to some versions of this narrative clearly articulates the didactic import of this *jātaka*, emphasizing that it should be cited in order to praise the qualities of "fine speech" (*kalyāṇa-vacana*), "good friendship" (*kalyāṇa-mitra*), and the longstanding relationship between Ānanda and the *bodhisattva* during multiple lifetimes as an apt embodiment of these ideals (Meiland 2009: 76-79).[13]

The Sanskrit version of the *Haṁsa Jātaka* found in the *Mūlasarvāstivāda-vinaya* (see full text and author's translation included in the appendix) diverges substantially from the Pāli

[13] Note that there remains some question as to whether or not these epilogues found in manuscripts of the *Jātakamālā* and dating to the medieval period belong to the hand of Āryaśūra; see Schopen 1999: 323 n. 112 and the sources cited therein.

examples as well as that in the *Jātakamālā*, but still retains both the same setting and most of the central protagonists, including King Brahmadatta, the goose-king Dhṛtarāṣṭra, and a fowler, although in this variant of the narrative it is a group of fowlers dispatched to capture the goose-king instead of only one. The storyline, however, centers not on the goose-king Dhṛtarāṣṭra, but on his two sons, Pūrṇa and Pūrṇamukha. The former is the eldest who is cruel and violent, while the latter, the *bodhisattva* in a former birth, is younger and virtuous. Concerned for the well-being of his flock, Dhṛtarāṣṭra is understandably loathe to appoint his elder son heir to the throne, and consequently devises a plan to ensure that his youngest son rightfully becomes king. He sends them both on a journey to survey all of the lakes, ponds, and streams in the region of Varanasi, promising that the first to return would be established as king. The eldest son becomes diverted by his own enjoyment at an especially beautiful lotus pond on the outskirts of Varanasi named Brahmavatī, while the dutiful son Pūrṇamukha returns promptly and becomes king. Subsequently, Pūrṇamukha returns to his flock at the Brahmavatī pond, and in doing so attracts the attention of the local people who become beguiled at his physical beauty and inform the king. Brahmadatta then orders fowlers to capture the bird and bring it before him. As in the other versions of this *jātaka*, the fowlers snare the goose-king and when the flock of geese flees, only one remains by his side. Fearing retribution from the king, the fowlers attempt to bring only the captured goose to the royal court, but the other follows them. Seeing the two geese, the king realizes that the one who was not captured is a female and understands that it is Pūrṇamukha's wife. Deeply moved by this act of bravery and loyalty, King Brahmadatta orders the fowlers to set them both free and proclaims that no aquatic birds are to be killed in his kingdom. Although this version of the *Haṁsa Jātaka* is clearly in certain narrative details markedly different from the other Sanskrit and Pāli versions, it is nevertheless evident that the familiar theme of "good friendship" (*kalyāṇa-mitra*) as embodied in the relationship between Ānanda and the *bodhisattva* still takes precedence, yet is exemplified here not by a Ānanda's selfless loyalty to the *bodhisattva* in a former life as the goose-king's general, but by his loving devotion to him as the goose-king's wife.

The extant art historical record from India has yielded as many as eight possible representations of the *Haṁsa Jātaka* in sculpture and painting, but several are only partially preserved and remain uncertain. The earliest example may date to the first century BCE and is found on a medallion fragment from Bharhut, but as little survives it is difficult to confirm the identification (Coomaraswamy 1956: 80, pl. XXXV). Another early representation of this *jātaka* has been found on a railing pillar from Bodh-Gayā which shows, in an unfortunately damaged roundel sculpture, a figure identifiable as a fowler carrying a bird on a pole over his shoulder in front of a seated king — a method for the conveyance of the geese described in both the Pāli and *Jātakamālā* versions (Coomaraswamy 1935: pl. 37; Schlingloff 2013: 84-85).[14]

The first unequivocal representation of the *Haṁsa Jātaka* dates to the Sātavāhana period and was only relatively recently discovered on an inscribed drum slab once adorning the *stūpa* at Kanaganahalli (Poonacha 2013: pl. LXV); the label inscription clearly reads "*Haṁsa Jātaka* above" (*hasa jātaka upari*) (Hinüber and Nakanishi 2014: 90, no. 17). This relief sculpture condenses two narrative scenes into a single square frame and depicts a seated king and queen in front of which is a figure holding a bird, clearly the fowler displaying the captured goose-king. Another goose is shown standing on the ground at the king's feet with wings outstretched. The fowler and the two geese also appear again in the upper right of the scene, which perhaps illustrates the goose-king being captured; the second goose is shown flying in the air, likely intended to indicate its refusal to leave the side of the captured

[14] A possible second bird may have been represented but this part of the relief is not extant.

one. The depiction of the second bird in this manner, flying in the air and then standing in front of the king, strongly suggests a close association with the Sanskrit version — or at least one related to it — of the *Haṁsa Jātaka* now contained in the *Mūlasarvāstivāda-vinaya*, as this is the only version to describe a second bird following the fowler and the captured goose-king "on its own accord" because it was "ensnared by the snare of love" (*snehapāśapāśitaḥ svayam eva gataḥ*). In all of the other versions both birds are transported by the fowler to the king together.

Another possible representation of the *Haṁsa Jātaka* dating to the Sātavāhana period may appear on the upper portion of another sculpted *stūpa* drum slab, this one from Amarāvatī, though as it only depicts a seated king and a single, unidentifiable bird, this interpretation is more than a little suspect (Knox 1992: 142; Schlingloff 2013: 85). Two elaborately painted examples of the *Haṁsa Jātaka* also survive at Ajantā, both on the interior of *vihāras* (nos 2 and 17) excavated during the Vākāṭaka period. These have been treated in extensive detail by Schlingloff (2013: 81-87), who has noted that while the literary source for the Cave 17 painting is ambiguous, the particular scenes incorporated in the version in Cave 2 "clearly indicate[s] ĀJM [Āryaśūra's *Jātakamālā*] as [*sic:* the] literary source of this painting (85)." Two additional examples of the *Haṁsa Jātaka* have been found, one a small sculpture of two seated geese with two male interlocuters forming part of an assemblage of *jātakas* on a doorway lintel from the early Cāḷukya period Buddhist temple at Aihoḷe (Melzer 2010: 696-98 no. 4), and another sculpture found on a dispersed slab with a label inscription clearly reading "*Haṁsa Jātaka,*" possibly from Bihar and dated to the Pāla period, showing two geese seated on thrones in front of a king kneeling in *añjali-mudrā* (Bautze-Picron 1987: fig. 1; Leoshko 1989: fig. 1).

As this body of imagery demonstrates, there was considerable variation in regard to how the *Haṁsa Jātaka* was depicted visually in Indian art, and it would seem entirely plausible that the sculpture in question (*fig.* 2.2) from Nālandā Site no. 2 should be added to this rather sizeable corpus. This relief sculpture depicts three human figures enclosed within a decorative arched niche. The figure in the center of the sculpture is shown standing and holding what appears to be a pole with a net or a snare attached to it in his right hand, and an unidentifiable object in his left. There can be little question that this was intended to represent a fowler. The two other human figures, possibly also fowlers, are shown seated on the ground, each holding a bird with their hands. The birds seem reasonably recognizable as geese and the one on the viewer's right is noticeably smaller. This typical convention was frequently employed in Indian art in order to differentiate status. The inscribed Pāla period sculpture referred to above, for example, exhibits a particularly pronounced instance of this visual strategy to emphasize hierarchical distinction. In the Nālandā sculpture, although subtler, the intent may have been to distinguish either between the goose-king and his general, or perhaps, between the goose-king and his wife. Although a depiction of a king is not included in this relief, the presence of the other central protagonists shared across all versions of the *Haṁsa Jātaka* is certainly strongly suggestive that this is the narrative represented. There remains, however, some ambiguity in regard to what specific scene may have been intended. One possibility is that this sculpture depicts the moment after the fowler agrees to release the goose-king, and shows the two geese in dialogue with the fowler during which the *bodhisattva* requests to be taken to the king. It is also possible that this sculpture was informed by, or even derived from, the version in the *Mūlasarvāstivāda-vinaya*, and that this scene was intended to depict the release of the two geese by a trio of fowlers on the order of the king, as it is only this version that refers to a group of fowlers.

If the identification of this sculpture as a representation of the *Haṁsa Jātaka* stands, then this would seem to provide the impetus to look anew at the sculpture from Nālandā Site no. 2 in order to ascertain if other specifically Buddhist elements in this corpus may have been missed. It might now be more cogent, perhaps, to see the sculpture depicting the story of the "loquacious tortoise" (*fig.* 2.3) as an intent to express the specifically Buddhist orientation of this narrative as recorded in the *Kacchapa Jātaka*, rather than those which may have been derived from the other possible literary sources referred to in the beginning of this paper.[15] Regardless, even the potential inclusion of one Buddhist *jātaka* should raise new questions about how specific narratives may have functioned in conjunction with the eclectic panoply of both narrative and non-narrative sculptures on the plinth of the structure at Nālandā Site no. 2, and what implications this may have for reconstructing its original cultic context. In this regard, it may be important to remember that Prof. Robert L. Brown, in his typically erudite manner, has not long ago firmly established that *jātaka*s in Buddhist art were demonstrably unusual as a form of narrative expression, that they:

> ... cannot be considered merely illustrations of a word text; they are not reminders to start a mental telling of ... the narrative stated in words; and they were not used to teach others. Rather ... [they] all share meanings and uses rooted in the context of the monuments with which they are associated. Considered in these terms, the *jātaka*s on the monuments worked as icons, units of meaning and reverence, expressions of an aspect of the Buddha's nature and life that is (more) fully expressed by the entire monument. One might say that a story is being told on these monuments, but it is told in a different way than through a narrative as read from a word text. – 1997: 99-100

[15] This sculpture, unfortunately not noticed in Yuyama 1991, merits further study. The narrative representation of the demise of the turtle, for example, may differ in significant details from the textual account preserved in the *Pañcatantra*, which appears to have been the source for an early sculpture depicting this story from Mathurā; see Vogel 1909: 529 and fig. 32. Another sculpture from the Nālandā Site no. 2 corpus that has been identified as a narrative drawn from the *Pañcatantra* (Majumdar 1970: 156) seems also in need of re-examination, as this association is more than a little dubious.

While the "story" on the monument at Nālandā Site no. 2 is certainly far from being revealed, it can, perhaps, be suggested by way of a conclusion that its details should be sought — at least in part — by following Prof. Brown's lead, in considering more carefully the potentially "iconic" or rather emblematic function of the thematic orientation of its narratives. It may not be too difficult, for example, to perceive the ways in which the quality of loyal, selfless service embodied by Ānanda in his actions towards his teacher, the *bodhisattva*, so visible in the *Haṁsa Jātaka*, could have been deployed with some valence visually in a seventh century CE ritual environment that may have already begun to absorb the influences of early Tāntric ideals, in which "an emphasis on secrecy, loyalty, allegiance, and unbreakable trust" between teachers and disciples had moved to the forefront (Davidson and Orzech 2004: 820). For now, however, this particular narrative can only remain incomplete, but its hesitant outlines gestured to here are offered *in medias res* as a small expression of gratitude from an erstwhile student to a venerable teacher.

An unusual Sanskrit version of the *Haṁsa Jātaka* from the *Saṅghabhedavastu* of the *Mūlasarvāstivāda-vinaya* in which Ānanda appears as the wife of the Buddha [Gnoli (pt II) 1978: 192.21–194.31; translation by N. Morrissey]

bhūtapūrvam bhikṣavo 'navatapte mahāsarasi dhṛtarāṣṭro nāma haṃsādhipatir babhūva; tasya dvau putrau pūrṇaś ca pūrṇamukhaś ca; pūrṇo jyeṣṭhaḥ pūrṇamukhaḥ kanīyān; tayoḥ pūrṇaś caṇḍo rabhasaḥ karkaśaḥ; nityam eva haṃsān bhartsayati; keṣāṃcit pakṣān utpāṭayati; keṣāmcit nakharikābhiḥ kṣataṃ karoti; etāni cānyāni ca upadravaśatāni karoti; te haṃsāḥ pratidinam āgamya dhṛtarāṣṭrasya haṃsādhipater nivedayanti; sa saṃlakṣayati: pūrṇaś caṇḍo rabhasaḥ karkaśaḥ; yady aham enaṃ yauvarājye pratiṣṭhāpayāmi, mamātyayād eṣa haṃsayūthaṃ nāśayiṣyati; tad upāyasaṃvidhānaṃ kartavyam iti; tena pūrṇaḥ pūrṇamukhaś ca ubhāv apy uktau: yaḥ utsān, sarāṃsi, taḍāgāni cāvalokya agrato matsakāśam āgacchati, tam ahaṃ haṃsādhipatim sthāpayāmi iti; tāv anyonyam spardhayā pañcaśataparivārau prakrāntau; tāv itaś cāmutaś ca utsān, sarāṃsi, taḍāgāni ca avalokayantāv anupūrveṇa vārāṇasīṃ nagarīm anuprāptau; tena khalu samayena vārāṇasyāṃ brahmadatto nāma raja rājyaṃ kārayati ṛddhaṃ ca yāvad ākīrṇabahujanamanuṣyaṃ ca; tena vārāṇasyāṃ udyānasya nātidūre brahmāvatī nāma puṣkariṇī saraḥprativiśiṣṭatarākhyā; tasyāṃ nānāvidhāni jalajāni puṣpāṇi ropitāni; tire samantāt caturṣv api pārśveṣu anekāni puṣpaphalavṛkṣasahasrāṇi ropitāni; sā utpalakumudapuṇḍar īkasaṃcchannā, anekataruṣaṇḍamaṇḍitā, bahuvividhavihaganikūjitā; tasyās tāṃ vibhūtiṃ dṛṣtvā pūrṇo haṃsaḥ pañcaśataparivāraḥ avatīrya yatheṣṭagatipracāratayā krīḍitum ārabdhaḥ; pūrṇamukho'pi svayūthyair ucyate: tvam apy avatīrya krīḍa iti; sa kathayati: rājyam tāvat pratīcchāmi; tataḥ paścād āgamya krīḍiṣyāmi iti; tena laghu laghv eva gatvā rājyaṃ pratīṣṭam; tataḥ pañcaśataparivāraḥ vārāṇasīm āgamya brahmavatīm puṣkariṇīm avatīrya krīḍitum ārabdhaḥ; taṃ tathā pramodavihāriṇam dṛṣtvā janakāyaḥ saṃśayaṃ āpannaḥ: aho paramadarśanīyo haṃsādhipatiḥ kuto'pīha saṃprāptaḥ, brahmāvatīm puṣkariṇīm alamkṛtya, sarvajalacarān pakṣiṇo rūpaśobhayā abhibhūya lokasya spṛhām utpādayati; yatheṣṭam ca viharati iti; śrutvā sarva eva vārāṇasīnivāsī janakāyaḥ samantāt brahmāvatīm puṣkariṇīm parivārya, tasya visrabdhavihāratām rūpaśobhām ca nirīkṣamāṇaḥ avasthitaḥ; amātyai rājño niveditam: deva kuto'pi haṃsādhipatir āgataḥ; sa brahmāvatīm puṣkariṇīm avatīrya anekahaṃsaśataparivāraḥ sarvān jalacarān pakṣiṇo rūpaśobhayā abhibhūya, lokasya spṛhām utpādayan visrabdhavihāratayā tiṣṭhati iti; rājā kathayati: bhavantaḥ yady evam āhūyantām śākunikāḥ iti; tair āhūtāḥ; rājā kathayati: bhavantaḥ śrūyate brahmāvatyām puṣkariṇyām atiparamadarśanīyavigraho haṃsādhipatiḥ kuto'py āgataḥ; sa yuṣmābhir eka eva akṣataḥ pāśair badhvā matsakāśam āneyaḥ; iti; sa taiḥ paramasukumāreṇa pāśena baddhaḥ; sa gāthām bhāṣate:

> *saṃsyandito 'smi baddho manuṣyavaśam āgato'ham* ।
> *acikitsya ādāya haṃsayūtham gacchata śighraṃ hy anavataptam* ॥
>
> *iti;*

ekonāni pañcaśatāni niṣpalāyitāni; eko na niṣpalāyitaḥ; tam eva ca baddhaṃ śocamāno'vasthitaḥ; śākunikās te dṛṣṭvā paraṃ vismayam āpannāḥ; rājabhayān na badhnanti; nāpi praghātayanti; te taṃ haṃsādhipatim ādāya rājñaḥ sakāśam gatāḥ; sa dvitīyaḥ abaddhaḥ; snehapāśapāśitaḥ svayam eva gataḥ; sa haṃsādhipatī rājña upanītaḥ; rājā kathayati: bhavanto'yam dvitīyaḥ kimartham ānītaḥ? te kathayanti: deva nāsmābhir ayam baddhaḥ; api tu svayam evāgataḥ iti; rājā paraṃ vismayam āpannaḥ kathayati: nūnam asyeyaṃ bhāryā; gacchata; etam haṃsādhipatiṃ saha bhāryayā muñcata; na ca yuṣmābhiḥ kenacid <*api*> *etau praghātyau iti; śākunikāḥ kathayanti: deva anye praghātayiṣyanti; janakāyasya nivedyatām iti; rājñā amātyānām ājñā dattā: gacchata bhavanto vārāṇasyāṃ nagaryām ghaṇṭāvaghoṣaṇaṃ kārayata deva evam samājñāpayati, na kenacit madviṣayanivāsinā jalacarāḥ pakṣiṇo ghātayitavyāḥ iti; tair ghaṇṭavaghoṣaṇaṃ kāritam.*

kim manyadhve bhikṣavo? yo'sau pūrṇamukho haṃsādhipatir aham eva saḥ tena kālena tena samayena; yā sā tasya patnī sa evāsāv ānandaḥ tena kālena tena samayena; yāni tāni ekonāni pañca haṃsaśatāni, etāny eva tāni ekonāni pañca bhikṣuśatāni; tadāpy aham ebhir haṃsabhūtaiḥ parityaktaḥ; ānandena haṃsabhūtena na parityaktaḥ; etarhy apy aham ebhiḥ parityaktaḥ; ānandena bhikṣuṇā na parityaktaḥ; bhūyo'pi bhikṣavaḥ yathā aham ebhiḥ parityaktaḥ, ānandena bhikṣuṇā na parityaktaḥ tac chrūyatām.

Monks, in the past, at Anavatapta, the great lake, there was once a king of geese named Dhṛtarāṣṭra. He had two sons, Pūrṇa and Pūrṇamukha; Pūrṇa was the eldest brother, Pūrṇamukha the younger. Of the two, Pūrṇa was cruel, violent, and harsh. He continuously tormented the geese. Some he plucked the feathers of, others he injured with his claws. He committed these and hundreds of other grievous acts. Having come on a daily basis, the geese made this known to Dhṛtarāṣṭra, the king of geese. He thought to himself: "Pūrṇa is cruel, violent, and harsh. If I formally establish him as heir to the throne, then after my death he will destroy the flock of geese. Therefore, an expedient plan must be undertaken." He spoke to both

Pūrṇa and Pūrṇamukha — "The one who, having surveyed all the lakes, ponds, and springs [in the region] returns to me first, him I will install as the king of geese." In competition with each other, the two brothers set out, each with a retinue of five hundred. Surveying in all directions the lakes, ponds and springs [throughout the region], the two in due course arrived at the city of Varanasi. At that time there was as king named Brahmadatta ruling in Varanasi, which was prosperous, flourishing, etc., and filled with many inhabitants. Not far from the royal garden in Varanasi was a lotus pond called Brahmavatī, the most renowned amongst bodies of water. Numerous varieties of water-borne flowers grew there. Indeed, on all four sides of its shore, many thousands of fruit trees and flowering plants grew; it was entirely covered with blue, red, and white lotuses, adorned with many stands of trees, and filled with the songs of numerous varieties of birds. Having seen the natural abundance of the place, Pūrṇa, along with a retinue of five hundred, descended and began to frolic, freely behaving as was their wont. Pūrṇamukha's relatives then addressed him: "You too, having descended, must frolic!" He replied: "First I will seek kingship, then, after having returned, I will frolic!" Having departed quickly, he was formally established as king. Afterwards, having returned to Varanasi and having descended at the Brahmavatī pond, he, along with a retinue of five hundred, began to frolic. Then, people, having seen the joyous frolicking of that king of geese, wondered: "Aho! From where has this most beautiful king of geese arrived here, who, adorning the Brahmavatī pond, surpasses with his beauty and splendor all the aquatic birds there, causing the envy of the world! And there he sports freely, as is his wont!" When they heard this, the people residing in Varanasi surrounded all sides of Brahmavatī pond and remained there admiring the splendor of the king of geese's form and his confident sporting. The king's ministers announced to the king: "Lord, a king of geese has arrived from somewhere! Having descended with a retinue of several hundreds of geese at Brahmavatī pond, he, having surpassed with his beauty and splendor all aquatic birds, causing the envy of the world, remains there confidently sporting." The king replied, "Sirs, if that is so fowlers must be summoned!" They were summoned by them. The king said: "Sirs, it has been heard that a king of geese, supremely beautiful, has arrived here from some other place. Having captured this very one with snares, unharmed, he must be brought to me by you all unharmed!" He was captured by them with a supremely delicate snare. He spoke this verse:

> Undoubtedly I am captured! Fallen into the dominion of men I cannot be saved! Having gathered the flock of geese, go at once to Anavatapta!

Except for one the five hundred geese fled. The only one that did not flee remained grieving for that one who was captured. Having seen this, those fowlers were thoroughly filled with amazement. Fearing the king, they did not capture nor kill it. Having gathered up the king of geese they returned to the king. Though that second one was not captured, it, being ensnared by the snare of love, went along on its own accord. The king of geese was presented to the king. The king said: "Sirs, why have you brought this second one?" They replied: "Lord, this one was not captured by us, but came along on its own accord." The king, filled with amazement, said: "Surely this is his wife! Go! Release this king of geese along with his wife! And under no circumstances are these two to be killed by you!" The fowlers replied: "Lord, others will kill them! The people must be informed!" The king then issued an order to his ministers: "Sirs, go to the city of Varanasi and have a proclamation made accompanied by the ringing of bells: 'No aquatic birds residing in my kingdom are to be killed!' " A proclamation accompanied by the ringing of bells was made by them.

What do you think monks? At that time, on that occasion, I was that very one who was Pūrṇamukha, king of geese. At that time, on that occasion, that one who was his wife was this very one, Ānanda. Those who were the five hundreds of geese save one, those were these very five hundred monks save one. Just so at that time I was abandoned by them when they were geese. Yet I was not abandoned by Ānanda when he was a goose. Now too, I was abandoned by them, but I was not abandoned by the monk Ānanda. Moreover, monks, as I was abandoned by them, I was not abandoned by the monk Ānanda, so it must be known.

References

Amar, Abhishek, 2012, "Buddhist Responses to Brāhmaṇa Challenges in Medieval India: Bodhgayā and Gayā," *Journal of the Royal Asiatic Society*, series 3, 22(1): 155-85.

Asher, Frederick M., 1975, "Vikramaśīla Mahāvihāra," *Bangladesh Lalit Kalā*, 1: 107-13.

——, 1980, *The Art of Eastern India 300–800*, Minneapolis: University of Minnesota Press.

——, 2015, *Nalanda: Situating the Great Monastery*, Mumbai: Marg Publications.

Bautze-Picron, Claudine, 1987, "A Unique Haṃsajātaka Representation from Bihar," in *Investigating Indian Art: Proceedings of a Symposium on the Development of Early Buddhist and Hindu Iconography Held at the Museum of Indian Art Berlin*, ed. M. Yaldiz and W. Lobo, pp. 31-38, Berlin: Museum für Indische Kunst.

——, 1996, "From God to Demon, from Demon to God: Brahmā and Other Hindu Deities in Late Buddhist Art of Eastern India," *Journal of Bengal Art*, 1: 109-35.

——, 1998, "La représentation des *jātaka* en Birmanie et dans l'inde orientale à l'époque médiévale," in *Études birmanes en homage à Denise Bernot*, éd. P. Pichard and F. Robinne, vol. 9, pp. 129-45, Paris: École Française de l'Extrême Orient, Études thématiques.

Brown, Robert L., 1997, "Narrative as Icon: The Jātaka Stories in Ancient Indian and Southeast Asian Architecture," in *Sacred Biography in the Buddhist Traditions of South and Southeast Asia*, ed. J. Schober, pp. 64–101, Honolulu: University of Hawai'i Press.

Coomaraswamy, Ananda, 1935, *La Sculpture de Bodhgaya (Ars Asiatica XVIII)*, Paris: Les Éditions d'Art et d'Histoire.

——, 1956, *La Sculpture de Bharhut*, tr. Jean Buhot, Paris: Les Éditions d'Art et d'Histoire.

Cowell, Edward B., ed. 1895–1913, *The Jātaka or Stories of the Buddha's Former Births*, 6 vols., Cambridge: Cambridge University Press.

Dalton, Jacob, 2011, *The Taming of the Demons: Violence and Liberation in Tibetan*

Buddhism, New Haven: Yale University Press.

Davidson, Ronald M. and Charles D. Orzech, 2004, "Tantra," in *Encyclopedia of Buddhism*, ed. Robert E. Buswell, pp. 820-26, New York: Macmillan.

Deva, Krishna and V.S. Agrawala, 1950, "The Stone Temple at Nālandā," *Journal of the Uttar Pradesh Historical Society*, 23: 198-212.

Dresden, Mark J., 1955, "The Jātakastava or 'Praise of the Buddha's Former Births': Indo-Scythian (Khotanese) Text, English Translation, Grammatical Notes, and Glossaries," *Transactions of the American Philosophical Society*, 45(5): 397-508.

Gail, Adalbert J., 1999, "On the Maṇḍalaic Structure of the Pahāṛpur Temple," *Journal of Bengal Art*, 4: 131-39.

Gnoli, Raniero (ed.) (with the assistance of T. Venkatacharya), 1978, *The Gilgit Manuscript of the Saṅghabhedavastu. Being the 17th and Last Section of the Vinaya of the Mūlasarvāstivādin*, Part II, Rome: Instituto Italiano per il Medio ed Estremo Oriente.

Hermann-Pfandt, Adelheid, 2008, "Maṇḍala Elements in Tantric Buddhist Architecture in India, Tibet, and Indonesia," in *The Heritage of Nalanda*, ed. C. Mani, pp. 52-67, New Delhi: Aryan Books International.

Hinüber, Oskar von and Maiko Nakanishi, 2014, *Kanaganahalli Inscriptions*, supplement to the *Annual Report of the International Research Institute for Advanced Buddhology at Soka University* for the Academic Year 2013, vol. 17, Tokyo: International Research Institute for Advanced Buddhology, Soka University.

Huntington, John and Chaya Chandrasekhar, 2000, "Architecture: Buddhist Monasteries in Southern Asia," in *Encyclopedia of Monasticism*, ed. William M. Johnston, pp. 55-66, Chicago/London: Fitzroy Dearborn.

Huntington, Susan L., 1984, *The "Pāla-Sena" Schools of Sculpture*, Leiden: E.J. Brill.

Karashima, Seishi and Margarita I. Vorobyova-Desyatovskaya, 2015, "The Avadāna Anthology from Merv, Turkmenistan," in *Buddhist Manuscripts from Central Asia: The St. Petersburg Sanskrit Fragments (StPSF)*, vol. 1, ed. Seishi Karashima and Margarita Vorobyova-Desyatovskaya, pp. 145-524, Tokyo: The Institute of Oriental Manuscripts of the Russian Academy of Sciences and The International Research Institute for Advanced Buddhology, Soka University.

Knox, Robert, 1992, *Amaravati: Buddhist Sculpture from the Great Stūpa*, London: British Musuem Press.

Lefèvre, Vincent, 2012, "Pahāṛpur, une œuvre de circonstances?," in

Orientalismes. De l'archéologie au musée. Mélanges offerts à Jean-François Jarrige, 9, pp. 237-53, Turnhout, Belgium: Brepols.

——, 2014, "The Hindu Sculptures from Pahāṛpur Reconsidered," in *South Asian Archaeology and Art: Changing Forms and Cultural Identity: Religious and Secular Iconographies*, pp. 131-42, Turnhout, Belgium: Brepols.

Leoshko, Janice, 1989, "A Rare Jātaka Relief from the Pāla Period," in *Nalinīkānta Śatavārṣikī. Studies in Art and Archaeology of Bihar and Bengal, Dr. N.K. Bhattasali Centenary Volume, 1888–1988*, ed. D. Mitra and G. Bhattacarya, pp. 29-34, Delhi: Sri Satguru Publications.

Linrothe, Rob, 1990, "Beyond Sectarianism: Towards Reinterpreting the Iconography of Esoteric Buddhist Deities Trampling on Hindu Gods," *Indian Journal of Buddhist Studies*, 2(2): 16-25.

Majumdar, Ramprasad, 1969, "Some Inscribed Slabs of Stones in the Neighbourhood of Nalanda Stone Temple Ruins," *Journal of the Asiatic Society*, 11(1-4): 122.

——, 1970, "A Note on a 'Lion-Jackal' Piece of Sculpture in Nālandā Stone Temple," *Journal of the Asiatic Society*, 12(1-4): 156.

Mallinson, James (tr.), 2007, *The Ocean of the Rivers of Story by Somadeva*, vol. 1, New York: New York University Press/JJC Foundation.

Mallmann, Marie-Thérese de, 1964, "Divinités hindoues dans le tantrisme bouddhique," *Arts Asiatiques*, 10(1): 67-86.

——, 1968, "Hindu Deities in Tantric Buddhism," *Zentralasiatische Studien*, 2: 41-53.

Meiland, Justin (tr.), 2009, *Garland of the Buddha's Past Lives by Āryaśūra*, vol. 2, New York: New York University Press/JJC Foundation.

Melzer, Gudrun, 2010, "Jātakamālā Scenes at the Buddhist Temple of Aihoḷe: An Early Experiment with Ambiguity (*śleṣa*)," in *From Turfan to Ajanta: Festschrift for Dieter Schlingloff on the Occasion of His Eightieth Birthday*, ed. Eli Franco and Monika Zin, pp. 691-714, Kathmandu: Lumbini International Research Institute.

Page, J.A., 1923, "Nalanda Excavations," *Journal of the Bihar and Orissa Research Society*, 9(1): 1-22.

Pal, Pratapaditya, 2007, "A Pāla Period Peacock Jātaka Panel in the Norton Simon Museum," in *Kalhār (White Water-Lily): Studies in Art, Iconography, Architecture, and Archaeology of India and Bangladesh. Professor Enamul Haque Felicitation Volume*, ed. G. Bhattacharya and Enamul Haque, pp. 213-16, New Delhi: Kaveri Books.

Panglung, J.L., 1981, *Die Erzählstoffe des Mūlasarvāstivāda-Vinaya Analysiert auf Grund der tibetischen Übersetzung* (Studia Philologica Buddhica. Monograph Series 3), Tokyo: Reiyukai Library.

Poonacha, K.P., 2013, *Excavations at Kanaganahalli*, Delhi: Archaeological Survey of India.

Prasad, Birendra Nath, 2013, "Cultic Relationships Between Buddhism and Brahmanism in the 'Last Stronghold' of Indian Buddhism: An Analysis with Particular Reference to Votive Inscriptions on Brahmanical Sculptures Donated to Buddhist Religious Centres in Early Medieval Magadha," *Buddhist Studies Review*, 30(2): 181-99.

Samuel, Geoffrey, 2002, "Ritual Technologies and the State: The Mandala-Form Buddhist Temples of Bangladesh," *Journal of Bengal Art*, 7: 39-56.

Sastri, Hiranand, 1942, *Nālandā and Its Epigraphic Material*, Delhi: Archaeological Survey of India.

Schlingloff, Dieter, 2013, *Ajanta: Handbook of the Paintings/Narrative Wall Paintings*, vol. 1: *Interpretation*, New Delhi: Indira Gandhi National Centre for the Arts and Aryan Books International.

Schopen, Gregory, 1999, "The Bones of a Buddha and the Business of a Monk: Conservative Monastic Values in an Early Mahāyāna Polemical Tract," *Journal of Indian Philosophy*, 27(4): 279-324.

Seyfort-Ruegg, David, 2008, *The Symbiosis of Buddhism with Brahmanism/Hinduism in South Asia and of Buddhism with "Local Cults" in Tibet and the Himalayan Region*, Vienna: Austrian Academy of Sciences Press.

Spooner, D.B., 1915-16, "The Royal Asiatic Society's Excavations at Nalanda," *Archaeological Survey of India Report, Eastern Circle*, pp. 33-38, Calcutta: Bengal Secretariat Book Depot.

——, 1916–17, "The Royal Asiatic Society's Excavations at Nalanda," *Archaeological Survey of India Report, Eastern Circle*, pp. 40-47, Calcutta: Bengal Secretariat Book Depot.

Tucci, Giuseppi, 1949, *Tibetan Painted Scrolls*, Roma: La LibreriadelloStato.

Vaidya, P.L., 1959, *Avadāna-Kalpalatā of Kṣemendra*, vol. 1, Darbhanga: Mithila Institute.

Verardi, Giovanni, 2003, "Images of Destruction: An Enquiry into Hindu Icons in Their Relation to Buddhism," in *Buddhist Asia 1: Papers from the First Conference of Buddhist Studies Held in Naples in May 2001*, ed. G. Verardi and S. Vita, pp. 1-36, Kyoto: Italian School of East Asian Studies.

Vogel, Jean-Phillipe, 1909, "Études de Sculpture Bouddhique," *Bulletin de l'École française d'Extrême-Orient*, 9: 523-32.

Yuyama, A., 1991, "The Kacchapa-Jātaka in Bas-Relief at the Caṇḍi Mĕndut in Central Java," in *Maeda Egaku Hakushi Shōju Kinen Ronshū (Studies in Buddhism and Culture: In Honour of Professor Dr. Egaku Mayeda on His Sixty-fifth Birthday*, ed. by the Editorial Committee of the Felicitation Volume for Professor Dr. Egaku Mayeda, pp. 251-65, Tokyo: Sankibo Busshorin.

3

Śāntideva's Buddhism of the Pāla Period
Poetics of Voice and Image

Mary Storm

And now as long as space endures,
As long as there are beings to be found,
May I continue likewise to remain
To drive away the sorrows of the world.
— *Bodhicaryāvatāra* 10.55[1]

Introduction

THE aesthetic and religious practices of eighth-century India developed during a period of special vitality in religious thought, poetry, and imagery. This study of Śāntideva's *Bodhicaryāvatāra* explores how the text's poetics and vivid imagery are used to set a tone for the understanding of new philosophical ideas and values. The *Bodhicaryāvatāra* also develops a link to the Pāla period world of Śāntideva: what he saw, which deities he worshipped, how his doctrinal and ritual needs were met, and how his aesthetic priorities were shaped. For example, by reading the many references to the *bodhisattva*, we see that Śāntideva had special devotion to Mañjuśrī; we know from historical descriptions of the place, that as a resident of Nālandā, Śāntideva must have been surrounded by paintings and sculptures, and his words reflect this aesthetic environment. Most

[1] All quotes in this article from the *Bodhicaryāvatāra* are taken from Śāntideva, 1997, *The Way of the Bodhisattva: A Translation of the Bodhicaryavatara*, tr. Padmakara Translation Group, Boston: Shambala.

specifically, the text reveals how Śāntideva used robust descriptive visuals in attempts to clarify difficult abstract concepts, such as "self" and "emptiness."

This essay first provides contextual background to Śāntideva's *Bodhicaryāvatāra.* It then examines the poetry and layered imagery of the text, showing how Śāntideva used both to highlight key aspects of his Buddhist metaphysics and philosophy. Specifically, the essay focuses on Śāntideva's views regarding the central tenants of Mahāyāna Buddhism, the *bodhisattva* vow, Mādhyamaka philosophy, meditative practices, and how those concepts were enhanced with visual poetics.

Background to Śāntideva's Bodhicaryāvatāra

The seventh and eighth centuries were a time of intellectual and artistic ferment in Buddhist India, and the monastic scholar Śāntideva wrote the *Bodhicaryāvatāra* in an atmosphere of creativity, prosperity, and stability supported by dedicated Indian, and even foreign, patronage. At that time, Indian Buddhists were exploring new ideologies and methods of religious practice. From the most abstract metaphysical speculation to the simplest charismatic devotion, Buddhism was changing from earlier forms. Buddhist philosophy had evolved into a system of subtle intellectual maturity. The rise of Tantrism (a diverse set of esoteric heterodox beliefs and practices) and *bhakti* (charismatic devotionalism) had profound effects on the development of devotional/ritual practice in many Indian religious traditions, producing new expressions of text, aesthetics, imagery, ritual, architecture, and even political structures.

Eastern India, in particular, was experiencing an upsurge of creative genius, supported by the patronage of both monastic and lay Buddhists and the Buddhist rulers of the Pāla dynasty (750–1174 CE).[2] The monastic centers were hubs of creativity and innovation

[2] This period is often referred to as the Pāla-Sena period in recognition that the Hindu Sena Dynasty, which overlapped and followed the Pālas

with lavish donations and political support. Nālandā University, specifically, was a place of intellectual and artistic creativity. It was probably here that the *Bodhisattvacaryāvatāra* or *Bodhicaryāvatāra* or *The Way of the Bodhisattva* was written in the seventh or eighth century by Śāntideva.

Buddhism declined in the centuries that followed the eighth-century heyday of monastic power. Many factors combined to bring about Buddhism's gradual disappearance from India (Sarao 2012), including loss of royal patronage, rise of Hindu reformist movements, religious persecution, and depredations of war. At the same time that Buddhism was declining, Purāṇic Hinduism was beginning a gradual rise. Under the inspirational impetus of the Hindu theologian Śaṅkara in the ninth century, devotional Hinduism was to emerge as the dominant religious force in India, and this was not always a peaceful transition (Bhattacharyya 2012: 46-49). However, during the time of Śāntideva, Hinduism and Buddhism still coexisted as separate, but mutually influential doctrines. There were nevertheless tensions that we see reflected in Śāntideva's text; for example, he is not reluctant to dismiss the Hindu penchant for vows and extremist forms of asceticism as useless and karmically destructive forms of self-violence (*Bodhicaryāvatāra* 8: 78).

The physical destruction of monastic institutions was particularly devastating to the organization of Buddhist life. The earliest Muslim military expansion into India had already begun in Śāntideva's day; the earliest incursion was in 710 CE with an assault into Sindh, although this event is usually assessed as a northwest frontier border incursion rather than an attempt for empire (Storm 2004). In the eighth century, eastern India was not yet under organized attack, and Indians were blissfully ignorant of the

---

in territory and chronology, often shared the same patronage efforts and continued the same styles, although the Senas were concerned more with Hinduism than Buddhism. Pāla feudatories, such as the Varmans and the Candras, were also patrons and helped to spread the Pāla aesthetic.

tumultuous 400 years to come; a future that would witness a series of increasingly destructive invasions, so that by the late twelfth century, Buddhism was in tatters in its birthplace: monks and nuns had perished, libraries had burned, and although Buddhism had expanded across North and East Asia, within India, Buddhist institutions had collapsed (Singh 2013).

The older interpretation that Buddhism also fell under its own "degenerate" Tāntric doctrines has long since been refuted (Wayman 2000: 361-62). This was a Victorian era response based upon prudish sensibilities and a misunderstanding of Tantrism as a corrupted form of Buddhism (Newell 2010: 390-94; Schopen 1991: 1-23). On the contrary, the high quality of poetic texts, metaphysical speculation, and refined, powerful art works all attest to a period of vitality and creativity. It is also evident that Tāntric forms of Buddhism invigorated the religion and arts of Japan, Nepal, Bhutan, Tibet, and Mongolia for centuries after the collapse of Buddhism in India (Huntington and Huntington 1990: 117).

It is perhaps because we have this bittersweet historical perspective that we can see this time in the eighth century of eastern India for what it was: a halcyon summer before a long dark winter of decline, destruction, and exile. It is therefore worth exploring the legacy of this creative period.

The Distinctive Quality of Śāntideva's World

Śāntideva wrote during the Pāla dynasty, which controlled much of eastern India from the eighth to the twelfth century. At the peak of its power in the late eighth and ninth centuries, the Pāla Empire covered most of the northern subcontinent, stretching into what are now Nepal, Pakistan, Bangladesh, and Myanmar, with diplomatic links to Tibet, Java, Śrīvijaya (Sumatra), and the Arab Abbasid Caliphate (Iraq). The religious culture of Buddhism at this time was distinctive; it inspired new schools of Buddhism and Buddhist aesthetics to develop in India, and then also find root in other areas of Asia, leading to the creation of a golden age of Buddhist culture across borders. From a religious perspective, the ideas and images of Pāla period Buddhism were attractive as the culmination of centuries of deep philosophical thought and artistic refinement; rulers from China, Tibet, Java, Cambodia, and Myanmar sent requests for Indian scholars to come and teach in their kingdoms based on the appeal of art and doctrine (both religious and political).[3]

This period of Buddhism presented the seductive combination of sophisticated philosophical ideas, dramatic rituals and exquisitely articulated sculpture, painting, and architecture. It satisfied the need for dramatic, ritualistic, and aesthetic delight, but put those gratifications on a firm moral foundation of intellectual subtlety. Surprisingly and unfortunately, this nexus of the sensual and the cerebral does not happen often in human history. Wisdom, morality, power, and aesthetics are not separate areas of life; they are each most effective when they are integrated. This was the significant element of Śāntideva's world and a good part of the basis for Buddhism's international appeal (Kossak 2002; Neelis 2011).

The Bodhicaryāvatāra: The Text

Śāntideva's *Bodhicaryāvatāra* is a Mahāyāna Buddhist exhortation to end suffering for both one's self, and for others. It is also a window into the aesthetic ideals of the Pāla period, which shaped Buddhist expression in India and beyond (Sarkar 1977-78).

The *Bodhicaryāvatāra* was influential in India from the eighth to the late twelfth centuries and throughout the decline of Buddhism in north India. It remains immensely popular in Tibet; the current Dalai Lama has written commentaries on it (1999), as have many

[3] For example, King Yeshe-Od, the ruler of Guge (Western Tibet) invited the Nālandā scholar-monk Dīpaṁkara Śrījñāna Atīśa (984–1052) to teach in Tibet, where Atīśa became greatly influential in the formation of Vajrayāna Buddhism. Atīśa previously spent twelve years in Śrīvijaya studying Tantrism under Dharmakīrtiśrī and is considered one of the major apologists for Tāntric Buddhism (Chattopadhaya 1981).

other Tibetan Buddhist teachers. It is still read by millions of Buddhists as an essential guide for the development of wisdom and compassion. The text is both accessible and at times highly esoteric, and much of the text resonates with common sense and compassion. Most of the text is written as a refined scholarly debate, typical of the rhetorical debates held in many Buddhist monasteries to the present day.

The *Bodhicaryāvatāra* was originally written in Sanskrit in ten chapters and 700 poetic stanzas. The text has since been translated many times; the earliest translations were from Sanskrit to Tibetan (Nelson 2016: 407). Allegedly, the ninth-century Indian monk Sarvajñadeva, translated and compiled the original Tibetan form of the text and then, many compilations and editions later, it reached its present Tibetan form. One of the earliest Tibetan versions, discovered by Wang Yuanlu and sold to Sir Aurel Stein at Dunhuang in the 1920s, dates from at least 1000 CE, if not earlier, but has not been fully translated into English (Crosby and Skilton 1995: xxx–xxxiv). There are at least twenty-five translations in contemporary Asian or European languages. The most widely used English translation is a poetic rendition by the Padmakara Translation Group from one of the later Tibetan recensions (1997). This Tibetan version may be from a text that was itself a translation from several earlier textual compilations from the original Sanskrit.

The *Bodhicaryāvatāra* is about awakening *bodhicitta* (a "wise heart") and perceiving the compassionate core of emptiness (*śūnyatā*). It rests on the principle that moral action must be guided by wisdom and analysis; it includes the idea that wisdom (*prajñā*) and compassion (*karuṇā*) together will lead to the flowering of *bodhicitta*. In other words, morality and intellect must be integrated.

The title may be translated in a number of ways, and it is often called *The Way of the Bodhisattva*. In Mahāyāna, *bodhisattva*s are portrayed as supra-human figures, who in some cases delay their own ultimate liberation until the last sentient being has been enlightened. In the *Bodhicaryāvatāra*, *bodhisattva* specifically refers to the individual practitioner who has committed to a life of aspiration towards liberation.

The *Bodhicaryāvatāra* is perhaps best translated as *Undertaking the Way to Awakening*. The Way, the Path, or the Road are terms used in many cultures to define the literature of a quest, a pilgrimage, or a romance ("romance", not in the modern sense of a courtship novel, but in a tale of journey that ends in self-discovery). The *Bodhicaryāvatāra* is not a story of knights, grails, dragons, and maidens, but in some important ways it parallels a European quest narrative. It uses poetics and visual description to outline an interior journey of commitment, hardships, struggles, and liberation. Also, like a European medieval romance, the *Bodhicaryāvatāra* describes an ideal world, potentially real, but remaining imaginary while lodged in the delusions of *saṁsāra.*

The Poetics and Visual Imagery of the Bodhicaryāvatāra

The text draws on vivid visual imagery; it is obvious that Śāntideva lived in a world of powerfully expressed aesthetics, but this never digresses into poetics without content. One of the distinguishing aspects of the text is that the author sees no conflict between poetic metaphor and incisive analysis. The ninth chapter, in particular, demands that the reader engage in acute metaphysical analysis and encourages rigorous thought, but uses the raw descriptions of the human body to drive home the concept of "voidness" (*śūnyatā*).

The *Bodhicaryāvatāra* uses visuals to describe the struggles of being human; it is sometimes comically, sometimes tragically, moving to see how similar the impulses of the eighth century and the twenty-first century remain. Judging by the *Bodhicaryāvatāra*, jealousy, anger, lust, impatience, sloth, arrogance, and fear of death all seem to be deeply ingrained in the human psyche. We can see our own foibles and recognize our own aspirations in Śāntideva's text.

However, there were distinctive cultural factors that distinguished Śāntideva's world view from our own contemporary concerns and that portray human existence as evanescent and often futile. One factor leading to this was a strong belief in the Buddhist "end of days," a kind of millennialism, a belief in an inevitable decline in the importance of the Buddha's teaching, which, in India at least, proved to be surprisingly accurate. It was taught in a number of *sūtra*s that the history of the Buddhist doctrine would be composed of three periods: the first was the phase of the Wonderful Law (*saddharma*) lasting for 500 years after the time of Śākyamuni, the second phase was the False or Imitative Law (*saddharma-pratirūpaka*) lasting for the next thousand years, and the third and final phase was the period of the Destruction of the Law (*saddharma-vipralopa*) (Huntington and Huntington 1985: 647). This last phase began as Buddhism declined in India. There was therefore a kind of poetic wistfulness and acceptance of human decline in the *Bodhicaryāvatāra*, which contrasts with Śāntideva's exhortations to strive for *bodhicitta*. Repeatedly, he acknowledges the pain of life that blinds us to the truth. He uses images of physicality to direct us to more abstract concepts. In chapter 10, Śāntideva repeatedly dedicates us to the task, but offers images of solace that acknowledge inevitable suffering, most easily understood in physical terms.

And may the blind receive their sight,
And may the deaf begin to hear.
And women near their time, bring forth
Like Māyādevī, free from pain. — 10.18

May those who lose their way and stray
In misery, find fellow travellers,
And safe from threat of thieves and savage beasts,
Be tireless, and their journey light. — 10.25

In this verse, Śāntideva uses powerful images of physical sensory perception: sight, hearing, pain, birth, struggle, fear, exhaustion, and realization. In contemporary society, we tend to think that life will inevitably improve from outside sources: discoveries in science, improvements in education, universal health care, and establishment of democratic process will bring us to an Arcadia of societal harmony. In this perhaps self-delusional cheeriness we believe that the weaker individual will be buoyed along by the improvements of society. Śāntideva was not so sanguine; he believed that it was only by acknowledging the struggle, pain of life, and the need for the individual awakening, that there was hope for the birth of *bodhicitta.* He uses these visual devices to make his arguments accessible. Even though Śāntideva was one of the great apologists of Mādhyamaka theory and could have written only in the remote abstractions of a scholar, here he is using accessible poetic metaphor to draw us in to awakening. In the passages below, Śāntideva encourages us to use the shame caused by hurting others to motivate ourselves to acknowledge failings and to struggle along the *bodhisattva* path:

All that I possess and use
Is like the fleeting vision of a dream.
It fades into the realms of memory;
And fading will be seen no more. — 2.36

And even in the brief course of this present life
So many friends and foes have passed away,
Because of whom, the evils I have done
Still lie, unbearable, before me. — 2.37

In this atmosphere of self-reliance, Śāntideva is not afraid of asking us to get out of the dream (*māyā*) and acknowledge guilt and shame, the bêtes noires of psychotherapy. Using accessible everyday imagery, he exhorts us to metaphorically "pull it together".

Bodhicaryāvatāra Influence on Mahāyāna Buddhism and the Bodhisattva Vow

The *Bodhicaryāvatāra* is also an essential explanation of the development of Mahāyāna views within Indian Buddhism. These schools of Buddhism emphasized the ideal that the practitioner strives not just for his own enlightenment as an *arhat*,[4] someone who "has laid down his burden" upon achieving *nirvāṇa*, but as a *bodhisattva*, one who also strives for the release of delusion in all living beings. Mahāyāna offered the appealing concept that laity and monastic, male and female,[5] could achieve enlightenment. Śāntideva presents *nirvāṇa* in practical terms of Awakening, and like most Buddhists, he tells us it is ineffable, but gives images to clarify his theory. *Nirvāṇa* is not suffering, it is relinquishment of emotional possession, and it is the expression of *maitrī* (loving-kindness, benevolence). In the following verses the author uses vivid imagery to help the reader understand the compassionate nature of *bodhisattvas*.

Nirvāṇa is attained by giving all,
Nirvāṇa the objective of my striving,
Everything therefore must be abandoned,
And it is best to give it all to others. — 3.12

May I be a guard for those who are protectorless,
A guide for those who journey on the road.

---

[4] The term *arhat* first appeared as a reference to the Buddha himself. An often-recited Theravāda liturgical reference is the Pāli homage: *namo tassa bhagavato, arahato, sammā-sammbuddhassa* (Homage to him, the Blessed One, the Worthy One, the perfectly enlightened Buddha). This verse is found in several of the Pāli texts including the *Dīgha Nikāya* (21.8).

[5] The idea that females could achieve *nirvāṇa* is explicitly admitted in the *Lotus Sūtra*: in chap. XI a young *nāginī* (a snake deity) princess is transformed into a male and instantly achieves *nirvāṇa*. In chap. XII, Yaśodharā, the mother of Rāhula, and the former wife of the Buddha, along with the nun Gautamī, the aunt of the Buddha, are both told that they will become *bodhisattvas* (*Saddharmapuṇḍarīka* 1884). The female *bodhisattva* Tārā is, of course, the perfect example of a female realized being. The Buddha himself was a virtuous woman in previous births. In the fifth century *Jātakamālā* by Haribhaṭṭa the *bodhisattva* (the Buddha-to-be) was the self-sacrificing woman Rūpyāvatī, who cut off her own breasts to feed a starving woman and child (Khoroche 2017).

For those who wish to go across the water,
May I be a boat, a raft, a bridge. - 3.18

May I be an isle for those who yearn for landfall,
And a lamp for those who long for light;
For those who need a resting place, a bed;
For all who need a servant, may I be their slave. — 3.19

May I be the wishing jewel, the vase of plenty,
A word of power and the supreme healing;
May I be the tree of miracles,
And for every being the abundant cow [Kāmadhenu]. — 3.20

When the aspirant takes the *bodhisattva* vow, he/she is on a path to becoming a "wise being." The *bodhisattva* strives for liberation but withdraws from his/her own *nirvāṇa* until the last sentient being is released from suffering. The *bodhisattva* doctrine changed the goal of religious life, and it also had profound influence on many aspects of secular Asian history. The *Bodhicaryāvatāra* is both a "how to" text on following the path of the *bodhisattva*, and also an exegetical text of Mādhyamaka theory presented in accessible and reassuring imagery.

Bodhicaryāvatāra Influence on Mādhyamaka Philosophy

Whatever is the source of pain and suffering,
Let that be the object of our fear.
But voidness will allay our every sorrow
How could it be for us a thing of dread? — 9.55

Mahāyāna gave rise to various subtle philosophical schools, the most influential of which was Mādhyamaka, or the middle path of philosophy, first described by Nāgārjuna in the second century CE. Śāntideva is considered one of the primary exponents of later Mādhyamaka thought. Mādhyamaka explores the concept of emptiness (*śūnyatā*); and the concept that *bodhicitta* is only true when it is acknowledged within emptiness.

Mādhyamaka is the mid-point between two extreme views:

1. "Eternalism," the idea that phenomena exist forever and can be immutable and unique, and
2. Buddhist "Nihilism," the idea that all things are non-existent and illusory.[6]

Mādhyamaka philosophy is the foundation of Zen, as well as the various forms of Esoteric Buddhism. Mādhyamaka theory espouses the idea that all phenomena (including the concept of the self and the perception of the ego) are empty of intrinsic independent reality.[7] Phenomena only *seem to exist* contingent upon various causes and conditions upon which they arise; those causes and conditions themselves are interdependent upon yet other causes and conditions, ad infinitum, so "reality" should be understood as constant flux. Phenomena are empty of self-nature (*svabhāva*) and are merely the play of our minds. "Reality" is the projected need for determinants that appear immutable for quotidian convenience. Despite its abstraction, this is not a form of inchoate mysticism, but a logical trope pushed to the edges of metaphysics and logic. Śāntideva may be speaking to other educated monastics, but he wants his text to read well; he uses common imagery and metaphors to give access. In verses 9.56-60 he repeatedly uses the gritty images of the body to describe the ineffable concepts of voidness.

If such a thing as "I" exists indeed,
Then terrors, granted, will torment it.

---

[6] Buddhist "Nihilism" should be distinguished from European Nihilism of the nineteenth and twentieth centuries. Buddhist Nihilism is not concerned with existentialism, or a refutation of idealism, morality, or theism. Sometimes, however, Buddhist and European Nihilism cross paths, such as with Schopenhauer's exhortation that the individual should separate himself from desire and turn away from the meaninglessness of life. As Nietzsche points out, the despair of European Nihilism is contradictory, as it implies a social connection and emotional response.

[7] "Ego," in the Buddhist context, is a different beast from the Freudian ego; in the Buddhist sense it implies the strength of the level of ignorance we attach to a sense of permanent self.

But since no self or "I" exists at all,
What is there left for fears to terrify? — 9.56

The "I" is not the body's grease or sweat,
The lungs and liver likewise do not constitute it.
Neither are the inner organs "I"
Nor yet the body's excrement and waste. — 9.57

He goes on in verses 9.74-75 to drive the point home that there is no self, no individual "I". He does this by using ordinary images, returning again later in the chapter in 9.82-86 to remind the reader we are not the individual or sum of our physical or mental parts.

For instance, we may take the banana tree —
Cutting through the fibers, finding nothing.
Likewise analytical investigation
Will find no "I," no underlying self. — 9.74

"If beings", you will say, "have no existence,
Who will be the object of compassion?"
Those whom ignorance imputes,
For whose sake we have pledged ourselves. — 9.75

Mādhyamaka, like all schools of Buddhist doctrine, accepts the notion of causal nexus. In the view of *pratīya-samutpāda* (conditioned arising), all physical and psychological phenomena are interdependent and conditioned upon each other. This is what entangles human beings in *saṁsāra*. Twelve links (*nidānas*) make up conditioned arising and lead to the continuation of rebirth. Mādhyamaka also accepts that there is no one intrinsic self and that there is no "me," no individual identity, and no eternal *ātman* (soul). There is thus no concept of a unique eternal soul. The personality/self/ego is composed of the five psychophysical aggregates called *skandhas*. These exist neither singly nor collectively to constitute a self-dependent ego-entity.[8]

---

[8] The *skandhas* are — First: body (*rūpa*), second: sensations (*vedanā*), third: discrimination/perception (*saṁjñā*), fourth: compound mental

Śāntideva accepted all of the above as basic tenets of Buddhist doctrine. He starts his particular Mādhyamaka discussion with these concepts firmly in place and does not need to explain them to his audience of educated monastics. In chapter 9, he expounds upon the nature of emptiness and the foundation of *bodhicitta* comprehension in this zone of illusory reality (9.4). It is this attachment to illusion and our clinging to the perception of the stone hard "realness" of reality and our individuality that causes us suffering and impels us into causal nexus. To eliminate attachment to the false, self-made perception of reality, we must analyse the objects of our projections; when doing this we find the object is not concrete in its many compounded aspects.

Mādhyamaka theory, with its intense emphasis on the abstract, needed a rich symbolic vocabulary for elucidation. We can see in the highly evolved and complex iconography of the period the need to make this metaphysical world visible in the sculpture, paintings, and architecture characteristic of the Pāla period (*fig.* 3.1). The abstractions of Mādhyamaka eventually led to stylistic opposites: the extreme detail of Tibetan Buddhism and the playful and nihilistic abstractions of Zen. Although two extremes, both aesthetic traditions were attempts to visually explore the transcendent expression of the elusive. It is in chapter 9, "The Wisdom Chapter," where Śāntideva puts forth his most specific ideas about Mādhyamaka. He describes the voidness (*śūnyatā*) of reality, but he still relies, not on academic abstractions but everyday imagery, he speaks of the body, bones, blood and sinew, guts, and excreta (9.56-60), as if to say, "let's not get too pleased with ourselves and our philosophy."

---

factors (*saṁskāra*). The *saṁskāras* are themselves made up of dependent phenomena such as mental or physical volitional impulses. The fifth *skandha* is consciousness (*vijñāna*). There are six forms of consciousness (those of the five sense organs and mental consciousness).

fig. 3.1: Mañjuśrī in Mañjuvajra Maṇḍala, Bangladesh or Bengal, India, *circa* eleventh century CE, black basalt

fig. 3.2: Śyāma Tārā/Cūṇḍā in *varada*- and *abhaya-mudrā*, Sirpur, Madhya Pradesh, India, *circa* eighth century CE, bronze inlaid with copper, silver

fig. 3.3: Standing Crowned and Jewelled Buddha (perhaps the Buddha Amoghasiddhi), Kurkihār, Bihar, India, *circa* early eleventh century CE, bronze with silver and copper inlay

fig. 3.4: Vairocana Buddha in *bodhiyaṅgī-mudrā,* Nālandā, Bihar, India, *circa* eleventh century CE, gilt bronze

Bodhicaryāvatāra Influence on Meditation, Ritual, and Art

The assumption that Buddhist monks and nuns spent most of their time in emptiness (*śūnyatā*) meditation is incorrect (Lopez 2004: xxxii–xxxiii). At certain times in Buddhist history, for example the eighth century, sitting emptiness meditation was not emphasized and, instead, visualization rituals took center place. This is evidenced in the vivid descriptions in the *Bodhicaryāvatāra* itself, as well as in the art and architecture of the period.

The small, but exquisite sculptures of Tārā, Amoghasiddhi Buddha, and Vairocana Buddha illustrated here (*figs.* 3.2-4) were not created to be decorative or generic Buddhist figures, but held specific docetic place in the complex and highly visualized *sādhana* (realization) rituals of Pāla Tāntric Buddhism.[9] These sculptures are delightful to look at, but they were not "art for art's sake"; they were tools for meditation. The esoteric Buddhist meditation techniques focused on a host of deities and their places in the diagrammatic hierarchy of meditation *maṇḍalas*. Practitioners spent years meditating upon and inculcating the attributes of the deities; finding realization through the interiorized visualization of the ideal attributes.

The struggle to articulate the concepts of *bodhisattva* and *śūnyatā* led to the complex *maṇḍalas* and imagery of esoteric Buddhist architecture and art, but is also expressed in the literature of the period, both poetry and image, reflecting the aesthetic ideals of Śāntideva's period. The iconography of the highly ritualized meditation and the looser poetic visualizations of Śāntideva's text were part of the same impetus — to make the ineffable conceivable.

The second chapter of the *Bodhicaryāvatāra* describes the kind of meditative rituals associated with medieval Buddhism.

---

[9] The *Sādhanamālā* (*Garland of Realization*) was a descriptive iconographic text written between the fifth and eleventh centuries. It gave specifics for the visualization of hundreds of Buddhist deities. It was translated by B. Bhattacharyya, 1958, *The Indian Buddhist Iconography*.

Rituals included visualization of the gifts of beautiful things to the *bodhisattvas* and Buddhas, as well as bathing the images with scented water, and the giving of food offerings, flowers, clothes, incense, lamps, and music. These are parallel to contemporary Hindu *pūjā* rituals. What strikes the reader of the *Bodhicaryāvatāra* is the intimate sensuality of these descriptions:

Lakes and meres adorned with lotuses,
All plaintive with the sweet-voiced cries of water birds
And lovely to the eyes, and all things wild and free
Stretching to the boundless limits of the sky; - 2.5

I hold them all before my mind, and to the supreme buddhas
And their heirs will make a perfect gift of them.
Oh, think of me with love, compassionate lords;
Sacred objects of my prayers, accept these offerings. — 2.6

In the *Bodhicaryāvatāra bodhisattva* specifically refers to the individual who has committed himself to liberation, however the term also references the divine figures, such as Mañjuśrī (*fig.* 3.1), Tārā (*fig.* 3.2), Amoghasiddhi (*fig.* 3.3), or Vairocana (*fig.* 3.4), who personify the virtues that Śāntideva invokes in the struggle for enlightenment. The cult of the *bodhisattva* developed in response to the charismatic ideals of *bhakti* and gave the impetus to visually personify Buddhist ideals, such as wisdom (Mañjuśrī), steadfastness (Amoghasiddhi), gnosis (Vairocana), and compassion (Tārā). Śāntideva wished us well. He spoke to both the educated monk and the layman. He was accessible; he believed his message was useful, and that through poetics and powerful images he could share the basic beliefs and the higher philosophy of Buddhism.

Throughout the spheres and reaches of the world,
In hellish states as many as there are,
May beings who abide there, taste
The bliss and peace of Sukhāvatī. — 10.4

May those who go in dread have no more fear.
May captives be unchained and now set free.

And may the weak receive their strength.
May living beings help each other in kindness. — 10.22

References

Barr, Nick, 2004 [unpublished], "Shantideva's Bodhisattvacharyavatara: The Way of the Bodhisattva Ninth Chapter Analysis," Emory University, IBD Tibetan Studies Program, Dharamsala, India.

Bhattacharyya, Bedasruti, 1958, *The Indian Buddhist Iconography: Mainly Based on the Sādhanamālā and Cognate Tāntric Texts of Rituals,* Calcutta: K.L. Mukhopadhyay.

——, 2012, "Varman's Incursion and Sacking and Burning of Somapura Mahavihara (Varendri): An Enquiry into the Religious Atrocity in Early-Medieval Bengal," *Proceedings of the Indian History Congress*, 73: 46-49.

Bodhicharyāvatara, see Crosby and Skilton 1995.

Chattopadhaya, Alaka, 1981, *Atīśa and Tibet: Life and Works of Dīpaṁkara Śrījñāna,* New Delhi: Motilal Banarsidass.

Coomaraswamy, Ananda K., 1998 [first published 1935], *Elements of Buddhist Iconography,* New Delhi: Munshiram Manoharlal.

Crosby, Kate and Andrew Skilton (trs.), 1995, *The Bodhicharyāvatara,* Oxford: Oxford University Press.

Dalai Lama, 1999 [originally published 1994], *A Flash of Lightning in the Dark of Night: A Guide to the Bodhisattva's Way of Life*, Boston: Shambhala South Asia Editions.

Dīgha Nikāya, see Rhys Davids and Rhys Davids 1995 [1889, 1910, 1921].

Elliott, Neil (tr.), 2002, *Guide to the Bodhisattva's Way of Life: How to Enjoy a Life of Great Meaning and Altruism,* Ulverston, UK: Tharpa Publications.

Haribhaṭṭa, *Jātakamālā*, see Khoroche 2017.

Huntington, Susan L. and John C. Huntington, 1985, *The Art of Ancient India: Buddhist, Hindu, Jain*, New York and Tokyo: Weatherhill.

——, 1990, *Leaves from the Bodhi Tree: The Art of Pāla India (8th–12th Centuries) and Its International Legacy*, Dayton, O: Dayton Art Institute with the University of Washington Press.

Kern, H. (tr.), 1884, *Saddharmapuṇḍarīka, or The Lotus of the True Law*, Sacred Books of the East, vol. XXI, Oxford: Clarendon Press.

Khoroche, Peter (tr.), 2017, *Once a Peacock, Once an Actress: Twenty-Four Lives of the Bodhisattva from Haribhatta's "Jatakamala"*, Chicago: University of Chicago Press.

Kossak, Steven M., 2002, "Pāla Painting and the Tibetan Variant of the Pāla Style," *The Tibet Journal*, 27(3/4): 3-22.

Lopez, Jr., Donald S., 2004, *Buddhist Scriptures*, London: Penguin Classics.

Neelis, Jason, 2011, *Early Buddhist Transmission and Trade Networks: Mobility and Exchange within and beyond the Northwestern Borderlands of South Asia*, Leiden: Brill.

Nelson, Barbara, 2016, "Śāntideva's Bodhicaryāvatāra in Translation: A Century of Interpretation of a Sanskrit Mahāyāna Text," *Journal of Religious History*, 40(3): 405-27.

Newell, Catherine, 2010, "Approaches to the Study of Buddhism," in *The New Blackwell Companion to the Sociology of Religion*, ed. Bryan S. Turner, pp. 388-406, Chichester, UK: Wiley-Blackwell.

Padmakara Translation Group (tr.), 1997, *The Way of the Bodhisattva: A Translation of the Bodhicaryavatara*, Boston: Shambala.

Rhys Davids, T.W. and Caroline A.F. Rhys Davids (trs.), 1995 [first published 1889, 1910, 1921], *Dialogues of the Buddha*, 3 vols., Oxford: Pali Text Society.

Saddharmapuṇḍarīka, see Kern 1884.

Śāntideva, see Crosby and Skilton 1995; Padmakara Translation Group 1997; Wallace and Wallace 1997; Elliott 2002.

Sarao, K.T.S., 2012, *The Decline of Buddhism in India: A Fresh Perspective*, New Delhi: Munshiram Manoharlal.

Sarkar, Himansu Bhusan, 1977-78, "The Philosophical Matrix and Content of the Vajrayāna System as Practised by the Śailendra-Rulers of Central Java (c. 775–856 A.D.): A Search for Its Origin (A Literary and Inscriptional Approach)," *Annals of the Bhandarkar Oriental Research Institute*, 58/59: 921-38.

Shantideva [Śāntideva], 1997, *The Way of the Bodhisattva: A Translation of the Bodhicaryavatara*, tr. Padmakara Translation Group, Boston: Shambala.

Singh, Anand, 2013, " 'Destruction' and 'Decline' of Nālandā Mahāvihāra: Prejudices and Praxis," *Journal of the Royal Asiatic Society of Sri Lanka*, New Series, 58(1): 23-49.

Schopen, Gregory, 1991, "Archaeology and Protestant Presuppositions in the Study of Indian Buddhism," *History of Religions*, 31(1): 1-23.

Storm, Mary, 2004, "The Rise of the Pratiharas," in *Great Events from History: The Middle Ages, 477-1453*, ed. Brian A. Pavlac et al., pp. 156-59, Pasadena: Salem Press.

Wallace, Vesna and B. Alan Wallace (tr.), 1997, *A Guide to the Bodhisattva Way of Life*, tr. Vesna A. Wallace and B. Alan Wallace, Ithaca: Snow Lion Publications.

Wayman, Alex, 2000, "Observations on the History and Influence of the Buddhist Tantra in India and Tibet," in *Studies in History of Buddhism: Papers Presented at the International Conference on the History of Buddhism at the University of Wisconsin, Madison, USA, August 19–21, 1976*, 2nd edn., ed. A.K. Narain, Delhi: B.R. Publishing Corporation.

4

The Iconographic Distribution of Ninth to Twelfth Century Buddhist Imagery from Bihar and Odisha

Kurt Behrendt

SCULPTURE recovered from the sites of Nalandā, Kurkihār, and Antichak in north India and Ratnagiri on the east coast can be used to characterize the ninth to twelfth century CE Buddhist traditions. This study attempts to sort the material iconographically in an effort to better understand the main patterns of patronage. While excavations of the great *mahāvihāras* have brought to light many stone and bronze sculptures, this data set is, of course, incomplete as much of the religious imagery from the sacred areas and monasteries has not survived. I was nevertheless able to assemble more than 750 stone and bronze images that reveal some broad patterns of image production. The quality and large scale of some of these sculptures offer a means to characterize elite patronage.

I contend that these data indicate that esoteric deities associated with Tantra/Vajrayāna practices tend to be more numerous in the east, especially in Odisha. The sculpture of Bihar, in contrast, is much more conservative and reflects a greater interest in Mahāyāna and earlier Nikāya ideologies. I am not suggesting that esoteric practices were not important in the Bihar region, but compared to practices in centers farther east, they were less emphasized.

Nālandā

The monastic complex of Nālandā in Bihar is a good place to begin, as considerable sculptural material was recovered in the course of excavations (Huntington 1984: 108-09; Mani 2008; Stewart 2016). Various foreign monks visited this center, and the written accounts of Xuanzang and Yijing describe this complex in some detail (Beal 1969, vol. 2: 170-72; Takakusu 1896). According to Xuanzang's seventh-century account, Nālandā was a major center for the study of Nikāya and Mahāyāna Buddhism. Later Tibetan histories suggest that Vajrayāna and Tāntric traditions were also significant (Chimpa 2010). However, these histories were written either well before the ninth through twelfth centuries CE period or long after the collapse of these monasteries in the early thirteenth century. Moreover, these textual sources reflect the interests of foreign visitors, not those of the resident monks in these great monastic centers.

Many of the major images to survive from Bihar could have served Mahāyāna audiences or may have been the focus of esoteric ritual. Take for example the Jagdishpur Buddha, found two miles south of Nālandā (*fig.* 4.1), which is more than 12 ft (3.7 m) tall, making it the largest known ninth to twelfth century monolithic Buddha to survive. The massive scale, quality of carving, and use of expensive imported schist (Asher 1998: 313-28) all suggest a rich patron. The Buddha is shown touching the ground at the moment of his enlightenment; stylized *bodhi* tree branches above his head place this event at Bodh-Gayā. He is surrounded by seven scenes that show the great events of his life numbered among the *aṣṭamahāprātihārya* (eight great miracles). Each of these places was a Buddhist pilgrimage center active in north India at this time. Small images of the multi-armed goddess Marīcī placed on side panels of the base are also present (Bautze-Picron 2001: 270-72, figs. 9-11). The image would have been accessible to a variety of audiences coming out of both the lay and monastic communities, but how it was venerated remains an open question.

Given the clear link to the Buddha's life events that, at this time, were active places of pilgrimage, this kind of imagery is open to many levels of interpretation. Hence, it could have served Buddhists having a range of ideological interests, including those espousing ideas coming out of the Nikāya and Mahāyāna traditions. A Chinese translation of *Aṣṭamahāprātihāryastotra* indicates that by this time a Tāntric interpretation of the Buddha's life events had also been established (Woodward 1990: 18), so this kind of image could have appealed to Vajrayāna practitioners as well. This is important because Buddhists from all of these traditions were traveling great distances to visit the monasteries and pilgrimage sites of the Ganges basin, as well as to study and translate texts in an effort to understand the true nature of the Buddhist *dharma.*

To characterize the ideological interests of a specific site, or at least the interests of the donor community who was commissioning expensive images, I begin by considering the major sculptures from Nālandā. These stone images would have been part of the sacred area, being placed in shrines and on *stūpas,* though some of the smallest images may have been used by monks in their cells for personal devotion. A total of 168 stone images were brought to light by excavations at this site (List 4.1 and Chart 4.1). It is not surprising that images of the Buddha are most popular and make up 33 percent of the images and that a similar pattern is observed at all the north and east Indian sites under consideration. The fact that crowned Buddhas make up 5 percent of the recovered images is significant, though their specific meaning has been much debated (Bautze-Picron 2010: 1-7, 107-08). The prevalence of images of Avalokiteśvara speaks to the established significance of this important Mahāyāna *bodhisattva*; they make up 14 percent of the recovered sculpture. The other two relatively numerous deities are Tārā (8 percent) and Mañjuśrī (6 percent), both of whom must have been significant components of the religious life of the Nalāndā community.

While much less numerous, esoteric deities are also a significant

Buddha	38
Crowned Buddha	9
Eight great sites with central Buddha	8
Avalokiteśvara	23
Mañjuśrī	10
Tārā	14
Maitreya	1
Birth of Buddha	1
Descent at Sankasya	1
Parinirvāṇa	2
Nālandā Esoteric Iconography	
Marīcī	9
Vajrapāṇi	4
Aparājita	2
Trailokavijaya	1
Vajrasattva	1
Yamāntaka	1
Heruka	1
Multi-armed Avalokiteśvara	2
Manasara	1
Vasudhārā	3
Nālandā Popular Deities	
Jambhala	8
Nāgarāja	1
Nāginī	1
Nālandā Hindu Deities	
Viṣṇu	13
Liṅga	1
Pārvatī	1
Umāmaheśvara	2
Gaṇeśa	3
Cāmuṇḍā	2
Durgā	2
Revanta	2
Sūrya	2
Saptamātṛkās	2
Jain Images	
Ṛṣabhanātha	2
Pārśvanātha	1

List 4.1: Nālandā stone sculpture

component of the stone images from Nālandā. In this group, the most popular is the fierce protector Goddess Marīcī, a wrathful manifestation of Tārā, whose images make up 5 percent of the stone sculptures (Bautze-Picron 2001). This mirrors the general growing popularity of all forms of Tārā at this time. While other esoteric protectors occur as attendants, veneration of them in the form of large independent stone images is limited; three Vajrapāṇi images and a large sculpture of Heruka merit notice (Linrothe 1999: 33, 307-08). Based on this stone image count, it would seem that esoteric deities were important, though they make up only 15 percent of the stone devotional images recovered at Nālandā.

Popular deities, in particular Jambhala, are important and make up 6 percent of the image production, following a long-established pattern going back to the earliest Buddhist sites. More difficult to interpret are the thirty Hindu devotional images, which comprise 18 percent of the image production. Were these deities venerated by the Buddhist community or did the site possibly have a period of Hindu occupation (Verardi 2011: 363-64)?

A great many bronzes were found at Nālandā, and I began with the assumption that this group would be iconographically more esoteric, as they would seem better suited to private veneration by monks. Typical of this group are seventeen bronzes found in Monastery 9. In all, 233 bronzes were found at Nālandā (List 4.2 and Chart 4.2). Again, the Buddha, Avalokiteśvara, and Tārā are most common; together they make up 63 percent of the images. The emphasis on the female deities Tārā and Prajñāpāramitā is noteworthy as representations of them are only slightly less numerous than those of male *bodhisattvas.*

The fifteen esoteric deities found at the site constitute only 6 percent of the bronzes recovered at Nālandā; in contrast, esoteric images make up 15 percent of the stone image production at this

Buddha	77	Four-headed Avalokiteśvara	1
Crowned Buddha	1	Multi-armed Avalokiteśvara	1
Avalokiteśvara	37	Multi-armed Tārā	3
Mañjuśrī	9		
Bodhisattva	20	**Nālandā Bronze Hindu Images**	
Tārā	33	Viṣṇu	5
Prajñāpāramitā	15	Śiva	2
Birth of Buddha	1	Pārvatī	2
Maitreya	2	Sarasvatī	1
		Gaṇeśa	2
Nālandā Bronze Esoteric Images		Umāmaheśvara	1
Ṣaḍakṣarī Lokeśvara	1	Sūrya	2
Bhṛkuṭī	1		
Trailokavijaya	1	**Nālānda Bronze Popular Deities**	
Vajrasattva	3	Jambhala	12
Vasudhārā	1	Hārīti	2
Cūṇḍā	1	Nāgarāja	1
Marīcī	2		

List 4.2: Nālandā bronze sculptures

site. In general, most of the bronze esoteric deities appear as single examples, though Vajrasattva, Marīcī, and multi-armed Tārās are each represented by two or three images. While I had guessed that the portable bronzes would have been more esoteric in character, as they could have been used in private contexts, this does not appear to be the case. The fact that the bronzes reflect mainstream, longstanding iconographic patterns suggests they were instead given as acts of pious devotion.

This emphasis on the Buddha, Avalokiteśvara, and Tārā occurs at many earlier sites across India and is especially evident at the western Deccan sites of Ajantā, Ellorā, Nasik, and Kānherī. While we can only speculate about the reasons for donating bronzes of these specific subjects at Nālandā, it would seem that this site was aligned with mainstream ideological sentiments already established centuries earlier.

Given the expense of donating a stone or bronze image, it seems clear that this pattern reflects powerful elite interests. In this light, the emerging Vajrayāna tradition appears to have been only a small part of this overall picture. For example, a spectacular twelve-armed Amoghapāśa Avalokiteśvara of the eighth or ninth century CE from Nālandā is the only example of its type in Bihar and does not represent a major image category. Nevertheless, large icons like this or the Heruka from Nālandā clearly signal the importance of emerging Vajrayāna practices. I wondered if the Nālandā data reflected a regional trend so I expanded the scope of inquiry to include the excavated site of Antichak and the hoard of bronzes found near Nālandā at the site of Kurkihār. Expanding the data set also has the potential of providing better statistical results.

Kurkihār

In 1847 Markham Kittoe first noticed the site of Kurkihār and at that time collected "ten cart-loads" of stone images, some of which are in the Indian Museum in Kolkata (Patil 1963: 221). This initial discovery led to surveys by Alexander Cunningham and later Aurel

Buddha	23	Trailokavijaya	1
Crowned Buddha	18		
Avalokiteśvara	19	**Popular Deities**	
Mañjuśrī	5	Jambhala	1
Bodhisattva	5	Hārīti	1
Tārā	18		
Prajñāpāramitā	1	**Hindu Deities**	
		Viṣṇu	3
Esoteric Images		Umāmaheśvara	1
Hayagrīva	1	Balarāma	1
Multi-armed Tārā	1	Pārvatī	1
Parṇaśabarī	5	Saptamātṛkās	1
Vasudhārā	3		

List 4.3: Kurkihār bronze sculptures

Stein. Then in 1930, a hoard of 226 bronzes was found (Patil 1963: 221-26). Though scholars have addressed individual objects from this large group, no systematic publication of these bronzes exists. However, the most important works are on view in the Patna Museum, and many of the significant bronzes appear together in the American Institute for Indian Studies photo archive, which documents 109 of these metal sculptures (List 4.3 and Chart 4.3). The iconographic distribution of these bronzes follows a pattern similar to that observed at Nālandā. One noteworthy difference is the appearance of many crowned Buddhas, 15 percent of the total recovered imagery (Bautze-Picron 2010: 70). Buddhas and crowned Buddhas form the largest group, together comprising 73 percent of the images, followed by large numbers of Avalokiteśvara and Tārā images. As at Nālandā, images of Mañjuśrī consistently appear as a small group. Esoteric deities make up 10 percent of the documented images, which falls between the Nālandā stone and bronze percentages. Some Hindu images are part of the Kurkihār group, but the significance of these data is hard to interpret given our limited understanding of this site. Thus, while this hoard came out of an uncontrolled excavation and only part of it was available for study, the proportionate distribution of imagery nonetheless mirrors that observed at Nālandā.

Antichak

Another site that offers useful data is the massive *mahāvihāra* of Antichak in eastern Bihar, which was likely the site of Vikramaśilā discussed in the Tibetan sources (Asher 1975: 107-13; Verma 2011). This fortified monastic enclosure is more than 1,000 ft on each side, making it the largest surviving monastery in all of South Asia. We know about the destruction of Vikramaśilā from the 1234 CE account of the Tibetan translator and pilgrim Dharmasvāmin (Verma 2011: 5, 431; Sanderson 2009: 88).

Compared to Nālandā, far fewer sculptures were excavated, but the eighty recovered stone and bronze images constitute a small yet significant group (List 4.4 and Chart 4.4) (Verma 2011: 235-308, 337-45). The presence of twenty-five Hindu deities, 31 percent of the total, would seem to indicate Hindu practitioners later occupied the site (Verardi 2011: 366). Some of these images, however, may date to the period of Buddhist occupation.

Antichak Bronze Images	
Buddha	2
Crowned Buddha	1
Avalokiteśvara	3
Tārā	1
Mañjuśrī	1
Vajrapāṇi	1
Antichak Stone Images	
Buddha	10
Crowned Buddha	3
Eight Great Life Events	4
Tathāgata Buddha	3
Avalokiteśvara	9
Tārā	6
Antichak Stone Esoteric Deities	
Ṣaḍakṣarīlokeśvara	2
Manasā	2
Mahākāla	1
Aparājita	1
Bhairava	1
Acala	2
Antichak Stone Popular Deities	
Jambhala	2
Antichak Stone Hindu Images	
Sūrya	7
Viṣṇu	3
Liṅga	2
Umāmaheśvara	1
Durgā	1
Cāmuṇḍā	1
Pārvatī	1
Gaṇeśa	4
Agni	1
Kāma	1
Vaiṣṇavī	1
Kumārī	1
Vāyu	1

List 4.4: Antichak bronze and stone sculptures

The breakdown of devotional Buddhist images reveals patterns that seem related to Nālandā and Kurkihār; the Buddha, Avalokiteśvara, and Tārā are the most prevalent Buddhist deities, making up 81 percent of the recovered Buddhist images. Relative to the total number of Buddhist images a slightly greater proportion of the deities are esoteric; they compose 17 percent of the total. Although this would seem to agree with Tibetan sources that describe Vikramaśilā as a center for Vajrayāna practice, they are nevertheless a small component of the total extant corpus.

While some scholars have characterized Bihar as being primarily Mahāyāna in orientation, extant palm-leaf manuscripts and Tibetan translations of north Indian Tāntric Sanskrit texts, indicate that Vajrayāna was an important component of north Indian Buddhist literature (Kinnard 1996: 281-300). Given the dominance of the Vajrayāna tradition in Tibet, especially after the thirteenth century, there has been a tendency to see Bihar as being similarly focused on esoteric practices. While it must be the case that Tāntric texts existed, and that Vajrayāna ritual was taking place, it would seem that this was only a secondary component of a large, relatively conservative Buddhist tradition that emphasized Mahāyāna and Nikāya ideas related to the historical Buddha Śākyamuni and his actions. Certainly, the evidence of durable image production listed above suggests that esoteric Vajrayāna practice was limited in importance; this kind of imagery occurs about as frequently as popular gods like Jambhala or the Hindu deities present at all the north Indian monasteries.

Following Tibetan tradition, it seems that Tāntric ritual could have been done in secret. If this were the case, it would naturally require the production of portable devotional imagery such as painted cloth *paṭas*, which could easily be rolled up and removed from view. Indian Sanskrit texts such as the *Mañjuśrīmūlakalpa* and *Viṣṇudharmottara Purāṇa* describe *paṭa* painting techniques in detail and speak of their religious efficacy, so it is reasonable to assume that *paṭa* painting was a component of image production (Kossak

2010: 26-27, 45-46). This may help us to understand why *tangka* painting on cloth became important to the Buddhist communities in Nepal and Tibet starting in the eleventh century CE. Because no *paṭa* paintings survive from north India, however, we have no way to assess this tradition, but it is interesting that the earliest Tibetan *tangkas* are not particularly esoteric in character. Rather they tend to follow the aforementioned trends emphasizing the Buddha (in the form of the various *tathāgatas*), Avalokiteśvara, and Tārā.

Ratnagiri

Farther to the east, in Odisha and Bangladesh, many esoteric deities have been recovered, and it seems that Tantra was more important to these Buddhist communities. Fortunately, the site of Ratnagiri in Odisha was systematically excavated, and the large body of recovered sculpture provides a useful point of comparison with the Bihar sites. This center is outside of the Buddhist heartland characterized by pilgrimage places, such as Bodh-Gayā or the massive monastic complexes. Scholars have understood Ratnagiri to be Vajrayāna in orientation, but a consideration of the recovered imagery can help us to understand the significance of this ideology. The 163 images recovered here broadly correspond to the pattern observed at the Bihar sites (List 4.5 and Chart 4.5); images of the Buddha, Avalokiteśvara, Tārā, and Mañjuśrī make up 75 percent of the devotional sculpture from the sacred area and monasteries. The esoteric images, as in Bihar, appear to be of secondary importance because they compose only 14 percent of the production. In contrast, however, the Ratnagiri sculptural forms are iconographically more complex, especially the secondary figures, and the iconography is less standard than that observed in Bihar. Certainly, the imagery is open to a much broader range of ideological interpretations. Interestingly, images of Hindu deities make up only 4 percent of the total, fewer than any of the Bihar monastic sites.

fig. 4.1: The Buddha reaching enlightenment at Bodh-Gayā surrounded by the additional seven Great Pilgrimage sites associated with the life of Śākyamuni, *circa* tenth-eleventh centuries CE, stone

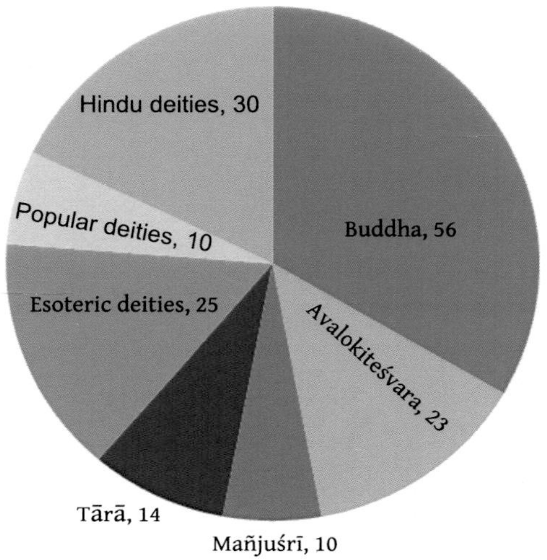

Chart 4.1: Nālandā stone sculptures (168 images)

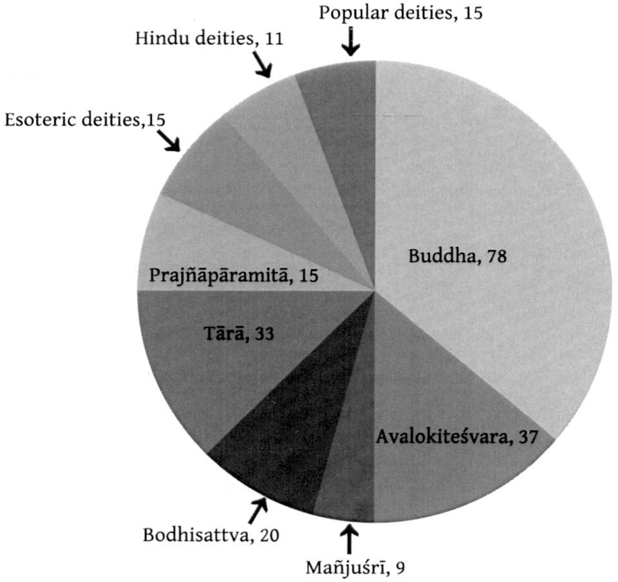

Chart 4.2: Nālandā bronze sculptures (233 images)

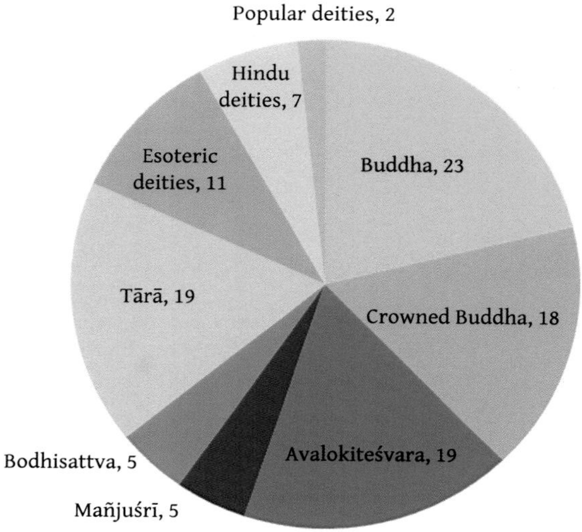

Chart 4.3: Kurkihār bronze sculptures (109 images)

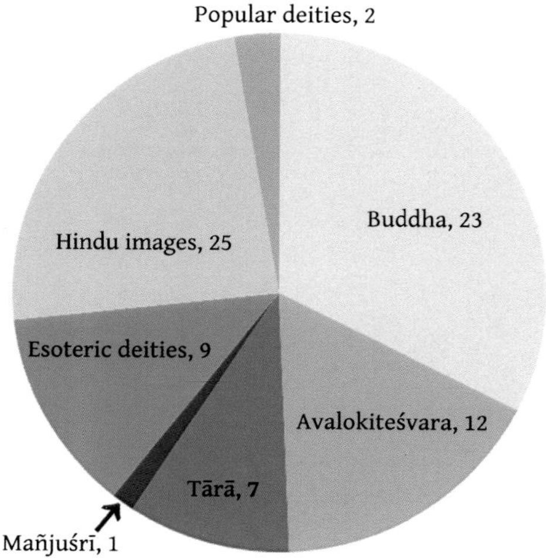

Chart 4.4: Antichak stone and bronze sculptures (72 images)

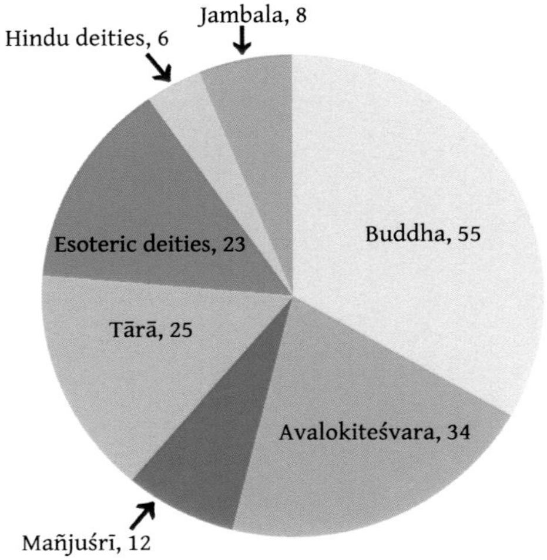

Chart 4.5: Ratnagiri stone and bronze sculptures from the sacred area and monasteries (163 images)

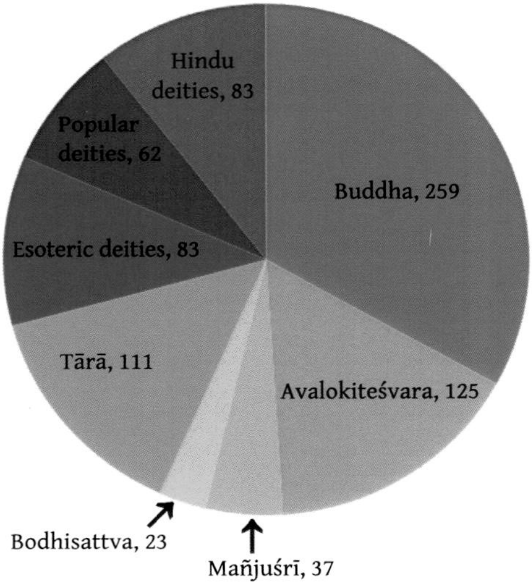

Chart 4.6: Total stone and bronze sculptures from Nālandā, Kurkihār, Antichak, and Ratnagiri (759 images)

Buddha	45
Crowned Buddha	1
Avalokiteśvara	33
Tārā	23
Mañjuśrī	9
Maitreya	1
Esoteric Stone Images	
Multi-armed Avalokiteśvara	8
Multi-armed Tārā 1	
Aṣṭamahābhaya Tārā 2	
Cūṇḍā	3
Vajrasattva	2
Mañjuvajra	2
Vajrapāṇi	2
Uṣṇīṣavījayā	1
Saṁvara	1
Mahākāla	1
Heruka	1
Aparājitā Tārā	1
Popular Deities	
Jambhala	8
Bronzes	
Buddha	9
Avalokiteśvara	1
Mañjuśrī	3
Maitreya	1
Yamāri	1
Jambhala	2
Hindu Stone Images	
Liṅga	3
Gaṇeśa	2
Durgā	1

List 4.5: Ratnagiri stone and bronze images

Combined Data

A clear and repeating pattern emerges among the bronzes and the stone devotional images that survive in considerable numbers across the Buddhist centers of Nālandā, Kurkihār, Antichak, and Ratnagiri. Moreover, the fact that a recurring subject matter distribution exists across multiple sites suggests that the stone and bronze image data are statistically relevant and reveal the dominant interests of the patron groups responsible for the expensive images found in the sacred areas. If all of the above data are compiled, the 759 stone and bronze images provide a distribution that mirrors that of the individual sites (Chart 4.6). This consistency across sites suggests that the large data set is valid and representative. Also telling is the fact that combining the small bronzes with the large stone devotional images did not significantly change the overall distribution pattern. Therefore, it seems that the iconographic distributions of stone and bronze images are broadly similar.

A few tentative conclusions can be drawn from these data.

Clearly, north Indian Buddhist practice overwhelmingly involved the veneration of Buddha images. I want to emphasize that the exact identification of some of these Buddhas is not always clear. In some instances, as with the Jagdishpur Buddha, there is no question that it is Śākyamuni. However, many of the Buddha figures could be one of the five *tathāgatas* (Vairocana, Amitābha, Ratnasambhava, Akṣobhya, and Amoghasiddhi). The veneration of Avalokiteśvara appears to have been extremely important and, among the esoteric images, there are many variations of this deity. Mañjuśrī was also important; while images of him represent only 5 percent of the total, they consistently appear in significant numbers at all of the north Indian sites. Like Avalokiteśvara, this *bodhisattva* had considerable popularity in Nepal and Tibet. In contrast, Maitreya is hardly ever represented; only three images of this deity appear in the overall sample. Tara's importance is attested by the fact that her images make up 15 percent of the corpus. Representations of Prajñāpāramitā are also common. Among the esoteric deities, many are ferocious manifestations of Tārā, with Marīcī being especially common. The fact that esoteric deities account for only 11 percent of the total is significant. Aside from Marīcī, Vajrapāṇi, Vajrasattva, and Cūṇḍā, most of the esoteric deities are known from only one or two examples. The great diversity of different esoteric deities indicates that they were known from texts even if they were not regularly depicted in sculpture. Identification of them is only possible because the images adhere to descriptions provided in Tāntric or other Vajrayāna textual sources. Popular deities, especially Jambhala, but also including Hārīti and *nāgas*, consistently appear at all of the monastic centers. Perhaps this is not surprising, as they have a long history in the Buddhist tradition.

Representations of Hindu gods make up 11 percent of the total. While the Buddhist sites could have later been occupied by Hindu communities, thus explaining the presence of these images, in some instances the sculptures were found in monasteries or other contexts that indicate they were being venerated by the Buddhists.

The fact that so many Hindu images were found and that they appear at all of the Buddhist centers is significant. In Nepal and Tibet, Hindu deities were incorporated into the Buddhist canon and often appear as secondary figures. Perhaps this practice started in India, where the ideological function and efficacy of these deities were well understood.

While the nature of the Buddhist traditions of Bihar and Odisha as gleaned from the imagery from the *mahāvihāras* of north India remains incomplete, this evidence suggests that we must be cautious with regard to the relative importance of north Indian Tāntric or Vajrayāna practices. It is clear, however, that long-standing image practices remained important to the Buddhist communities active from the ninth to twelfth centuries CE. How all of this went on to impact the Buddhist communities in places like Nepal, Tibet, or Myanmar is beyond the scope of this paper, nonetheless these data raise a host of interesting questions that merit further research.

References

Asher, Frederick, 1975, "Vikramasila Mahavihara," *Bangladesh Lalit Kala — Journal of the Dacca Museum*, 1(2): 107-13.

——, 1998, "Stone and the Production of Images," *East and West*, 48(3/4): 313-28.

Bautze-Picron, Claudine, 2001, "Between Śākyamuni and Vairocana: Mārīcī, Goddess of Light and Victory," *Silk Road Art and Archaeology*, 7: 263-310.

——, 2010, *The Bejeweled Buddha from India to Burma: New Considerations*, New Delhi: Sanctum Books.

——, 2014, *The forgotten Place: Stone Images from Kurkihar, Bihar*, New Delhi: Archaeological Survey of India.

Beal, Samuel (tr.), 1969 [first published 1884], *Si-Yu-Ki, Buddhist Records of the Western World Translated from the Chinese of HiuenTsiang* A.D. *629*, 2 vols., Delhi: Munshiram Manoharlal.

Chimpa, Alaka Chattopadhyaya (tr.), 2010 [first published 1981], *Tāranātha's History of Buddhism in India*, Delhi: Motilal Banarsidass.

Hiuen Tsiang (Xuanzang), see Beal 1969.

Huntington, Susan, 1984, *Stone Sculptures of Bihar*, Leiden: Brill.

I-Tsing (Yijing), see Takakusu 1896.

Kinnard, Jacob, 1996, "Reevaluating the Eighth–Ninth Century Pāla Milieu: Icono-Conservatism and the Persistence of Śākyamuni," *Journal of the International Association of Buddhist Studies*, 19(2): 281-300.

Kossak, Steven, 2010, *Painted Images of Enlightenment: Early Tibetan Thankas, 1050–1450*, Mumbai: Marg Publications.

Lalou, Marcelle, 1930, *Iconographie des étoffes peintes (paṭa) dans le Mañjuśrīmūlakalpa*, Paris: Geuthner.

Linrothe, Rob, 1999, *Ruthless Compassion*, Boston: Shambhala Press.

Mani, C. (ed.), 2008, *The Heritage of Nalanda*, New Delhi: Aryan Books.

Mitra, Debala, 1981 and 1983, *Ratnagiri*, 2 vols., New Delhi: Archaeological Survey of India.

Nath, Birendra, 1983, *Nalanda Murals*, New Delhi: Cosmo Publications.

Patil, D., 1963, *The Antiquarian Remains in Bihar*, Patna: Kashi Prasad Jayaswal Research Institute.

Sanderson, Alexis, 1995, "Meaning in Tantric Ritual," in *Essais sur le rituel: Colloque du centenaire de la Section des sciences religieuses de l'École pratique des hautes études*, vol. 3, ed. Anne-Marie Blondeau and Kristofer Schipper, pp. 15-95, Bibliothèque de l'École des hautes études, Section des sciences religieuses, no. 102, Louvain: Peeters.

——, 2009, "The Śaiva Age: The Rise and Dominance of Śaivism during the Early Medieval Period," in *Genesis and Development of Tantrism*, ed. Shingo Einoo, pp. 41-350 , Tokyo: Institute of Oriental Culture University of Tokyo.

Schopen, Gregory, 1987, "Burial 'Ad Sanctos' and the Physical Presence of the Buddha in Early Indian Buddhism: A Study in the Archaeology of Religions," *Religion*, 17: 193-225.

Stewart, M., 2016, *Nalanda Mahavihara: A Critical Analysis of the Archaeology of an Indian Buddhist Site*, Delhi: Manohar Publishers.

Takakusu, J. (tr.), 1896, *A Record of the Buddhist Religion as Practised in India and the Malay Archipelago (A.D. 671–695)*, Oxford: Clarendon Press.

Verardi, Giovanni, 2011, *Hardships and Downfall of Buddhism in India*, New Delhi: Manohar Publishers.

Verma, B.S., 2011, *Antichak Excavations-2 (1971–81), Memoirs of the Archaeological Survey of India*, no. 102, New Delhi: Archaeological Survey of India.

Woodward, Hiram, 1990, "The Life of the Buddha in the Pala Monastic Environment," *Journal of the Walters Art Gallery*, 48: 13-27.

5

Rasa and Darśana in Indian Temple Sculpture

Debashish Banerji

THE early pioneers of Indian Art History, such as E.B. Havell (1861–1934) and Ananda Coomaraswamy (1877–1947), conceived of a distinct identity for "Indian Art," theorizing it as "spiritual" in contrast to a "naturalistic" Western canon (Guha-Thakurta 1995: 78). As an important part of this representation, they pointed to *rasa* theory as the foundation of its aesthetics (Coomaraswamy 1918: 30-37; 1934: 51, 55).[1] Nationalist artists and ideologues, such as Abanindranath Tagore (1871–1951), his disciples, and art critics related to his school of art followed this characterization (Guha-Thakurta 1992: 100). Later scholars, including Western Indologists such as Stella Kramrisch (1896–1993) and Indian art historians to this day, such as B.N. Goswamy (b. 1933), have persisted in this categorization of Indian art (Goswamy 1986: 17-30, 1994: 188-92; Kramrisch 1994: 270).[2]

Undoubtedly, the importance of *rasa* theory cannot be denied in Indian culture and it is pervasive to this day, but it is important to unravel the various registers and nuances in what has been

[1] Coomaraswamy (1918: 30) attributes the theory of *rasa* to "poetics and drama" but claims its extension to "all arts alike."

[2] Kramrisch considers *rasa-citra* from the traditional *śilpa* text *Śilparatna*, which she translates as "pictures of emotion," relating different emotions to specific colors. Goswamy consistently narrativizes Indian painting within the discourse of *rasa* aesthetics.

universally categorized as Indian art. Does *rasa* mean the same thing in the context of courtly painting and temple sculpture? Is it even appropriate to think of the latter context in terms of *rasa*? In the cultural experience of temple visits in India, the term *rasa* is seldom used, while the term *darśana* is ubiquitous. How does *darśana* work in the visual aesthetics of a temple visit? Does it have any relationship with *rasa*? This paper is an attempt to explore some of these questions and in particular, how *rasa* and *darśana* may have worked in the Indian temple context. As is well known in Indian anthropology, there are many cultural practices which lack textual formalization, yet are ubiquitous (Parker 2003: 5-8). Indian religious sculpture, particularly in the temple context, finds its reality at the confluence of elite patronage, art-making canons, ritual demands, and popular use. What I propose here is the development of oral practices in popular use and perhaps art making, based on the translation of popular philosophemes into specific cultural environments. I use the term "philosopheme" here in the sense given by Jacques Derrida and R. Klein (1981: 2) to refer to conceptual complexes which move out of their original context and enter into the cultural imaginary in a variety of contexts, creating unauthorized hybrid realities. Philosophemes are not "owned" by ideologies and freely translate across ideological borders (if they are utilized by an ideology as an identity factor, they turn to "ideologemes"). Early contemplative texts, such as the Upaniṣads, provide us with many examples of philosophemes which are pervasive across Indian culture to this day. It is not easy to trace the history of movement of philosophemes, because they belong to oral culture, and thus follow the unmarked translations of "spoken language". Yet the slippage between textual authority and popular culture will remain invisible unless oral processes such as the operation of philosophemes are theorized and probed. This paper is a speculative attempt to trace the combined working of *rasa* and *darśana* in Indian religious visual practice, through the mediation of a philosopheme.

The Rasas and the Visual Arts

In a simple (though inadequate) translation, *rasa* could be called "taste" and/or "emotion". We will consider the nuances of this term in greater detail later. Its origins are found in the *Taittitrīya Upaniṣad,* whose second chapter, Ānanda Vallī (II.7.1), ends with the line *raso vai saḥ* (He is *rasa* itself); but its theoretical foundations were laid in the sixth chapter of Bharata's *Nāṭyaśāstra*, a text dated between the second century BCE and first century CE (Ghosh 1950). Bharata established the canon for eight *rasas* (expressed and experienced emotions) and their corresponding *bhāvas* (states) of subjective being. We may enumerate these *rasas* and associated *bhāvas* as:

- *Śṛngāraṁ* (श्रृंगारं) : Love, attractiveness. *Bhāva*: *Rati* (Eros)
- *Hāsyaṁ* (हास्यं): Laughter, mirth, comedy. *Bhāva*: *Hāsya* (Humour)
- *Raudraṁ* (रौद्रं): Fury. *Bhāva*: *Krodha* (Anger)
- *Kāruṇyaṁ* (कारुण्यं): Compassion, mercy. *Bhāva*: *Śoka* (Sorrow)
- *Bībhatsaṁ* (बीभत्सं): Disgust, aversion. *Bhāva*: *Jugupsā* (Repulsing)
- *Bhayānakaṁ* (भयानकं): Horror, terror. *Bhāva*: *Bhaya* (Fear)
- *Vīraṁ* (वीरं): Heroic mood. *Bhāva*: *Utsāha* (Enthusiasm)
- *Adbhutaṁ* (अद्भुतं): Wonder, amazement. *Bhāva*: *Vismaya* (Amazement)

Sometime between the sixth and ninth centuries, a ninth *rasa*, *śāntam* (peace) was added to this system. The tenth-century Śaiva *yogī*, philosopher, and aesthetician from Kashmir, Abhinavagupta (*c*.950–1020) wrote a definitive commentary on Bharata's *Nāṭyaśāstra* in which this ninth *rasa* was conceived as the most important in the set, necessary for coexistence with any of the others to effectuate its spiritual function (Schechner 2001: 27-50). He identified the *bhāva* of *śāntam rasa* as *ātman*, the presence of the divine self in the human. It is important to note here that Bharata's characterization of *rasa* theory pertained mainly to dramaturgy and dance drama. By

Abhinavagupta's time, *rasa* had come to encompass theater, dance, and poetry, both spoken and read (Pollock 2018: 6). One cannot be sure if Bharata meant for *rasa* to be the profoundly spiritual transmission that Abhinavagupta interpreted it to be.

Rāmacandra and Guṇacandra, the twelfth-century Jaina authors of *Nāṭyadarpaṇa* interpreted *rasa* as a "worldly" experience and eschewed the "other-worldly" (*alaukika*) or spiritual sense given to the theory by Abhinavagupta and others of that persuasion (Trivedi 1966). It is also not clear whether Bharata's theory is related primarily to an aristocratic class. In Abhinavagupta's characterization, *rasa* is clearly a courtly and aristocratic phenomenon, a receptive connoisseurship of the trained *rasika* (enjoyer of *rasa*) or *sahṛdaya* (well-educated sympathetic spectator). It should also be noted that neither in Bharata nor in Abhinavagupta is *rasa* theory applied explicitly to static visual arts; it is concerned with the performance arts. This does not mean that the treatises or oral practices of art making did not include references to *rasa* theory, but its adaptations are not as obvious as Indologists have concluded.

Darśana and Temple Sculpture

Relating these ideas to temple sculpture, one must note important deviations. Although aristocratic patrons may have been involved in sponsoring temple construction, temple sculpture — which is mostly featured on the outer walls — is generally available to all visitors without class expectations.[3] Moreover, sculpture is not a performative form,[4] and exists primarily for religious relation. Particularly for modern Hindus, a visit to the temple is not one

[3] The point here concerns the popular nature of temple worship and access to figurative representations of deities. Some temples have caste restrictions for inner entry and some refuse entry to non-Hindus, yet there are many instances of known relations of authorized and unauthorized worshipers with surface images, with the temple itself or with "invisible" deity-forms in the proximity of the temple.

[4] I qualify this proposition later in the text.

they associate with *rasa*. This could, of course, be due to changes in practice and expectation; or it could be that *rasa* is a mistaken category to apply to the encounter with Indian temple sculpture.[5] More prevalent in the common temple experience is the idea of *darśana*, which literally means "sight." In the Indian spiritual context, it can mean one of four things: a spiritual philosophy, a visit to a spiritually realized person (often one's *guru*), a visit to a sacred pilgrimage site — which may or may not include a built structure (*tīrtha darśana*) — and a visit to a temple (Eck 1998: 3). In the case of a visit to a spiritually realized person, *darśana* means to see and be seen, a reciprocity of consciousness, with the possible eventuality of a loss of personal ego and the experience of a state of non-duality. In the case of the temple, a similar reciprocity and experience is often sought, with the difference that here "the other" is physically not a human or living being yet is considered as such by the devotee (ibid.: 6-7).

Hindu temple culture works on the assumption that the temple is a space of divine consciousness centered in the principal deity but pervading all the objects, deities, and the structure of the temple itself (Davis 2000: 61–64). Of course, the visual order of the temple space is also a ritual order, and the relationship between devotee and deity is a ritually mediated one. This mediation is performative (more of this later) with its climatic event staged as the exchange between devotee and deity mediated by the *pūjā* in the *garbhagṛha*. However, this ritual mediation is not absolute or exclusive, as independent agency is assumed for both deity and devotee,[6] which might result in a moment of *darśana* at any point in the visit. A devotee may visit a temple or attend a *pūjā* for a variety of reasons, ranging from the acquisition of material, emotional, and/or social benefits to the gaining of spiritual merit, freedom

[5] In the next section, I will consider the elite inscription of *rasa* theory in texts and examples of temple sculpture.

[6] This is particularly true for the deity, whose agency, as grace (*anugraha*) subsumes all else and is absolute (Davis 2000: 160-62).

from *karma,* cessation from rebirth (*punarjanma*), and/or spiritual freedom (*mokṣa*) through relation or identity with the deity.[7] In all these cases, however, this aim forms part of the devotee's relationship to the independent cosmic agency of the deities, and the devotee seeks for confirmation of this relationship through physical (*sthūla*) or "subtle" (*sūkṣma*) experiences of reciprocity and at its limit, non-duality. In a specialized sense, *darśana* is an optically mediated experience of this kind.

Though such a conjecture relates more properly to the premodern temple experience, a residue of these attitudes continues within the modern temple imaginary.[8] As part of this continuing expectation, temple visitors speak of their visit synonymously as "going for *darśana*" of the deity, usually referring to the principal shrine (*garbhagṛha*) image; but sometimes a niche image on the outer walls; an entity, physical or "subtle" (*sūkṣma deha*), in or around the temple; or the temple itself, seen as a three-dimensional geometric representation (*yantra*) of the deity (Eck 1998: 62-63; Kramrisch 1976: 165). In the case of an iconic or anthropomorphic form of embodiment (*arcā*), it is the eyes that become the medium of exchange and identity, which is why Hindu deities in anthropomorphic form are typically depicted frontally with large staring eyes. The most prominent example of this is the

[7] Śaiva Āgama texts divide temple visitors into two types, those that seek worldly enjoyment (*bubhukṣu*) and those that seek spiritual liberation (*mumukṣu*) (Davis 2000: 46).

[8] It is difficult to fix a time period when such a practice may have originated. Even Diana Eck in her eponymous text (1998) has been unable to provide direct textual sources for the origins of temple *darśana*. One could speculate that it might be related to the idea of the *arcā* (physical embodiment of deity in an image), which made its appearance in Pāñcarātra sectarian practice around the second century BCE and is referred to in the *Mahābhārata*. Today, at sites and among people with a stronger continuity with the past and less impacted by modernity, such as those belonging to rural ontologies, the social reality of *darśana* is more living than among urban populations.

Jagannātha triad at Purī, three images which are almost all eye (Eck 1998: 7). This is also the case with several Devī images, such as those of Kālī at Kālighāṭ or Dakṣiṇeśvara or of Durgā during the seasonal Durgā-Pūjā in Bengal. This specialized sense of *darśana* depends on figurative representation and the literalism of iconic embodiment of the deities. The reciprocal gazing of devotee and deity then becomes a form of physical contact through the eyes (Pinney 2004: 9). Theorizing this optical phenomenology for visual culture, Christopher Pinney (ibid.: 8) has coined the term "corpothetics," characterizing it as "embodied, corporeal aesthetics — as opposed to 'disinterested' representation, which over-cerebralizes and textualizes the image."

However, in popular practice, the term *darśana* is not used exclusively in this specialized sense, but, as mentioned above, synonymously with any temple visit. For the purpose of this essay, I will use this broader popular sense of *darśana*. *Garbhagṛha* deities are often represented in non-anthropomorphic form. In the case of Śiva, the *liṅga* is the most prominent form of the central image, while anthropomorphic images are usually found in the niches of the outer walls.[9] In the case of Viṣṇu or Devī, non-anthropomorphic forms such as the *śālagrāma* (ammonite fossil) for Viṣṇu or a natural object for Devī usually coexist with the anthropomorphic image. The idea of *darśana* in the case of non-anthropomorphic or symbolic forms lacks the mimetic reciprocity of anthropomorphic images with eyes, yet they are also seen as embodiments of divinity capable of communication, energy exchange, and the bestowal of gifts, including experiences of identity and/or non-duality (Davis 2000: 132-34, 160-61). The principal differences in experience, however, can be understood if we relate these forms to the soteriologies of which they are the center. The telos of Śaivism is liberation

[9] A striking exception is the image of the dancing form of Śiva (Naṭarāja) in the main shrine of the Śiva Temple at Cidambaram. However, there is supposed to be an invisible "astral" (*ākāśa*) *liṅga* form within the main shrine and a sub-temple with a *liṅga* in this temple complex.

(*mokṣa*) attained through identity (*yoga*) with Śiva (George 2008: 259-93).[10] The goal of *darśana* in this case is to see the object of *darśana* within and as oneself.[11] The telos of Vaiṣṇavism is to enjoy relationship with Viṣṇu/Kṛṣṇa (ibid.: 226-58).[12] The liberation (*mukti*) here is thought of as arising from proximity (*sāmīpya*) through residence in the same world (*sālokya*) and sharing likeness (*sādṛṣya*) and nature (*sādharmya*) with Viṣṇu/Kṛṣṇa seen as one's object of love. The telos of Śāktism is to be possessed by Devī. The liberation (*mukti*) here is to be related to Devī as her child and portion, yet also to be her instrument (*yantra*) through whom she may enjoy her world (*bhukti*) and in whom the fullness of her powers (*siddhi*) may manifest (Kempton 2013: 12-21, 28-30). From this we may imagine that *darśana* in the case of anthropomorphic forms belongs to soteriologies of relational nondualism that are world-affirming; while *darśana* in the case of non-anthropomorphic forms belong to soteriologies of monistic identity. However, the matter is more complicated than this, since the temple system for each of these deities includes both iconic and aniconic images in each case, with variant priorities. In the case of Viṣṇu or Devī, *darśana* may entail contemplation and realized relation with non-anthropomorphic forms in the *garbhagṛha*, but anthropomorphic relational exchange coexists with this. In the case of Śiva, *darśana* includes relation with anthropomorphic forms of Śiva as depicted in

---

[10] This is true for both of the major temple traditions of Śaivism, monistic Kashmir Śaivism, and pluralistic Śaiva Siddhānta. The goal of the first is attainment of identity with Śiva as transcendental and universal Consciousness, while that of the second is to realize one's true essence as "a Śiva," identical with the essence of Śiva though a different entity.

[11] "*Yogins* see Śiva in the soul and not in images. Images are meant for the imagination of the ignorant" (*Jābāladarśana Upaniṣad* III.59 as quoted in Eck 1998: 45).

[12] One may note the different schools of Vaiṣṇavism such as Viśiṣṭādvaita, Dvaita, Śuddhādvaita, Acintya Bhedābheda, and Puṣṭimārga. Though there are differences of doctrine and approach, all these schools hold their goal to be in intimate relation with Kṛṣṇa.

the outer wall niches (*devakoṣṭha*), but these may be thought of as a preparation for the final *darśana* of the non-anthropomorphic *liṅga*, entailing contemplation and identity arising from the awakening within oneself of the divinity, aided by ritual (Davis 2000: 62).[13] To include these variant forms of experience, *darśana*, then, cannot be restricted to figurative optical exchange, but one must expand its scope to "subtle" or "spiritual" vision and contact (*sūkṣma darśana*).

Rasa and Temple Sculpture

This returns us to *rasa*. Though Bharata and Abhinavagupta conceived of *rasa* as applicable to the performing arts, one of the earliest texts on visual art, the *Citrasūtra*, part of the *Viṣṇudharmottara Purāṇa*, carries a chapter enumerating the nine *rasa*s as emotive themes of painting, whether secular or religious. It is difficult to date this part of the *Citrasūtra* (chapter 43). It could be as early as the fifth century and as late as the ninth, but it is clear that an adaptation of *rasa* theory translated itself to the visual arts as well (Mukherji 2001). In a sense, this is not hard to imagine, because temple sculpture has always been known to have had a close relation to dance. Indian dance itself may be thought of as a continuum relating stillness and movement. Staccato postures alternate with flowing transitions. On the other hand, as I argue later here, the temple experience needs also to be seen as performative, the visitor encountering static images during circumambulation (*pradakṣiṇā*), thus experiencing a similar succession of movement and stillness in the process. Moreover, the production of *rasa* in performance is taken by Bharata to be achieved through three principal means: speech (*vācika*), gestures or actions (*āṅgika*), and costume (*āhārya*) (Ghosh 1950, VI.23). Of these, temple images re-enact only the *āṅgika*

13 Liberation (*mokṣa*) as identity with Śiva is common to all Śaiva schools though its nature and the means through which it arises in the case of *liṅga darśana* and ritual (*pūjā*) differs from sect to sect, such as the Śaiva Siddhānta, Mahāvratin, Pāśupata, Kāpālika, or Kashmir Śaiva schools (Davis 2000: 85).

visual aspects of facial expressions (*abhinaya*), body bends (*bhaṅga*), and coded gesture (*mudrā*). Starting with Cāḷukyan temples of about the eighth century but proliferating in number and complexity from the eleventh century, particularly in regions of major dance traditions such as Coḷa controlled Tamil Nadu, Hoysaḷa controlled Karnataka, as well as Odisha and Bundelkhand in eastern Madhya Pradesh, these elements are seen, manifesting mobile intermediate coded postures related to *rasa*s, called *karaṇa*s in the *Nāṭyaśāstra* (Nandagopal 1990). The *Nāṭyaśāstra* lists 108 *karaṇa*s, and the temple that depicts these most systematically and prominently is, as one might expect, the Naṭarāja Temple at Cidambaram.

This translation of *rasa* theory to the visual arts, however, finds less overt description and analysis in most Rasaśāstra texts and may thus be thought to include an unauthorized element. The elite "classical" tastes of patrons meet ritual traditions and popular practices in a negotiated space; and, we must think of less conventional ways to understand this hybrid adaptation to a religious use.[14] Courtly painting, though not performative, may more justifiably lend itself to the kind of reception response and theory of aesthetics and elite spirituality implied by Abhinavagupta. However, even there the use of *rasa* theory is not textually unequivocal. Though Stella Kramrisch translates *rasa-citra*, occurring in the twelfth-century *Śilparatna*, as "pictures of emotion," this is a questionable translation, the term being used as a designation for murals using paint (Kramrisch 1994: 270). Here the term *rasa* is more probably used in its sense as "liquid"

---

[14] The strong oral component of Indian culture must be considered to account for such slippages in the textual record in comparison to anthropological practice, as in Saussure's distinction between *langue* and *parole*. The lack of textual injunction in the case of visual practice in temples may also be seen in the more ubiquitous case of *darśana*. Narrative anthropological records may be found at some point to establish evidence. However, my essay is not evidentiary in nature; rather it makes a speculative or hypothetical case based on the virtual field of cultural potential and present practice.

or "wetness" to refer to the nature of paint, since *rasa-citra* is contrasted with *dhūli-citra*, meaning paintings made with "dust" or powdered paints (*Śilparatna* 46.143). The term *rasa-citra* is used similarly in a classification of paintings in another *śilpa* text of the twelfth century, the *Mānasollāsa* of King Someśvara III. This text, however, adds a classification type of *bhāva-citra*, which, more properly than *rasa-citra*, could be translated as "pictures of emotion" (Shrigondekar 1939: 79). This goes to show that the term *rasa* is less doctrinally defined in the context of art than in performative contexts.

In its most common sense, *rasa*, as a substance, means "flavorful juice" or "sap"; and as a subjective state, "taste." A kitchen is called *rasoī* in Hindi, after the flavoring substances used to add taste to food, and the sciences of alchemy and chemistry are known as *rasāyana* as they deal with liquids and salts, called *rasas*. The sense of flavor and fluidity is seen to predominate in all these cases. Highlighting these meanings, Victor Mair has presented a compelling argument for the derivation of the six canons of Chinese painting from the six limbs of painting (*ṣaḍaṅga*) from India (2004: 81–122). Although the earliest extant version of the *ṣaḍaṅga* comes from a thirteenth-century commentary on the *Kāmasūtra* by Yaśodhara (*Jayamaṅgalaṭīkā*), it is believed to have its origin in the fourth or fifth century CE, the period in which the Indian temple was formalized and both sculpture and painting developed a standard aesthetic (Agrawala 1981: 9, 16). The *ṣaḍaṅga* includes *bhāva* as one of the "limbs" of painting, but couples it with *lāvaṇya* rather than *rasa*, a word which today is taken to mean "gracefulness." Mair points to the synonymous connection between *lāvaṇya* and *rasa*, since *lavaṇa* means "salt" or "flavoring substance" (2004: 101). *Lāvaṇya* also connotes fluidity of the body. This gives us a key to the principal aesthetic means of Indian painting and sculpture, which is the fluid or rhythmic line. The quality of linear rhythm harmonizes the elements of the visual depiction, both body and environmental setting, and structures the characteristic *rasa*. We have already seen how such an aesthetic evolved by incorporating the *karaṇas* of "classical" dance based on the *Nāṭyaśāstra* into its visual vocabulary.

Another way in which *rasa* may be evoked in temple sculpture is through the dramatic presentation of climactic moments in narratives, drawing seamlessly on cultural imaginary. As with the *karaṇas* of dance, such representations function as metonyms of theatrical performance. Summarizing these forms of *rasa* experience in temple sculpture, one sees at least four ways in which *rasa* may have been meaningful in the temple context:

1. the visual experience of emotion carried by the fluid line;
2. the representations of *karaṇas* translated from performances of dance;
3. dramatic representations of climactic moments in narratives, translated from performances of theater; and
4. successive encounters with static images in the performance of circumambulation (*pradakṣiṇā*).

Temple Sculpture and the Rasa-Darśana System

Given these meanings, the combined working of *rasa* and *darśana* in the case of the visual arts of painting or sculpture in temple experience may be explored. The key to this thinking is that *rasa* is a mobile element of concentrated feeling in expression, *bhāva* is the static (*sthāyī*) "being" of the *rasa* in viewer experience and *darśana* is a reciprocal transpersonal relationship through "seeing" with the being expressed by the *bhāva* and *rasa*, opening to relational intimacy and identity. The social phenomenology of temple experience develops in a negotiated space of ritual convention, elite aesthetic convention, and popular understanding and expectation. As mentioned earlier in this text, there is a slippage between text and practice, particularly in the case of popular culture in India. Cultural philosophemes percolate to crystallize popular uses without formal textual authorization. An important philosopheme

fig. 5.1: *Mahākapi Jātaka*, Vedikā roundel, Bharhut Mahāstūpa, Bharhut, Madhya Pradesh, India, 100-80 BCE, sandstone

fig. 5.2: Durgā battling Mahiṣāsura, north wall, Mahiṣāsuramardinī Cave Temple, Māmallapuram (Mahābalipuram), Tamil Nadu, India, *circa* seventh century CE, granite

fig. 5.3: Viṣṇu-Anantaśayana, outer south wall, Viṣṇu Temple, Deogaṛh, Uttar Pradesh, India, *circa* early sixth century CE, sandstone

fig. 5.4: Nara–Nārāyaṇa, outer east wall, Viṣṇu Temple, Deogaṛh, Uttar Pradesh, India, *circa* early sixth century CE, sandstone

fig. 5.5: Gajendramokṣa, outer north wall, Viṣṇu Temple, Deogaṛh, Uttar Pradesh, India, *circa* early sixth century CE, sandstone

of this kind, derived from *yoga*, which has developed pervasive cultural currency in India is the three-step formula for identity in consciousness (*yoga*) of the *guru-śiṣya* transmission developed during the earliest phase of the Upaniṣads, *circa* eighth century BCE. We find this formula in the *Bṛhadāraṇyaka Upaniṣad*:

> *ātmāvā are dṛṣṭavyaḥ śrotravyomantavyonididhyāsitavyomaitreyi ātmanovā are darśanenaśravaṇenamantayāvijñānenedaṁ sarvaṁ viditam* ।
> — II.4.5.6
>
> It is the *ātman* that is meant to be seen, heard, cogitated about and realized, Maitreyī; By seeing, hearing, cogitating about the *ātman*, all here comes to be known.[15]

As one may see, this is a contemplative trope bridging a dualistic sensory experience having a soteriological goal of non-duality with the universal Self (*ātman*). In popular repetition in a variety of cultural contexts, it takes the formulaic form "*śravaṇa* [listening], *manana* [cogitation], *nididhyāsana* [realization of identity in consciousness]." This three-step process has taken on quasi-canonical cultural status in popular usage over the centuries.[16] The ritual context of temple worship is included among these. We find, for example, in the *Śiva Purāṇa*:

---

15 Translation by the author.

16 Various authorities of different schools of Vedāntic interpretation have referred to this Upaniṣadic formula as central to the *yoga* discipline (*sādhanā*) of their respective schools. For example, Śaṅkara (*c.*788–820), founder of Advaita Vedānta refers to it as a means to its monistic realization in his *Aparokṣānubhūti* (verse 100), as do other proponents of Advaita such as Vācaspati Miśra (*circa* ninth/tenth century); while Mādhavācārya (*c.*1238–1317), founder of Dvaita, holds it as a means to his relational dualism. Devotional temple culture has been strongly influenced by Dvaita ideas. Mādhava has also referred to the importance of this formula to Pāśupata Śaivas in his compendium of spiritual philosophies (*Sarvadarśanasaṁgraha*). Some variation of this three-step formula forms the pedagogical cornerstone of education in many traditional lineages of cultural transmission, such as in schools of singing, dance, and Āyurveda.

> The attainment of Śiva's region is the Achievable.... Listening to the glory of Śiva [*śravaṇa*], glorifying him by means of words [*kīrtana*], and deliberation in the mind [*manana*], these constitute the greatest of the means. — Younger 1995: 219

The actual lines from the Upaniṣad, include *darśana* (seeing) along with *śravaṇa* (listening) (see above). "Listening" has been privileged in the cultural imaginary in keeping with the oral culture which formed the setting of the lines.[17] The disciple heard the Upaniṣadic (intimate) *mantra* from the teacher and focused his/her mental and vital attention on it. Through thinking about, repeating and holding the idea in one's mind, one came into the living presence of its consciousness, and at a certain point, became identified with the consciousness of, or referred to, in the *mantra*.

In the visual context of the temple, one may replace hearing with seeing (*dr̥ṣṭi*), cogitation (*manana*) by the build-up of emotion (*rasa-bhāva*), and identity in consciousness (*nididhyāsana*) with non-dual seeing (*darśana*) of the type indicated by the soteriology of the deity and its depiction. Given the early provenance of this text and its pervasive use in oral transmission, I hypothesize that popular use of images in Indian temple contexts assimilated the ideas of *rasa* and *darśana* with such a practice, from an early stage in the performative use of these terms (*circa* second century BCE).[18] Whether this practice was actually the case in antiquity, when it may have begun historically and whether it is bounded in terms of

---

17 "Upaniṣad" literally means "sitting near" and refers to a class of oral communications between the *guru* and disciples in an intimate hermitage setting. Such communications include the *mantra* of initiation, which is uttered in secret by the *guru* into the ear of the disciple. These texts are considered as one of the primary canonical sources of Hinduism.

18 There have been a number of possibilities suggested for the function of images on temple walls. These include a pedagogic function, an aesthetic function, and a hieratic function. These functions need not be thought of as exclusive. What I am suggesting here, an aesthetic anthropology of *darśana*, could very well include all these functions, as discussed below.

sectarian use, are questions for which we lack sufficient evidence at this point; I posit it as a plausible hypothesis to explain the visual phenomenology of popular temple experience through a *rasa-darśana* complex.

I see four ways in which *rasa* works as a mobile element in this scheme to produce an experience of *darśana* in the sense posited here. We have already considered the first of these ways: the rhythmic mobility of the line forming a characteristic means of the "classical" Indian aesthetic, which crystallized *circa* fifth century CE and developed further specificity with the *karaṇas* of "classical" dance from the eighth century onward. The eye, lingering on the movement of the line, partakes of the *rasa* being expressed and senses the *bhāva* behind it and may contact the being of the *bhāva* for *darśana*, either through the eyes or through the idea behind the depiction.

For the second of these ways, we may turn to instances of panels encapsulating multiple episodes in a single frame, early examples of which may be found in Buddhist art of the second century BCE to sixth century CE such as in the railings (*vedikā*) of Bharhut and Sāñcī.[19] The mobility of the sub-episodes constituting

[19] One may question such an early intention of *darśana* using *rasa* in a Buddhist setting, particularly since doctrinal evidence seems opposed to it. The absence of Buddha images at these *stūpa* sites combined with the doctrinal non-substantialism of *nirvāṇa* (*nibbāna*) and the non-acceptance of the *ātman* (the doctrine of *anātman* or *anattā*) would be factors of implausibility for the application of my hypothesis, more so since it rests on a philosopheme originating in an Upaniṣad, which couched its soteriology in terms of the realization of *ātman*. However, if we treat cultural practice not as ideologically bound but as a field of popular negotiation mediated by traditional factors such as philosophemes, the proto-possibility of *rasa* and *darśana* in early Buddhist practice is not at all unlikely. Attention to the presence of Vedic solar ideas in the symbolism and practice relating to *stūpas* has been brought by several scholars, including Coomaraswamy (1983) and Snodgrass (1992: 189-200). According to these conjectures, later Mahāyāna ideas such as that of *dhātu-garbha* may have been preluded in the *stūpa* seen as the eternal gestating germ of the Buddha, not unlike the union of *liṅga* and *yoni* in the Śaiva *garbhagṛha*

and narrativizing the theme amplifies the *rasa* (mood) leading to the totality of the emotional experience (*bhāva*), which the viewer mirror-embodies. Thus, the *bhāva* of the totality and the *rasa* of its parts coexist in the frame of the work of art as it is experienced. As the viewer "recollects" the episodes of the tale, the *bhāva* makes possible the contact with the being behind the narrative, thus amplifying the experience of a living relationship conducive to *darśana*. We may see examples of this in the Jātaka roundels on the railings (*vedikā*) of the *mahāstūpa* at Bharhut, such as that depicting the *Mahākapi Jātaka* (*fig.* 5.1). *Vedikās* of some early *stūpas* such as the *mahāstūpa* at Bharhut contain stories from the Buddha's past lives (*jātaka*) and episodes from his life story. Encountering these stories visually (*dṛṣṭi*), while circumambulating the *stūpa*, brings the long history of the Buddha's lives to mind (*manana*) making more real the contact with the presence of the Buddha's relics (*śarīra*) as his living presence. Each of these past lives or significant episodes from the present one is treated as a "whole" within the "whole" of the *stūpa* complex. The eye traces a continuity from episode to episode, marked by the repetition of the central character. At the same time, the containing frame of the narrative is sensed as a familiar unit, known in its totality, but amplified in its presence

---

(Snodgrass 1992: 192-94). Irrespective of the doctrinal erasure of the Buddha image, the presence of the Buddha in germinal form in the *stūpa* could well have been accepted in popular practice. The *stūpa* body itself, designated *aṇḍa* (egg), and the relics, termed *śarīra* (body), coupled with the solar performance of circumambulation (*pradakṣiṇā*), give credence to ideas of awakening a sense of identity with the Buddha within, which could be reinforced visually through looking at (*darśana*) and cogitating upon (*manana*) images of his past lives and incidents related to his present life. This is more distinctly the case in the fifth century at Ajantā.

Pia Brancaccio has made the case for *darśana*, within a coherent visual program, for the roundels at Bharhut (2010: 47, 51). According to her, the panels depicting incidents from the life of the Buddha are *darśana* images while the Jātaka roundels, which are privileged, are not. While her argument supports my view of *darśana* imagery at Bharhut, I see a more pervasive role for *darśana* which includes the Jātaka imagery.

with the sequential dwelling on its episodes.

In the *Mahākapi Jātaka* roundel the eye follows the rhythmic curve of the tree at the end of which the monkey protagonist stretches its body for the others of its band to cross over. One sees the last monkey poised to leap powerfully on its back, recollecting the heinous deed of the one who would later take birth as Devadatta. At the far end of the circle one catches a peripheral glimpse of the rest of the monkeys having reached safety at the bottom of the neighboring tree; but the centrality of one's gaze drops to the scenes directly below the extended monkey, where two other significant episodes of the *Jātaka* can be seen. The king's men, seeing the sacrifice of the monkey leader and his imminent fall, hold out a hunting net to break his fall; and below this, one sees the conclusion of the story, the fallen monkey on a seat teaching the king. The transition of moods (*rasas*) in the narrative, particularly along the central vertical axis, through heroism, odiousness, and compassion, amplifies the overall (*sthāyī*) affect (*bhāva*) of noble spiritual compassion (*karuṇā*) which is characteristic of the Buddha and awakens the viewer's memory in thought (*manana*) opening it to the metonymic presence that may be equated to *darśana* in the popular sense we are using for it. We see a similar effect orchestrated in some of the horizontal narrations of the architraves at Sāñcī, for example, the continuous narrative of the Great Departure of Gautama.

We see the third of these ways in Hindu art of a kind which is prominent from the fifth through ninth centuries, where, either in rock-cut caves or in small temples, monumental horizontal panels showing single episodes belonging to a larger thematic narrative are depicted. Examples may be the magnificent early fifth-century Varāha saving the Earth Goddess at Udayagiri or the late seventh-century Mahiṣāsuramardinī panel at Māmallapuram (*fig.* 5.2). The dynamic and dramatic quality of these depictions liken them to moments in a theatrical performance, evoking *rasa* as a result.[20] They also serve as metonyms for the larger narrative of which they form a part and evoke powerfully its wholeness in memory, relating to the larger content behind the depiction as the expression of the being in its *darśana*.

The fourth way is more specific to structural Hindu temples with niche images along the walls. Here, the mobile or performative element of *rasa*, apart from the expressive line, is served by the movement of the devotee in circumambulation (*pradakṣiṇā*) around the temple. Stopping before the niche images, one experiences the anthropomorphic individual deity-icon with minimal iconographic signage (*lakṣaṇa*) to recognize the specific role backgrounded by the invisible cultural memory of its episodes. What is visible highlights *bhāva* and *darśana* above *rasa*. The *rasa* is experienced in the build-up through successive encounters of such *darśana*s conceived as episodes within the frame of the temple and its central deity. The completion of the circumambulation leading into the temple and its central shrine (*garbhagṛha*) brings one face to face with the temple deity, whether iconic or aniconic, which becomes the focus of all the *rasa* and the occasion for the grand inclusive *darśana* of the deity, within and without the devotee.

We may consider two examples of this kind of *rasa-darśana* dynamic. The first is the fifth-century Daśāvatāra Viṣṇu Temple at Deogaṛh, where one follows a counterclockwise circumambulation (*prasavya*) encountering first the moment of creation, with Viṣṇu supine on his serpent bed (*fig.* 5.3). Lakṣmī attends his feet, while Brahmā sits on a lotus emerging from his navel and other gods are arrayed above his head. All have their eyes shut in repose. The sinuous lines heighten the *rasa*s of peace (*śānta*) and wonder

[20] I am indebted to Katherine Harper and Robert DeCaroli for pointing out that the patronage of theater in the seventh-century Pallava court is well known. The first king who converted to Śaivism and is responsible for initiating the cave temple excavations of Māmallapuram, Mahendravarman I, himself wrote and patronized plays.

(*adbhuta*) that seem to be evoked by the Creator. Moving on to the western panel, one encounters the twin sages Nara and Nārāyaṇa meditating for the welfare of the world (*fig.* 5.4). They also have their eyes closed and represent the preservation aspect of Viṣṇu. They may evoke the *rasas* of peace (*śānta*) and compassion (*karuṇā*) in the devotee. Finally, one moves to the southern niche, where one encounters a panel showing Viṣṇu on his eagle mount saving the elephant king (*gajendra*) from the clutches of the *nāga*, who adulates Viṣṇu along with his consort (*fig.* 5.5). Once again, all the characters have their eyes closed. The *rasas* evoked here would probably be experienced as peace (*śānta*) and power (*raudra*). These encounters with different episodes connected with the creative, preservative, and destructive power of Viṣṇu build up into a composite sense of the Supreme God. The deity in the shrine is absent, but it is most probable that this would have been a standing image of Viṣṇu with open eyes that would have facilitated the experience of *darśana* readied through the encounter with his varied powers.

The Bṛhadīśvara Temple at Thanjavur is a fine example of the massive architecture of the eleventh century that exposes a large amount of wall surface. Hindu temples after the eleventh century, under the patronage of powerful rulers, began to take on an architectural monumentality in a variety of locales, which reduced sculpture to a severely controlled sequential role within the whole of the temple. Images on the outer wall became constrained within limited spaces (*devakoṣṭha*) where only iconic depictions with little setting or episodic elaboration could be articulated. The walls of the Bṛhadīśvara Temple, however, are broken into several narrow niches, featuring different aspects of Śiva such as Dakṣiṇāmūrti, Bhikṣāṭana, Naṭarāja, Harihara, and Ardhanārīśvara. One encounters these in succession (*dṛṣṭi*) as one follows a circumambulation (*pradakṣiṇā*). Though not following a compact logical sequence or portraying associated details of the setting such as in the Daśāvatāra Temple, these images are recognizable by their iconography and are evocative through the careful delineation of rhythmic line. When one enters the shrine after circumambulation, the varied aspects of Śiva and the narratives associated with them are brought forward in one's mind (*manana*). At the center of the *garbhagṛha* is an enormous black stone *liṅga*, overwhelming in its presence. Though non-anthropomorphic, the devotee has a *darśana* of Śiva literally present in stone and is open to subtle communication with the being, which grants reality to all his powers, symbolized in the outer walls. As this experience deepens, the *liṅga* is felt to be living within the subtle (*sūkṣma*) body of the devotee and an experience of non-dual identity (*darśana*) may be had.[21] This subjective identity explains the layers of objectivity, as if all form has emanated from the formless (Davis 2000: 63-65).

The above descriptions have been simplified to isolate the visual component of the experience. In reality, the experience inside the temple is accompanied with chanting and ritual offerings, and sometimes with offerings of singing, instrumental music, and/or dancing. These are meant to heighten the sensory transmission of living consciousness in the deity and the devotee, sensitive to this multisensory power, is brought more potently into *darśana*. One may also speculate about the enhanced mediating role of the cadre of temple priests in premodern temples. Hindu families are organized according to regional heredity lineages and major temples are equipped with priests who service regional families. Such priests (*paṇḍā*) become the guides of devotees belonging to the family lineage (*kula*) which they service. Whereas in smaller temples there is no such differentiation and an individual or family may be serviced by any priest, in more canonical temples, which service large numbers of visitors, the *pāṇḍā* system is prominent. In a premodern context, one of the functions of these priests may have been to serve as "*darśana* docents," leading the devotee(s) along the circumambulation path, identifying the images in

---

[21] "Non-dual identity" is a broad term for a field of experiences that has been applied to varieties and degrees of non-duality, including but not restricted to Advaita.

subsidiary temples or niches and evoking the *rasa* of relating to the transcendental episodes of the deity or his/her associates through narration, chant, or song.[22] This process would deepen the relationship awaking a sense of reciprocity and exchange through eye contact and leading to the possible experience of *darśana* in the *garbhagṛha*. At present, hints of this process may still be encountered sometimes, though the temple visit has become largely a material transaction in which the priest and devotee have reduced their relation to one of a propitiation ritual with little imagination or agency. This is part of the transformation wrought through modernity with its dominantly materialist ontology.[23]

Conclusion

In conclusion, the reality of images in Indian temples needs to be understood as being at the negotiated intersection of elite patronage, ideological/ritual convention, traditions of architecture and sculpture, and popular use. Cultural memes, such as mythemes and philosophemes, constitute an important oral component of this space of negotiation, particularly in mediating popular use and modifying tastes and conventions of art making/ritual. I have hypothesized a combined *rasa-darśana* sequence of subjective states, as a visual replication of the three-step formula *darśana* (seeing),

---

22 Hindu temple viewers even today will attest to a large variation among *pāṇḍās*, some of whom explain the imagery of the temple with storytelling and even with songs. The author has encountered several such intermediaries, at various places such as the Viśvanātha Temple in Varanasi (mediated by an unidentified *pāṇḍā* in 2000, the Jagannātha Temple at Purī (mediated by Mahadeb Paṇḍa in 2001) and the Kālī Temple at Kālighāṭ, Kolkata (mediated by Kashinath Bhattacharya in 2003 and 2016).

23 This is not meant to be a nostalgic gesture towards "tradition." It is to acknowledge the creative power integral to "becoming," which served and was served by the re/presentations of the gods. It is at the same time to acknowledge the problems of our times (or space-times) as a response to materialism in both of its ontological and cultural senses.

manana (cogitation), *nididhyāsana* (identity in consciousness) originating in the *Bṛhadāraṇyaka Upaniṣad* and operating as an unauthorized philosopheme in the aesthetic phenomenology of temple visits. I have enumerated four organizations of visual space and popular practice as examples of this phenomenology and suggested some additional mediating devices. The use of the term *darśana* in the context of temple worship is much more pervasive in Indian temple practice than the term *rasa*. It is also less doctrinally inscribed. Combined with *rasa* in the visual organization of temple space, it could very well be a convenient popular mnemonic for this three-step formula leading towards an aesthetically mediated intimate communication and non-dual experience between devotee and deity.

References

Agrawala, Prithvi Kumar, 1981, *On the Sadanga Canons of Painting,* Indian Civilisation Series, no. 22, Varanasi: Prithivi Prakashan.

Bharata Muni (attrib.), *The Nāṭyaśāstra*, see Ghosh 1950.

Brancaccio, Pia, 2010, "The Making of a Life: Re-reading Bhārhut Sculpture," *South Asian Studies,* 21(1): 47-52.

Bṛhadāraṇyaka Upaniṣad, see Sivananda 1985.

The Citrasūtra of the Viṣṇudharmottara Purāṇa, see Mukherji 2001.

Coomaraswamy, Ananda, 1918, "Hindu View of Art: Theory of Beauty," in *The Dance of Shiva: Fourteen Indian Essays,* New York: The Sunwise Turn, pp. 30-37.

——, 1934, *The Transformation of Nature in Art*, New York: Dover Publications.

——, 1983, *Symbolism of Indian Architecture: The Skambha and the Stupa*, Jaipur: Historical Documentation Research Program.

Davis, Richard, 2000, *Worshiping Śiva in Medieval India: Ritual in an Oscillating Universe*, New Delhi: Motilal Banarsidass.

Derrida, Jacques and R. Klein, 1981, "Economimesis," *Diacritics,* 11(2): 2-25. doi:10.2307/464726.

Eck, Diana L., 1998, *Darśan: Seeing the Divine Image in India*, New York: Columbia University Press.

Ganapatisāstrī, T. and K. Sāmbaśivaśāstrī (eds.), 2008, *Śilparatnaṁ*, Nāgarakovila: C.B.H. Publications.

George, Vensus A., 2008, *Paths to the Divine: Ancient and Indian*, Washington D.C.: Council for Research in Values and Philosophy.

Ghosh, Manomohan (tr. and ed.), 1950, *The Natyashastra: A Treatise on Hindu Dramaturgy and Histrionics*, Calcutta: The Royal Asiatic Society of Bengal.

Goswamy, B.N., 1986, "Rasa: Delight of the Reason," in *Essence of Indian Art*, pp. 17-30, San Francisco: Asian Art Museum.

——, 1994, "Another Past, Another Context: Exhibiting Indian Art Abroad", in *Interpreting Objects and Collections*, ed. S.M. Pearce, pp. 188-92, London and New York: Routledge.

Guha-Thakurta, Tapati, 1992, "Images of Nationalism and Modernity: The Reconstruction of Indian Art in Calcutta at the Turn of the Century," in *Modernization of Culture and the Development of Political Discourse in the Third World*, Occasional Paper 5, pp. 89-114, Roskilde, Denmark: International Development Studies Roskilde University.

——, 1995, "Recovering the Nation's Art," in *Texts of Power: Emerging Disciplines in Colonial Bengal*, ed. P. Chatterjee, pp. 63-92, Minneapolis: University of Minnesota Press.

Kempton, Sally, 2013, *Awakening Shakti: The Transformative Power of the Goddesses of Yoga*, Boulder, CO: Sounds True.

Kramrisch, Stella, 1976 [first published 1946], *The Hindu Temple*, 2 vols., Delhi: Motilal Banarsidass.

——, 1994 [first published 1983], *Exploring India's Sacred Art: Selected Writings of Stella Kramrisch*, ed. B. Stoler Miller, New Delhi: Motilal Banarsidass.

Mair, Victor H., 2004, "Xie He's 'Six Laws' of Painting and Their Indian Parallels," in *Chinese Aesthetics: The Ordering of Literature, the Arts and the Universe in the Six Dynasties*, ed. Zong-qi Cai, pp. 81-122, Honolulu: University of Hawai'i Press.

Mānasollāsa, see Shrigondekar 1939.

Mukherji, Parul Dave (ed.), 2001, *The Citrasūtra of the Viṣṇudharmottara Purāṇa*, Delhi: Motilal Banarsidass and Indira Gandhi National Centre for the Arts.

Nandagopal, Choodamani, 1990, *Dance and Music in the Temple Architecture*, New Delhi: Agam Kala Prakashan.

Nāṭyaśāstra, see Ghosh 1950.

Parker, Samuel K., 2003, "Text and Practice in South Asian Art: An Ethnographic Perspective," *Artibus Asiae*, 63(1): 5-34.

Pinney, Christopher, 2004, *Photos of the Gods: The Printed Image and Political Struggle in India*, New Delhi: Oxford University Press.

Pollock, Sheldon (ed.), 2018, *A Rasa Reader: Classical Indian Aesthetics*, New York: Columbia University Press.

Saussure, Ferdinand de, 1998 [first published 1959], *Course in General Linguistics*, Peru, IL: Open Court.

Schechner, Richard, 2001, "Rasaesthetics," *The Drama Review*, 45(3): 27-50.

Sharvananda, Swami (tr. and ed.) 1921, *Taittirīyopaniṣad*, Chennai: Ramakrishna Math.

Shrigondekar, G.K. (ed.), 1939, *Mānasollāsa*, Part II, Baroda: Gaekwad Oriental Series.

Sivananda, Swami, (tr. and ed.), 1985, *The Brihadaranyaka Upanishad: Sanskrit Text, English Translation, and Commentary*, Shivanandanagar, Tehri-Garhwal: Divine Life Society.

Snodgrass, Adrian, 1992 [first published 1985], *The Symbolism of the Stupa*, Delhi: Motilal Banarsidass.

Srikumar (attrib.), *Śilparatnaṁ*, see Gaṇapatiśāstrī and Sāmbaśivaśāstrī 2008.

Taittirīya Upaniṣad, see Sharvananda 1921.

Trivedi, K.H., 1966, *Natyadarpana of Ramachandra and Gunachandra: A Critical Study*, Ahmedabad: L.D. Institute of Indology.

Younger, Paul, 1995, *The Home of Dancing Śivan̲: The Traditions of the Hindu Temple in Citamparam*, New York and Oxford: Oxford University Press.

Part II
South Asia after 1400 CE

6

Relics, Icons, and Portraits in Hindu Institutions

An Examination of the Worship of the Teacher

Nalini Rao

Relic veneration has been practiced in many religions, particularly Buddhism, in the form of *stūpas* and *caityas*, but relics have typically been considered polluting or even non-existent in Hinduism. The remains of a Hindu person are usually cremated and the ashes immersed in a river, preferably in the Ganges. However, a paradoxical phenomenon can be found in some Hindu monasteries where the "relics" of the head monk are enshrined. The head is normally a philosopher-monk known variously as an *ācārya*, *svāmī*, *tīrtha*, or simply as a *guru* who has renounced the world (*saṁnyāsin*). The relics of the *guru* are deposited in a container, known as the *vṛndāvana*. However, the *vṛndāvana* does not merely consist of post-cremation remains, like those of the Buddha, but the entire embalmed body of the *saṁnyāsin*. In some sectarian Hindu monasteries *vṛndāvanas* are immovable non-figural stone structures that are considered very sacred.

The aim of the paper is to understand the role and function of the *vṛndāvana* within Hindu monastic culture by investigating its multivalent meanings and its transformation from relic to a portrait. The focus is on the *vṛndāvana* of Śrī Rāghavendra Svāmī in Mantralaya, which has grown to be a large pilgrimage site in the state of Karnataka, India. Worship of the *vṛndāvana* invites numerous questions regarding the nature of the relic and its function as a portrait, along with its central role in a sectarian monastery. This paper is an investigation into the meaning of a *vṛndāvana* that recalls some Buddhist practices and casts light on the interplay between relic and portrait, death and sacredness, God and *guru*.

Although enshrinement of the physical remains of a *saṁnyāsin* has been practiced in Dvaita Hindu monasteries for the past 500 years, it has yet to spark scholarly interest (Stoker 2016). Until now studies on the *vṛndāvana,* such as those by Deepak Sarma and B.N.K. Sharma, have been largely focused on the philosophy of Madhvācārya or on his teachings, such as those of Hayavadana Rao and Acharya Bannanje Govindacarya (Govindacarya 2002; Rao 2010; Sarma 2003; Sharma 1986 and 2008). Cenkner's publication *The Teaching Tradition* focuses on Ādi Śaṅkarācārya and his monasteries, while the focus of Tamara I. Sears is on monastic architecture (Cenkner 1983; Sears 2014). There are no textual descriptions or writings about the *vṛndāvanas*. There are uncommonly scant textual records and inscriptions to cast any light on these sacred objects. In addition, the texts, in the form of commentaries on the Vedas and Upaniṣads written by the monastic heads are philosophical in nature, rather than describing the funerary practices for monks. I found that even the popular musical works in Sanskrit and Kannada that are composed by disciples of the Dvaita tradition extoll the former *gurus* without mentioning any after-death practices. On the other hand, the monthly Kannada journal *Sudha* provides brief descriptions of monastic pilgrimage sites and the *vṛndāvanas*, the teachings of Dvaita philosophy as well as the miracle stories of *gurus* (*Sudha*).

In regard to the problems of research, because *vṛndāvanas* are considered extremely sacred, close examination and photography of these objects are prohibited. The art historian's task is further complicated by the fact that religious sanctuaries do not keep detailed reports about conservation or new constructions at these sites. One, therefore, has to rely on cultic memory, oral tradition, and interviews with heads of *maṭhas*. Studies on the visual, historical, and religious dimension of the *vṛndāvana* have yet to be conducted. This paper will rectify the situation by providing details about funerary practices and the worship of the deceased body of the teacher, where the boundaries between the dead and living, aniconic and iconic are crossed.

Description of a Vṛndāvana

A *vṛndāvana* is an impressive, solid, cubical, non-figural, stone container, about 8 ft by 8 ft (2.4 sq. m). The term refers both to the structure and the deceased body that is placed inside. It may be installed either near a river, monastery (*maṭha* or *mutt*), or a temple. However, for the past thirty years or so, a permanent structure is typically built around the *vṛndāvana* and daily worship is offered to it.

Ranging from simple to decorative, *vṛndāvanas* are varied in form. A typical *vṛndāvana* is an impressive, simple, immovable stone sculpture in the form of a closed cubical shrine or box. It is aniconic and built by placing horizontal slabs of stone on a platform. It can be divided into three parts, consisting of a base, body, and top, adorned with a running leaf design.

Above the *vṛndāvana* is placed a small metal image of Kṛṣṇa.[1] The *vṛndāvana* is related to the *tulasīvṛndāvana,* a sacred pot that holds the *tulasī* (Holy Basil) plant, which is worshiped by women in many Hindu households (Simoons 1998: 7-40).[2] Etymologically, *vṛndāvana* means "the garden (or orchard) of Vṛndā," the wife of Viṣṇu. In this garden of Vṛndā, Kṛṣṇa, the main deity for many Vaiṣṇavites, is said to have danced with his female devotees, *gopīs* (Pintchman 2005).

---

[1] The image of Lord Kṛṣṇa was installed in the "temple" at Udipi in 1250 CE by Madhvācārya.

[2] *Tulasī* is particularly sacred to Vaiṣṇavites for the worship of Viṣṇu.

Vṛndāvanas (meaning the aniconic object with the saint's relic), appear only during the late medieval period, around the fifteenth century CE. Due to the importance accorded to the worship of *vṛndāvanas*, these objects have become a part of *maṭha* architecture associated with sectarian Hindu Vaiṣṇavite monasteries. Through the transformation of the profane remains of a past *guru* into a sacred death marker, *vṛndāvanas* have become sacred icons of intense veneration and they are accorded daily devotion similar to the worship of a deity in a Hindu temple.

Growth of Hindu Maṭhas

A brief examination of the history of *maṭhas* will provide a background to the simultaneous growth of *vṛndāvanas* and Vaiṣṇavite Dvaita *maṭhas*. The Hindu term for a monastery is *maṭha*, although it is used in a broad sense. A *maṭh*, or *maṭha*, *mutt* or *matam* is a religious, philosophical, and educational institution. The word *maṭha* has been defined variously, but most scholars agree that it refers to a religious institution that is a residential school of learning. *Maṭhas* are often attached to temples and are headed by a monk/teacher who is an ascetic (*saṁnyāsin*) and often a celibate *guru*.[3] The head may be known by various terms, such as *guru* or *jagadguru* (world teacher). The title *jagadguru* is often used in the *maṭhas* that follow the precepts of Ādi Śaṅkarācārya, although he is also known by other titles, such as *ācārya*, *svāmī*, *ānanda*, or *tīrtha*. Here, we will use the term *guru* to refer to the head of a monastery.[4]

Although Jaina and Hindu *maṭhas* have been known to exist since the fifth century CE, independent Śaivite, Pāśupata, Kālāmukha, and

[3] There are approximately ninety monastic orders in Hinduism, and about seventy of them impose celibacy.

[4] Many in the West are familiar with the Rāmakṛṣṇa Maṭh, that follows the Advaita tradition of Ādi Śaṅkarācārya. Advaita, Dvaita, and Viśiṣṭādvaita are the principal schools of Vedānta, each representing a point of philosophical departure that emerged from their interpretations of the *prasthānatrayī* or the triune authority of the Vedānta in the medieval period.

Śaiva Siddhānta *maṭhas* flourished in different parts of India from the sixth through twelfth centuries CE, particularly in southern India. During the medieval period (tenth–fourteenth centuries CE), they grew into institutions of seminal importance and became an integral part of the community. They expanded into residential schools, places of ecclesiastical teaching, centers of worship, and they fulfilled the functions of feeding and lodging pilgrims/devotees. These dynamic institutions differ in their religious beliefs, rituals, philosophy, organizational structure, and imagery. They are varied in religious and philosophical ideologies, and cover a wide range of religious groups and organizations. Among the numerous Hindu monasteries, the three best-known traditional Vedānta *maṭhas* are the Advaita *maṭhas* which were established by Ādi Śaṅkarācārya, the Viśiṣṭādvaita *maṭha* of Rāmānuja, and the Dvaita *maṭha* of Madhvācārya (1238–1317) (Cenkner 1983: 109-10).[5] Each respectively represents the philosophical doctrines of Monism, Qualified Non-Dualism, and Dualism (or Realism/Pluralism).Today these *maṭhas* are still very popular religious and educational institutions, especially in southern India.

Only the Dualist or Dvaita *maṭhas* of Madhvācārya house the relics of the deceased *guru* in the *vṛndāvana*. In the post-Madhvācārya period, a voluminous literature grew around his works. Exponents of this school included Madhva, Jayatīrtha, Vyāsatīrtha, Vādirāja, and Vijayīndra among others. Due to certain negligible philosophical differences between his disciples, the Dualist *maṭhas*, which are also known as Madhva *maṭhas*, began to separate themselves and this led to the emergence of branch *maṭhas* in which former disciples took up the *saṁnyāsin* role and set up their own *maṭhas*.[6] The celibate disciples of the Dvaita *maṭha*

[5] Ādi Śaṅkarācārya, who established Advaita *maṭhas* at Purī, Dvārakā, Śṛṅgerī, and Badarī, revitalized the ten orders of Śaiva ascetics along monastic lines.

[6] Such was the case with the Vyāsarāja, who had established his *maṭha* on River Kabini, near T. Narasimhapura near Mysore. Śrī Vyāsarāja Maṭha split into Kundapura Vyāsarāja Maṭha and the Sosale Vyāsarāja Maṭha.

established their own lines of sectarian *maṭhas* and became the precursors for the *aṣṭa maṭhas* (eight *maṭhas*) in Udipi, on the west coast of India. They were, in later times, the *maṭhas* of Palimāru, Adamāru, Kṛṣṇapura Puttige, Śirūru, Sōdhe, Kaṇiyūru, and Pējāvara. The "married and renounced" disciples of Madhvācārya in northern Karnataka established their own *maṭhas* (called *deśastha maṭhas*). The disciples Śrī Padmanābha Tīrtha, Narahari Tīrtha, Madhva Tīrtha, and Akṣobhya Tīrtha founded other independent Madhva *maṭhas* that include the Uttarādi Maṭha, Śrīpādarāja Maṭha, Vysaraya Maṭha, Sosale Vyāsarāja Maṭha, Kundapura Vyāsarāja Maṭha, Rāghavendra Svāmī Maṭha, Mulabagilu Maṭha, Majjigehalli Maṭha, Kūḍli Maṭha, and Balegaru Maṭha (Tirumalai 2000: 402). However, each of the sectarian Madhva *maṭhas* adhered to the philosophy of Madhvācārya.

Each of the above *maṭhas* were and still are headed by an ascetic *guru*. After their demise, the bodies of these *gurus* are contained in the *vṛndāvana*, known as the *mūla* (original) *vṛndāvana*. In addition, like a Buddhist *stūpa*, a relic from the *mūla vṛndāvana* (where the original embalmed body is deposited) can be divided to be reinstated and form new "commemorative," "votive," or secondary *vṛndāvanas*. A particle of soil (*mṛtige*) from the *mūla vṛndāvana* of any of the numerous Madhva *maṭhas* can be reinstalled to create secondary *vṛndāvanas*, or *mṛtige vṛndāvanas*, and thereby a new branch *maṭha* (Flügel 2010: 391).[7] Hence, each Madhva *maṭha* that has a *mūla vṛndāvana* (with the body) is thus known as a *mūla maṭha*, and each *mūla maṭha* can have various branches in different geographical areas, called *mṛtige maṭhas*. For instance, the *mūla maṭha* of the Pējāvara Maṭhas is in Udipi, while its branches are scattered. If a (living) head of the Pējāvara Maṭha (in Udipi) dies, it is his body that would be contained in the *vṛndāvana*. The *mūla*

[7] The antecedents for the distinction between the original and secondary *vṛndāvanas* can be found in the terms *samādhi* (a relic shrine) and *smāraka* (a commemorative shrine), the former constructed for *pūjā* and the latter for *darśana* and meditation.

vṛndāvana of Rāghavendra Svāmī is in Mantralaya, while his *mṛtige* or votive *vṛndāvanas* are in various places and number about a hundred in southern India alone. Moreover, the deceased bodies of the succeeding heads of a *mūla maṭha* have also been entombed (and still continue to be enshrined) in the *maṭha* at Mantralaya, near the *vṛndāvana* of the first *guru*, Rāghavendra Svāmī. Thus, the multiplication of *vṛndāvanas* resembles the division of relics in Indian Buddhism, and was closely associated with the proliferation of *maṭhas*. With the growth of sectarian Madhva *maṭhas*, *vṛndāvanas* in the sanctum came to play a seminal role in the popularizing of the relic cult.[8]

Vṛndāvana as Relic and Icon

As mentioned above, the deposit in a *vṛndāvana* does not consist merely of post-cremation remains, like those of the Buddha, but rather the entire embalmed body of the *saṁnyāsin*, who was the head of the *maṭha* and upholder of the Dvaita (Dualist) school of philosophy propounded by Madhvācārya (1238–1317 CE) (Sharma 1986: 25, 79-83). The term relic has been used here with an expanded meaning to denote the entire embalmed body of the *guru* due to the lack of a proper equivalent term in Sanskrit or the local Kannada language.[9] They may be called tombs and sepulchral or mortuary icons but no matter the terminology, they have been venerated for the past 600 years in the innumerable Vaiṣṇavite Dvaita Madhva *maṭhas*. They are still popular institutions and the practice of enshrining the deceased body of the *saṁnyāsins* is still followed.

The Hindu burial practice for *saṁnyāsins* and *yogīs* in almost all parts of India consisted of a few simple practices. Because they

---

[8] There are also *vṛndāvana* for Śrī Vaiṣṇavite *gurus*, but the practice of relic worship and constructing *vṛndāvanas*, it appears, originated with the disciples of Madhvācārya.

[9] In the local language, Kannada, the dead body is called *śarīra* and only after the body has been transferred inside the container is it termed the *vṛndāvana*.

were understood to have performed their own cremation during initiation, there was no postmortem cremation and they were instead buried or immersed in rivers (De Marco 1987: 224). All formal burial feasts and *śrāddha* ceremonies were (and still are) normally avoided, as they were performed when an individual decided to become a *saṁnyāsin* (Pandey 1969: 271-73). In Madhva *maṭhas*, the funerary practice for the head monk, *saṁnyāsin*, or *guru* consists of two simple and distinct rituals performed by the members of the *maṭha* — the mummification or embalming of the body and its transfer into the *vṛndāvana*. After the death of the head monk, coconuts are broken, which symbolize the cracking of the skull and allows the imprisoned soul to be "liberated" from the body (Oman 1903: 158-61). The body is placed in a sitting posture, facing east or north-east, and sand and salt are piled over it. Three months later, on an auspicious day, it is transported in a procession, placed in a sitting posture (with its arms on a wooden frame) inside the container (*vṛndāvana*) and numerous *śālagrāmas*,[10] precious stones, beads, and gold objects are also placed in the container. The ritual deposition of the embalmed body is later followed by the enshrinement (or burial) ritual, called *pratiṣṭhāpana*. The *vṛndāvana* is then sealed, Vedic *mantras* are chanted and food is distributed to the devotees. It is only after forty-one days that the object is considered sacred; it can now be worshipped and called a *vṛndāvana*.[11] The transformation of a *vṛndāvana* into an icon is not merely the ritual of *pratiṣṭhāpana*, but the construction

[10] *Śālagrāmas* are round black stones, the aniconic symbol of Viṣṇu. According to personal communication to the author by the head of a *maṭha*, in other parts of India, when a *saṁnyāsin* dies, his body is buried in a grave like a pit, in which the body is made to sit up facing east or north-east with its arms supported on a wooden frame or support. In the branch (*mṛtige maṭha*) of Rāghavendra Svāmī, in Bengaluru, the objects include fifteen *śālagrāmas*, a conch (*śaṅkha*) that spirals to the right, garlands composed of nine gems and images of the gods Rāma, Kṛṣṇa, and Varāha.

[11] In Kannada, when a saint dies, he is referred to as *vṛndāvanastha ādaru*, probably referring to final *mokṣa* (liberation).

of a structure in the form of a pavilion or small room within the precincts of a *maṭha*.

Vṛndāvana as a Portrait

Ritual worship of a *vṛndāvana* is similar to the honors paid to a god in a Hindu temple with incense, flowers, lights, *namaskāras* (ritualized reverence), *japa*, music, and Vedic chants. Bathing consists of *pañcāmṛta* (a mixture of water, milk, honey, fruits, and butter) that is distributed as blessed food (*prasāda*). On festive occasions a portable image of God Kṛṣṇa is taken in procession around the premises of the *maṭha*. However, there are some forms of worship that are offered to a *vṛndāvana* and not to a god, such as dressing of the image with a saffron cloth. Furthermore, the *vṛndāvana* is anointed with sandalwood paste in the form of the symbols of Vaiṣṇavism, *śaṅkha* (conch), *cakra* (wheel), *gadā* (club), and *padma* (lotus), and it is further decorated with facial features, such as eyes, in addition to a *nāma*.[12] Ultimately, a silver plate engraved with a few facial features, such as eyes, is physically affixed to the stone *vṛndāvana*.

The *vṛndāvana* also functions as a miraculous image and is believed to have profound powers. The deceased *guru* is said to have performed miracles during his life, which justifies the high level of veneration accorded to his *vṛndāvana* which is a manifestation of the *guru*'s powers. Numerous miracle stories have been narrated and retold in the form of oral tradition. Rāghavendra Svāmī, for example, is said to have brought the dead to life, turned meat into fruits, healed the sick, and restored vision to the blind.

Conclusion

It appears that for many Hindus there was nothing objectionable about the worship of relics of saints and *saṁnyāsins*; from this

[12] The followers of Madhvācārya also wear a mark on the forehead. It is composed of two white perpendicular lines made with *gopīcandana*, a type of earth obtained on the west coast of India, and a dark line in the middle with a spot in the center. The two white lines are joined by crossline on the bridge of the nose.

perspective it does not violate the letter or spirit of Hindu teachings from the medieval period. Neither do the followers of Advaita Vedānta openly decry the worship of relics. In fact, the Rāmakṛṣṇa Maṭh in Beḷūr, which follows the Advaita doctrine, exhibits the relics of its founders. The transformation of the relic in the *vṛndāvana* into an icon and a portrait of a *guru* makes the image come alive. The attributions of power and life to the relic, which is treated as presence, is enacted through visual marks, decorations, and worship. In addition, the memories preserved in miracle stories reinforce the function of the *vṛndāvana* as an object of efficacy and sacredness. Acting as a renewal of devotion to the cultic personality of the past *guru*, it also stands for the idealism of an ascetic personality and the timelessness of a renunciate lifestyle.

The *vṛndāvana* is linked both to the world of the *guru* and to the gods; through its link to the image of Kṛṣṇa it gains a divine status. Whether one views it as the site of Kṛṣṇa's garden or as commemorating the life, teachings, and divinity of the *guru* as an *avatāra*, the ongoing invocation of the *guru* through Vedic *mantra*s and *pūjā* has stood as a testimony of the *vṛndāvana*'s efficacy for 600 years. It may be added that the efficacy of the *vṛndāvana* lies not in the connotations of death or the embalmed body, but rather in the life within the *guru* as well as in each of the devotees. Here the boundaries between the dead and living, sacred and unholy, aniconic and iconic are crossed. The *vṛndāvana* reveals the religious exchanges between the dynamic traditions of asceticism and concepts of bliss, between form and formlessness, and between the earthly and divine realms. Each can be attributed to the enigma that is the multivalent symbol of the *vṛndāvana*.

References

Cenkner, William, 1983, *A Tradition of Teachers: Sankara and the Jagadgurus Today*, Delhi: Motilal Banarsidass.

De Marco, Giuseppe, 1987, "The Stupa as a Funerary Monument: New Iconographic Evidence," *East and West*, 37(1/4): 191-246.

Flügel, Peter, 2010, "The Jaina Cult of Relic Stūpas," *Numen*, 57(3): 389-504.

Govindacarya, Acarya Bannanje, 2002, *Madhvacarya: Life and Works*, Udupi: Isavasya Pratishthanam.Kane, Panduranga Vamana, 1973, *History of Dharmasastra*, 2nd edn., vol. 4, Poona: Bhandarkar Oriental Research Institute.

Oman, John Campbell, 1903, *The Mystics, Ascetics, and Saints of India: A Study of Sadhuism, with an Account of the Yogis, Sanyasis, Bairagis, and Other Strange Hindu Sectarians*, London: T.F. Unwin.

Padmanabhacharya, C.M., 1983, *Life and Teachings of Sri Madhvachariar*, 2nd edn., Bombay: C.A. Pattabiraman and C.A.P. Vittal.

Pandey, Rajbali, 1969, *Hindu Samskaras: Socio-Religious Study of the Hindu Sacraments*, 2nd rev. edn., Delhi: Motilal Banarsidass.

Pintchman, Tracy, 2005, *Guests at God's Wedding: Celebrating Kartik among the Women of Benares*, New York: SUNY Press.

Rao, Hayavadana, 2010, *Poornaprajna Vijaya: Life and Teachings of Sri Madhwacharya*, tr. from Kannada by Dhadra Krishnamoorthy, Chennai: Sri Krishna Sri Raghavendra Trust.

Saraswati, Baidyanath, 1977, *Brahmanic Ritual Traditions in the Crucible of Time: Studies in Indian and Asian Civilizations*, Simla: Indian Institute of Advanced Study.

Sarma, Deepak, 2003, *An Introduction to Madhva Vedanta*, Aldershot: Ashgate.

Sears, Tamara I., 2014, *Worldly Gurus and Spiritual Kings: Architecture and Asceticism in Medieval India*, New Haven: Yale University Press.

Sharma, B.N.K., 1986 [first edition 1962], *Philosophy of Śrī Madhvācārya*, Delhi: Motilal Banarsidass.

——, 2008 [first edition 1961], *History of the Dvaita School of Vedanta and Its Literature*, Delhi: Motilal Banarsidass.

Simoons, Frederick J., 1998, *Plants of Life, Plants of Death*, Madison: University of Wisconsin Press.

Stoker, Valerie, 2016, *Politics and Patronage in the City of Victory*, Oakland: University of California Press.

Tirumalai, R., 2000, "The Maṭhas in Pāṇḍyan Townships," in *Narasiṁhapriyā (Prof. A.V.N. Murthy Felicitation Volume): Essays on Indian Archaeology, Epigraphy, Numismatics, Art, Architecture, Iconography, and Cultural History*, ed. I.K. Sarma, D.V. Devaraj, and R. Gopal, pp. 395-407, New Delhi: Sundeep Prakashan.

7

A Little More Fakīr and A Little Less Fanatic

Putting Aurangzeb's Deccani Architecture into a Sufi Context

Santhi Kavuri-Bauer

THE most commonly held view of Aurangzeb's architectural history is one of rapid decline precipitated by his turn to Sunni orthodoxy. Today he is remembered primarily for the Hindu temples he razed and the mosques he built over them, which are typically read as signs of his intolerance. This view of Aurangzeb (r. 1658–1707), as the bigoted Mughal builder, has gone uncontested since the time of the court historians writing for Aurangzeb's brother and rival aspirant to the throne Dara Shikoh (1615-59). British historians reiterated that image of Aurangzeb in their self-serving history of Mughal decline. James Wheeler's *History of India from the Earliest Ages*, published in several volumes from 1867 to 1881, provides an example of this representation:

> [Aurangzeb] exhausted the resources of the empire upon one design; — the dethronement of the Hindu gods and extension of the religion of the Koran over the whole of India. — 1881: 390-91

This sort of perspective was shared by the architectural historian James Fergusson and allowed him to conclude, "There are few things more startling ... than the rapid decline of taste that set in with the accession of Aurungzeb" (1899: 602). Besides supporting the colonial agenda, Fergusson's negative assessment of Aurangzeb can be attributed to an art historical interpretive framework that orders architecture by oppositional sectarian taxonomies, e.g. Hindu vs Saracenic and the assumed teleology of formal progress and decline.

Architectural historians continued for another hundred years to employ this colonial framework. Michael Brand was among the first to note the failure of this approach, and as a remedy proposed using a cyclical measure of classical revivals. Therefore, rather than using the measure of linear progression replete with notions of "perfection" and the inevitable "decline," he asked historians of Mughal architecture, "to investigate the deeper nature and causes" of what he perceived as recurrent building forms and practices (Brand 1993: 324). In the case of Aurangzeb's architectural program this would mean identifying both what he maintained of the past practices of his forefathers from Timūr to Shah Jahan, and how he sought to distinguish himself from his predecessors in order to maintain Mughal rule in light of the socio-economic realities he faced in late seventeenth-century India (Chandra 1989: 35-38).

Another problem specific to the study of Aurangzeb's architectural program is the political discourse and representation of the ruler as a bigoted religious fanatic who sought to dismantle the tolerant policies of Akbar and alienate the Hindu population. Art historians such as Catherine Asher questioned this representation and argued that Aurangzeb's motivations were not only driven by religion but also by retaliation against subversive Rājpūt kings that threatened the empire (1992: 252-91). Furthermore, because our understanding of the actual religious beliefs espoused by Aurangzeb are incomplete, an incorrect interpretation of his neglect of art and architecture can only be expected. Because Aurangzeb discontinued the practice of keeping a court historian, more stress is put on the interpretation of his other documents to uncover his thoughts on religion. In these archives the image of Aurangzeb that emerges is not always consistent and depends on the type of sources being consulted. For example, one kind of image, and the one popularly accepted, is based on the reports and announcements of his public policies in 1679 that show him engaging in the suppression of Hindus through the implementation of the *jizyā* (tax on non-Muslims), and the orders to destroy certain Hindu temples.

The second more multifaceted image of Aurangzeb is drawn from private documents such as letters to his princes and the hand-written responses to local administrators. These sources reveal a more measured, at times agonizing, but always judicious ruler. Katherine Butler Brown, in her seminal study of Aurangzeb's banning of music argued that the character of the emperor expressed in his private sources was less black and white than it appears in his public histories (2007: 109). As with his abolition of music, Aurangzeb's turn away from monumental architecture toward the end of his life needs to be put into a deeper context that is informed by his personal attitudes about governance and religion, as well as by the changing topography of the Mughal Empire in the late seventeenth century. This more nuanced understanding of the value of architecture is presented in his letters to his sons. Using these sources this paper will examine Aurangzeb's early architectural program in the Deccan with regard to how his religious beliefs and connection to Sufism came to influence his choices.

Aurangzeb's Connection to Sufism in the Deccan

From his time as a prince to his death, Aurangzeb (*fig.* 7.1) showed interest in reforming the imperial court's practice of Sunni Islam, which favored the mystical Sufism of previous Mughal emperors. This goal was neither paradoxical nor atypical for his place and time (Ernst and Lawrence 2002: 4). However, this attitude toward reforming instead of rejecting Sufi religious belief and practice has either been ignored or misrepresented in art historical writing. Instead, the narrative tropes of degeneration and opposition between heterodoxy and orthodoxy are employed to chart a path of Mughal decline starting in the late seventeenth century.

Aurangzeb's beliefs, imperial policies and the choices he made in his architectural programs were indeed shaped by his historical circumstances, family legacy, and feelings of failure toward the end of his life. Reading Aurangzeb's letters that describe meetings with mystics, visits to tombs, and reverence to the practices of his father, we see an emperor who pays as much attention to his Sufi beliefs as to his desire to reform Indian Islam. The letters reveal a complex and thoughtful figure, a stalwart supporter of kind and honest administrators, sheikhs, and noblemen. They also show how he never stopped thinking about how to be a just ruler to all his people even as his empire became unwieldy under the pressures of global trade, internecine quarrels among his administrators, and threats from neighbors like the Marāṭhās, Jāṭs, and Afghans.

When religious matters were discussed in letters to his sons, for example, one of his main concerns was to expose false sheikhs and to support true ones. In one missive to Prince Muhammad Azam he narrates a conversation he had with Abdul Latif, a Sufi sheikh of Burhanpur:

> Exalted son, I remember that one day I paid a visit to Sheikh Abdul Latif, may his tomb be sanctified. During the conversation he stated: ... "Fix monthly allowances on the mendicants, who put faith in God. ... Administer justice (carefully) to the oppressed in such a way that no one will be deprived of his rights. Don't allow the weak to be oppressed by the tyrants. (Then) you will see [an] increase in your happiness." Immediately these words of the [Sheikh] reminded me of the complaints of the inhabitants of your territory, and so involuntarily I wrote this letter to you. May you be happy! — Bilimoria 1908: 28

The recollection described in the letter indicates Aurangzeb's intimate bonds with Sufi sheikhs, which began when he ruled in the Deccan as viceroy to the Mughal emperor and which he maintained throughout his life.

The topography of the Deccan that Aurangzeb encountered when he began his rule there as governor in 1636 already contained a highly-developed network of living Sufi saints and saints' tombs. These saints were integral to the spread of Islam and rendering the otherwise Hindu-dominated population amenable to Islamic rule. As his ancestors had done before, Aurangzeb supported Sufis and provided financial support for the upkeep of their tombs. As viceroy of the Deccan, Aurangzeb engaged the Sufis of his province in regular intimate talks to acquire some of their wisdom (Sarkar 1912: 8). Even before that time, when Aurangzeb was leading armies into the Deccan for Shah Jahan, he spared the destruction of old Sufi tombs. For example, when Gulbargā, the previous capital of the Bahmanī Sultanate (1347–1425), was besieged the tomb of the famous Sufi sheikh Gesū Darāz was ordered to be spared (ibid. 1912: 276). Later, as emperor, he made several pilgrimages to this tomb to pray before battle. Before and after the capture of Golcoṇḍā, Aurangzeb visited and rewarded the attendants of Gesū Darāz's shrine (Green 2012: 152-53). When the living descendant of Gesū Darāz, Mir Sayyid Muhammad, predicted the capture of Aurangzeb's enemy the Marāṭhā Sambhājī, he was rewarded and Gesū Darāz's shrine was given an extra 10,000 rupees (Green 2012: 13). Such gifts and visits from Aurangzeb preserved the memory of the Chishtī Sufi saint, Gesū Darāz, whose importance in the Deccan stretched back to the Bahmanī (1347–1527) and 'Ādil Shāhī (1490–1686) Sultanate.

Aurangzeb's other acts of reverence for saints in the Deccan include the construction of a fortified stone wall to surround the Sufi center of Khuldābād. This wall was most likely built in 1668 when similar stone walls were constructed around nearby Auraṅgābād (Michell and Zebrowski 1999: 54). The wall of Khuldābād had seven portals and a ceremonial gateway with a *naqqārkhānā* (musicians' gallery) (*fig.* 7.2). Situated 20 km from Auraṅgābād, the town contained several tombs of prominent Chishtī Sufi sheikhs like Zainuddīn Shirāzī (1301-70) and Burhānuddīn Gharīb (d. 1344). It would also be the final resting place of Aurangzeb and members of the ruling class like Āzam Shāh, Aurangzeb's second son, and Nizām-ul-Mulk Āsaf Jah. Before Aurangzeb was buried next to Zainuddīn

Shirāzī's shrine, he collected money from selling copies of Koran and prayer hats that he made to pay for his simple open-air tomb. So that there would be no mistake he wrote how he wanted to be buried in his last will and testament:

> Let Hamid-ud-Din Khan, who is faithful and trusty, convey my corpse to the place of Shah Zen-ud-Din and erect a tomb over it in the same manner as is done for dervishes.
>
> — Bilimoria 1908: Letter CXXVI 22 n. 1

Until the time of his death in 1707 Aurangzeb deeply revered the Sufis of the Chishtī order. They had helped establish Islam in the Deccan since the fourteenth century. They provided advice on the ethics of rule, maintained a network of tombs and lodges to support Islamic faith and rule in the region, and through their prayers, predictions, and charms helped rulers like Aurangzeb succeed in battles.

Aurangzeb, the Timūrīd Builder

The patronage of Sufi tombs and emulation of their burial practices was thus not unique to Aurangzeb, but part of a larger Mughal culture of rule that dates back to his ancestor, Timūr (1336–1405). His support of the Sufi orders that drew him into their orbit in the Deccan happened in accordance with the practices of the Timūrīds. By following these precedents Aurangzeb communicated to the rest of the world that his empire was based on the same foundation as that of his predecessors. This connection was always a part of Mughal statecraft and lessons for the princes. Aurangzeb advised his sons and grandsons to respect their ancestors' practices and to use them to connect with their power in India. In a letter to his grandson Bahadur about showing kindness to his soldiers, an important trait of Mughal rulers, Aurangzeb writes of the Mughal's lineage and the values passed down from its progenitors:

> He of a happy disposition and of a high birth (i.e., you) should try his best to execute this affair according to the entire sound advice

fig. 7.1: The Emperor Aurangzeb carried on a Palanquin, *circa* 1705-20, opaque water color and gold on paper

fig. 7.2: The Naqqār Khānā Gate, Khuldābād, *c*.1668

fig. 7.3: The Bībī kā Maqbarā, Auraṅgābād, *c*.1653–61

> of his forefathers. Because on the continent of India, this [Mughal Empire] is a generous gift (to us) from Their Majesties, the Lord of the Happy Conjunction (i.e., Tamerlane) and the Resident of Heaven (i.e., Akbar). — Bilimoria 1908: Letter LXXXIII, 81

The Mughal connection to the Timūrīd culture of Iran and Central Asia has been the focus of recent studies, most notably by A. Azfar Moin in *The Millennial Sovereign*. Moin correctly argues that investigations into Mughal culture need to move beyond seeing the Mughals as a uniquely Indian phenomenon. Instead, we must broaden the context of influences to include their preternatural ancestry that proceeded from their messianic and powerful progenitor, Timūr (Moin 2012: 3-4). Mughal art and architectural programs, seen from this wider context, were shaped by the Timūrīd practice of fusing sovereignty with Sufi mysticism.

In his letters to his sons, Aurangzeb makes it clear that they are the sons of Timūr and the Indian branch of a larger family. Akbar and Shah Jahan are quoted or used as examples of proper governance brought to India from Central Asia. In his reprimands and praises it is this identity that is crucial to Mughal rulers and informs their every move. So, what did it mean to be a Timūrīd ruler? First and foremost, it meant to define one's rule by the same institutional forms founded by ancestors. One of the most important of these was Sufi sainthood. Timūr and the Mughals presented themselves as saints in order to displace the influence of powerful Sufi sheikhs and avoid the possibility of opposition to their authority. They began projecting themselves in court and in public as Sufi mystics known for curing the sick, having prophetic dreams, and performing miracles. Their time of birth was also written about as occurring when Jupiter aligned with Saturn, which is why Timūr, Akbar, Jahangir, and Shah Jahan called themselves by the title "Lord of the Auspicious Conjunction." This label enabled them to be venerated as worldly kings and "heaven sent saviors" (Moin 2012: 50).

Once the mystical was connected to the worldly function of rule, Timūrīd and by extension Mughal culture, became permeated by Sufi practices, which were conspicuously displayed in court. As Moin explains about the all-encompassing influence of the Sufi practices in the Mughal court:

> The 'messianic' and 'saintly' nature of their sovereignty was adduced by astrological calculations and mystical lore, embodied in court rituals and dress, visualized in painting, enshrined in architecture, and institutionalized in cults of devotion and bodily submission to the monarch as both saint and king. — 2012: 5

In his letters to his sons there is evidence that Aurangzeb distanced himself from some of the more outwardly questionable rituals of his predecessors, such as the bodily submission of nobles to the king, but maintained the ethical and self-possessed ways of the Sufi saints in his court and exhorted the princes to do the same.

In building practices, Aurangzeb also seemed to distance himself from monumental shrine building, but that was not until the end of his life. With the construction of the tomb for his first wife Rabiā Durrānī (1622-57), the Bībī kā Maqbarā, we see the same rationale and messianic symbolism in the practice of building monumental tombs that connected him back to Timūr and Shah Jahan. While Catherine Asher and others discount the importance of the tomb and Aurangzeb's part in its construction, I argue that his connection with the tomb was essential for taking over the Mughal Empire from both his father and favored older brother, Dara Shikoh, because it signified his dedication to the messianic beliefs of his ancestors.

The most well-known study of the messianic associations of Mughal architecture is of course Wayne Begley's article, "The Myth of the Taj Mahal" (1979: 7-37). While compelling, his analysis, which connects the shape and design of the tomb to depictions of God's throne in cosmological texts, made it seem unique that Shah Jahan viewed himself as the Universal Man and God's shadow on earth.

The infusion of architecture with the sacred and saintly culture of mystical Islam, however, had been a major part of Islamic building practices since the ninth century. According to Samer Akkach's study of the mystical component of Islamic architecture, these practices followed the principles of Sufi cosmogony and cosmology, and were founded on the core concept of emanation (2005: 159). The theory of emanation contends that, because God produced the world from himself, there is no temporal separation but only an ordering of things based on proximity to God that moves from the perfect to the less perfect. Knowing where everything belongs does not come from self-evident knowledge or reasoning but from access to that reality that comes only to great beings like Sufi sheikhs or certain rulers. Astronomers, builders, and city planners also had access to this esoteric knowledge and used Euclidian geometry to design spaces in which one could encounter gnosis of the mystical world. Indeed, many of the engineers were Sufis who were able to combine their knowledge of building with the mystical knowledge of their orders.

Tombs, gardens, and other monuments materialized Sufi beliefs about the origin of everything as God, or the Absolute, and that man's duty was to find his way back to the source using his intellect guided by reason and truth. In their completed form, these spaces symbolized the builder's gnosis or secret knowledge of mystical cosmological and cosmogonic orders and more importantly distinguished his singular ability to unite outer knowledge or reason with inner knowledge or the Way to God (Ardalan and Bakhtiar 1973: 5-10). This understanding of the function of architectural spaces helps us understand why the Mughals were drawn to precisely designed and proportioned monumental forms like gateways, gardens, throne rooms, and tombs, and how these spaces supported Mughal claims to be saintly sovereigns in India.

Bringing Mystical Content of Mughal Building to the Deccan

Because the Timūrīds and their Mughal descendants styled themselves as saintly rulers, God's Shadow on Earth or the Perfect Man, their built environments mirrored the Sufi principles for the ordering of space. This was as true for Babur's ceremonial four-part gardens and Akbar's city of Fatehpur Sikri, as it was for Shah Jahan's Taj Mahal and Aurangzeb's tomb for his first wife, Rabiā Durrānī, the Bībī kā Maqbarā (*fig.* 7.3). Laura Parodi was the first to examine the tomb as a monument not of decline but as another distillation of Mughal building principles (1998: 349-83). Parodi correctly argues that one must not judge Aurangzeb's tomb for his deceased wife against the Taj Mahal, wherein the assessment of decline emerges, but instead one should understand it as keeping with the Mughal's practice of synthesizing local and imperial styles. The Deccani tomb was the logical result of the Mughal building practice that sought to adapt itself to the topography instead of forcing a uniform imperial style into the southern dominions. Parodi meticulously charts the Deccan variation of the Bībī kā Maqbarā by comparing and contrasting the forms, design, auxiliary buildings, and ornamentation, to reveal the hybrid nature of Aurangzeb's architectural patronage. My contribution is to move the discussion into the area of the spiritual and to focus on how this tomb was consistent with local and Mughal Sufi spatial practices by looking at the design and form, as well as by examining the role of the engineer selected for this monumental project.

Started in 1653 and completed in 1661, the Bībī kā Maqbarā was built during Aurangzeb's second governorship of the Deccan when many crucial events took place that led to his enthronement.[1] The period included the conquests of Golcoṇḍā in 1656 and Bījāpur in

[1] According to the travel writings of Jean-Baptiste Tavernier (1889), 300 wagons of marble loaded on carts driven by twelve bullocks reached Auraṅgābād on 17 March 1653 for what appeared to be a monumental construction project.

1657, the war of succession, the imprisonment of Shah Jahan and Aurangzeb's fratricide of his brother, Dara Shikoh. Built at a critical juncture in his life, when Aurangzeb transformed from a prince into an emperor, the tomb was essential to proving that he was ready to rule. In his book on Mughal princes, Munis Faruqui states that, while Mughal princes fought in wars of succession, they also engaged in projects that helped them "articulate a vision of who they were and what they might bring to the empire as emperor" (2012: 12). The Bībī kā Maqbarā, built in the midst of the war of succession, gave a spatial dimension to Aurangzeb's claim to the imperial throne and transposed the pre-existing Sultanate's political and spiritual authority with that of the Mughal's in the Deccan.

Therefore, rather than seeing the Taj Mahal and the Bībī kā Maqbarā as marking Mughal architectural climax and decline, it would be more helpful to view them as part of the ongoing dynastic aim to give a material dimension to their claim of Timūrīd kingship, a claim based squarely on the cosmological principles of Sufism. The proximity in dates of the two tombs, built only ten years apart, suggests that the tomb in Auraṅgābād followed the same architectural practices used at the Taj, such as combining local forms with a design derived from a Timūrīd cultural legacy. For example, the dome, whose style originates in the Deccan, was resignified to symbolize Mughal rulership. This specific shape, as argued by Wayne Begely, "played an important symbolic role, along with other emblems of sovereignty and dynastic succession" (1979: n. 16). But the symbolism of the dome does not end with the meaning of dynastic succession. From the Sufi perspective, the dome represented the heavenly vault and the two arcs that send the soul up to the domain of God and back down to the domain of man. In addition to the dome, at the Bībī kā Maqbarā we see the other mystical symbols of Mughal tombs reiterated. For example, the eight heavens of the Islamic paradise, the *hashtbihesht*, serve as the organizing principle of the garden, with its four-part subdivision and axial water channels and walkways. It was not the style, material or beauty, but the precise spatial ordering of these symbolic parts into what Lisa Golombek identified as the Timūrīd grid, which unites the Bībī kā Maqbarā with other Mughal tombs and reveals, not a departure, but a full reiteration of the underlying Sufi-based design principles of Mughal building and rule (1995: 137).

Another clue, which supports the claim that Aurangzeb's architectural program at the Bībī kā Maqbarā followed Timūrīd symbolism and Sufi design principles, is the little discussed but very important figure of the *muhandis* (architect), that all Mughal rulers placed in their service and held in high regard. The *muhandis* was not only an architect but also someone who united the mystical knowledge of geometry, astronomy, and alchemy to design imperial mosques and tombs. The *muhandis* was part of a guild whose initiation ceremonies and organization followed the model of a Sufi lodge. The initiates of the architectural guilds were family members who learned the sacred art of building and design from elders, usually their father or brothers. The Persian Timūrīds of Herāt, Balkh, and Shirāz made use of the *muhandis* to build and lend cosmological significance to their tombs, caravanserais, markets, schools, and mosques. Following the precedent shaped by their Timūrīd ancestors, the Mughals too used the *muhandis* to organize and design their architecture according to the sacred science of numbers and geometry that informed part of the Sufi's mystical inner knowledge.

The *muhandis* of the Bībī kā Maqbarā was Attā Ullāh Rashīdī, the eldest son of Ustād Ahmad Lāhorī, Shah Jahan's honored architect and designer of the Taj Mahal in Agra and the Red Fort in Delhi. Attā Ullāh was also a respected intellectual in Dara Shikoh's court, but very little is known about him and what is known comes from a *masnavī* (poetic collection), written by his brother Lutfullāh. Attā Ullāh is described in this poem as a great teacher learned in mathematics, geometry, poetry, and all the crafts (Nadvi 1948: 87-99). As was customary for Persian and Central Asian architects, his father trained him in architecture, Euclidian geometry, alchemy, and astronomy. Court documents mention in passing that he assisted his father at the Taj Mahal and the Red Fort. The Bībī kā Maqbarā is Attā Ullāh's only well-known building project and his presence there confirms that the same mystical principles and symbolism that shaped the Taj were used to design the Bībī kā Maqbarā. Aurangzeb's first and only monumental tomb, was thus an extension of the Timūrīd legacy of mystical Islam into the Deccan.

The fact that Aurangzeb never built another monumental tomb after the one for his wife is often attached to his growing disenchantment with the Sufi practices of his predecessors and his turn toward Sunni reforms. This idea may have originated due its outward similarity to the Wahhabis and their critique of tomb veneration and building. However, this reformist view, which started in the mid-eighteenth century in Saudi Arabia, did not reach India until several decades after Aurangzeb's death. Therefore, there must have been another influence on his attitudes toward tomb building, namely the mystical, political, and legal principles of governance derived from Timūrīd beliefs in the divine nature of their sovereignty. Aurangzeb may indeed have grown critical of certain aspects of Sufism, such as music, the adoption of Hindu practices, and magic spells, however, his reverence for the truth of the Sufi sheikh's knowledge and Timūrīd practices of kingship never faltered as he grew older.

While there is so much more that needs to be investigated about the style and form of the Bībī kā Maqbarā, in this paper I initiate the process by taking a Sufic approach to the study of Aurangzeb's architecture. Wherever the Mughals ruled they built public spaces such as tombs, gardens, and mosques to help spread the nature of their charisma, prophetic calling, Timūrīd ancestry, and their connection with the principles of Sufism. Placing the Bībī kā Maqbarā in this religious and political context allows us, finally, to move not only beyond the representation of Aurangzeb's architectural program as solely guided by Sunni orthodoxy, but also beyond the tropes that structure Mughal art history based on teleology and oppositions. The Bībī kā Maqbarā tomb marked the beginning of Aurangzeb's Deccan rule and his own simple grave marked the end. Both conformed with Sufi cosmogonic and cosmographic beliefs based on emanation and the soul's return journey to the Absolute. Both spaces were meant to announce Mughal rule in the Deccan and the spread of Timūrīd culture based on the distillation of Sufi principles of the world and its ordering.

References

Akkach, Samer, 2005, *Cosmology and Architecture in Premodern Islam: An Architectural Reading of Mystical Ideas*, Albany: State University of New York Press.

Ardalan, Nader and Laleh Bakhtiar, 1973, *The Sense of Unity: The Sufi Tradition in Persian Architecture*, Chicago: University of Chicago Press.

Asher, Catherine B., 1992, *Architecture of Mughal India*, Cambridge, UK: Cambridge University Press.

Begley, Wayne E., 1979, "The Myth of the Taj Mahal and a New Theory of Its Symbolic Meaning," *The Art Bulletin*, 61(1): 7-37.

Bilimoria, Jamshid H. (tr.), 1908, *Ruka'at-i-Alamgiri, Or, Letters of Aurungzebe*, London: Luzac.

Brand, Michael, 1993, "Orthodoxy, Innovation, and Revival: Considerations of the Past in Imperial Mughal Tomb Architecture," *Muqarnas*, 10: 323-34.

Brown, Katherine Butler, 2007, "Did Aurangzeb Ban Music?: Questions for the Historiography of His Reign," *Modern Asian Studies*, 41(1): 77-120.

Chandra, Satish, 1989, "Reassessing Aurangzeb," *Seminar*, 364: 35-38.

Ernst, Carl W. and Bruce B. Lawrence, 2002, *Sufi Martyrs of Love: Chishti Sufism in South Asia and Beyond*, New York: Palgrave Macmillan.

Faruqui, Munis D., 2012, *The Princes of the Mughal Empire, 1504–1719*, Cambridge and New York: Cambridge University Press.

Fergusson, James, 1899, *History of Indian and Eastern Architecture*, Book VII, London: John Murray.

Golombek, Lisa, 1995, "The Gardens of Timur: New Perspectives," *Muqarnas*, 12: 137-47.

Green, Nile, 2006, *Indian Sufism since the Seventeenth Century: Saints, Books and Empires in the Muslim Deccan*, New York: Routledge.

——, 2012, *Making Space: Sufis and Settlers in Early Modern India*, New Delhi: Oxford University Press.

Michell, George and Mark Zebrowski, 1999, *Architecture and Art of the Deccan Sultanates*, Cambridge, UK: Cambridge University Press.

Moin, A. Azfar, 2012, *The Millennial Sovereign: Sacred Kingship and Sainthood in Islam*, New York: Columbia University Press.

Nadvi, Sayyed Sulaiman, 1948, "The Family of the Engineers Who Built the Taj Mahal and the Delhi Fort," *The Journal of the Bihar Research Society*, 34: 75-110.

Parodi, Laura E., 1998, "The Bibi-ka Maqbara in Aurangabad: A Landmark of Mughal Power in the Deccan?," *East and West*, 48(3/4): 349-83.

Ruka'at-i-Alamgiri, Or, Letters of Aurungzebe, see Bilimoria 1908.

Sarkar, Jadunath, 1912, *History of Aurangzib Based on Original Sources*, vol. 1, Calcutta: M.C. Sarkar.

Tavernier, Jean-Baptiste, 1889, *Travels in India*, vol. 1, London: Macmillan and Company.

Wheeler, James Talboys, 1881, *The History of India from the Earliest Ages*, pt. I: *Mussulman Rule*, pt. II: *Mogul Empire*, London: N. Trübner.

8

Kutch Silver
A Study of Stylistic Sources

Stephen Markel

> No part of India is more celebrated for its work in precious metals than Kach [Kutch]. — Mukharji 1888 [2000]: 168

As T.N. Mukharji exclaimed in his catalogue of the Glasgow International Exhibition in 1888, Kutch silver was indeed celebrated worldwide for its extraordinary artistic quality and technical expertise (Mukharji 1888: 168). Featuring sophisticated *repoussé* work, distinctive lush floral decoration, and a very high standard of purity (95-98 percent silver compared to the minimum standard of 92.5 percent required for Sterling silver) (Wilkinson 1999: 68), it was produced from the mid-nineteenth through the early twentieth centuries in Kutch (now known as Kachchh) in western Gujarat. Comparable masterpieces in gold were also fashioned in Kutch, although far fewer were produced because of its significantly higher price (Mukharji 1888: 169). Consequently, extant Kutch gold is extremely rare (*fig.* 8.3).[1]

The pre-eminent silversmith of Kutch was Oomersi Mawji, whose work and that of his sons are generally identifiable by the

---

[1] In addition, for a Kutch gold *pandan*, serving tray, and rosewater sprinkler, see *Arts of India* 2001: 158-61; lots 118-19.

maker's marks stamped in the bottom.[2] For an exceptional example, see a *Mug with Hunting Scenes*, now in the Los Angeles County Museum of Art (M.2017.98) (*figs*. 8.1–8.2). The mug is stamped on the base with "O.M | BHUJ", indicating that it was made by Oomersi Mawji and Sons in *c*.1890.[3] Mawji was active from around 1860 to 1890 in the Kutch capital city of Bhuj, where he was appointed the court silversmith to Mahārāo Śrī Khengarjī III (r. 1875–1942). Mawji's sons continued his workshop into the 1930s, with one son serving as the court silversmith to Mahārājā Sāyājīrāo Gāekwāḍ III of Baroda (r. 1874–1939).

At its height, Kutch silver achieved enormous demand in both domestic and international markets. It was sold in London by the well-known firm of Liberty & Co., as documented in catalogue advertisements from around 1890 (Wilkinson 1999: 12, fig. 12; Wilkinson and Hawkins 2000: 145, fig. 11). The handmade beauty of Kutch silver was very influential on the English Arts and Crafts Movement from 1860 to 1910. As Saloni Mathur has noted in her informative discussion of Liberty & Co., the Arts and Crafts Movement's luminaries William Morris (1834-96) and John Ruskin (1819–1900) were patrons of Liberty & Co., where they undoubtedly encountered Kutch silver, in addition to seeing it displayed at the various International Exhibitions in the late nineteenth century (Mathur 2007: 33). Kutch silver even inspired comparable styles in late nineteenth-century American silver, as evidenced by a vase made by the Whiting Manufacturing Co. around 1880 (Wilkinson 1999: 8, fig. 1) and a tea service made by the Gorham Manufacturing

---

[2] Although sometimes identified as a silver "smith" (*sunāra*), presumably Oomersi Mawji was technically a silver "chiseler" (*citerā*) responsible for creating only the *repoussé* work. For a discussion of the division of labor involved in Indian silversmithing, see Sharma 2008: 56-58. Wilkinson relates that Oomersi Mawji was a member of the "*mocī* or cobbler caste", some of whom had switched to silversmithing (Wilkinson 1999: 69).

[3] For an almost identical Oomersi Mawji and Sons maker's mark, see Wilkinson 1999: 90, fig. 134.

Co. in 1886-88 (Busch and Futter et al. 2012: 111, no. 75).

Kutch silver encompasses an immense range of decorative object types, known collectively in trade parlance as "silver plate" to distinguish it from silver jewelry. The broad spectrum of Kutch silver plate primarily consists of myriad vessels and housewares whose function and overall form derived from European decorative art traditions. Such well-known works include tea services and a wide range of tableware, toilet trays with silver-mounted mirrors and hairbrushes, and presentation cups that could be suitably engraved with monograms or commemorative inscriptions. The European-style Kutch silver was intended and often commissioned for the European market, as well as for Europeans residing in India and Westernized Indians who had, in particular, adopted the affection for tea (Kolsky 2009).

Although now much less known than the European-style Kutch silver, there was once an equally extensive tradition of making Indian-style vessels and assorted decorative and ceremonial objects in Kutch silver and gold. Relevant publications from the late nineteenth and early twentieth century typically list and often illustrate such works, especially rosewater sprinklers, betel leaf boxes and matching trays, scent vases, and water pots (for example, Baden-Powell 1894: 61, pl. 103; Gupte 1886: 126, 131, pl. "Silver Work. Baroda"; Hoey 1880: 184; Rivett-Carnac 1902: 37, pls. 67-69). Sumptuous ritual objects were also made in Kutch, such as a *repoussé* gold ball now in the Los Angeles County Museum of Art (M.2002.37a-b) (*fig.* 8.3). It was originally part of a set of ritual toys used in celebrating Kṛṣṇa's birth.[4]

[4] This gold ball was originally part of a set of ceremonial objects used to grace a Kṛṣṇa shrine. Other items in the set would have included golden rattles, bells, mirrors, fruits, and various toy animals and birds symbolic of Kṛṣṇa's pastoral origins. This ball and numerous other gold objects were officially sold by the Trustees of the Śrī Vaḍabācārya Temple Trust in Māṇḍvī in 2000 and legally exported in 2001. For related works possibly from the same set, see Aitken 2004: 58-59, nos. 14-15.

Transcending its plethora of object types, Kutch silver is stylistically unified through its renowned design hallmark of the Kutch flowering scroll, which has been described elegantly as "sinuous vines that coil and wind in infinite, undulating, swirling patterns. [...] Emerging from the vines are stylized poppies and other flowers; these curl and twist to reveal every stage of blossoming" (Wilkinson and Hawkins 2000: 137). Interspersed amongst the fertile fields of flowers are often stock images of animals attacking prey and the occasional human figure, particularly a hunter on horseback. Kutch silver is typically adorned with rows of stylized acanthus leaves that serve as elegant borders framing the lush fields of floral decoration.

Kutch silver has been the focus of several scholarly studies. It was most recently examined in 2008 in the excellent exhibition, catalogue, and website, *Delight in Design: Indian Silver for the Raj*, by Vidya Dehejia, with contributions by Dipti Khera, Yuthika Sharma, and Wynyard Wilkinson (Dehejia et al. 2008). Wilkinson is, of course, the pre-eminent specialist on colonial Indian silver. His chapter on Kutch silver in his *Indian Silver 1858–1947*, constitutes the principal modern source of information on the subject (Wilkinson 1999). There is also research contemporaneous with the production of Kutch silver, with the most important reference article being "The Silver Workers of Cutch (Western India)" (Baden-Powell 1894).[5] My remarks presented herein are heavily indebted to these outstanding publications and are intended to augment the discussions presented within them.

Even with this long history of scholarship on Kutch silver, a critical basic question remains to be fully addressed. Namely, what were the artistic sources for the distinctive Kutch flowering scroll, often interposed with animal and human figures? In attempting to begin to answer this question, I will be examining both general and

---

[5] Note the Preface declaration (59): "Based on a paper from India by Mr. B.A. Gupte". Balkrishna Atmaram Gupte (1851–1919) was an historian from Bombay and also associated with the Mayo School of Art in Lahore.

individual motif sources, as well as foreign and domestic sources, with a particular focus in the latter on western Indian antecedents and peer examples. Some of these stylistic sources were previously presented in the aforementioned publications, which I will certainly acknowledge, but I will also suggest some potentially fruitful areas of further research.

The scrolling tendrils festooned with flowers that epitomize Kutch silver have long been compared to the related lyrical designs of the well-known pierced stone windows of the Sidi Saiyyed Mosque in Ahmedabad dating to *c.*1572. Most recently, Wilkinson (1999: 66) and Wilkinson and Hawkins (2000: 139-40) discuss this apt comparison, while Sir George Watt (1903: 33) in his catalogue for the Delhi Exhibition of 1902-03 is representative of the early proponents for the resemblance. Although the aesthetic relationship between the Ahmedabad mosque windows and the decoration of Kutch silver is certainly close, I would like to observe a key difference. Whereas the writhing foliage on the mosque windows can all be traced back to a large trunk in the center of the composition, the scrolling flowers embellishing Kutch silver generally do not originate from a central stalk. Rather, as Watt noted, they have "no beginning or ending ... [and] a composite flower [that] recurs at repeated intervals" (1903: 33). Considering that these infinite scrolls were likely created by the silversmith from memory as an embodiment of regional artistic expression, as maintained by Yuthika Sharma in the *Delight in Design* catalog, it is likely that the Kutch flowering scrolls were based on stock images of scrolling vines and flowers that were utilized as needed to fill the space to be decorated rather than being derived from a specific source such as the Ahmedabad mosque windows (Sharma 2008: 56).

The existence of stock images of numerous motifs and vessel types for use by the Kutch silversmiths, and also functioning as sales catalogs for potential customers, has been documented in a fascinating essay by Vidya Dehejia and others in the *Delight in Design* catalog, "A Cache Uncovered: Workshop Drawings of Oomersee

Mawjee & Sons of Kutch" (2008: 38-47). She discusses sixteen drawings out of a group of some 300 drawings belonging to the collectors Elizabeth and John Sequeira, and a number of additional such drawings are illustrated throughout the catalogue's section on Kutch silver where they are paired with images of silver works to which they correspond. With the illustrations in the catalog and a large group of images sent to me directly by John Sequeira, I have now seen images of about 80 out of the 300 drawings. What has struck me so far about these workshop drawings — and this is still obviously a preliminary impression since I have seen less than a third of the works — is that even the complete vessels represented in the drawings are intended to be object types rather than the source models or representations of specific vessels. This can be deduced by a number of annotations on the drawings that offer customers variations in the size or overall weight of the silver of a given vessel, and even instructions from customers and retailers specifying the extent of desired ornamentation. Moreover, there is also a marked difference in the treatment of the design elements between the drawings and the actual physical objects. In the drawings the floral scrolls are generally even denser than on the silver objects, and the animal and human figures are frequently emphasized by being shown proportionally larger.

What is important in the present context of studying the sources for the flowering scrolls and interspersed figures found on Kutch silver is that, apart from certain annotations identifying a particular geographical vessel form or overall design style, such as a drawing of a so-called "Arabian shape Claret Jug," there are no annotations naming or identifying the origin of the scrolling vines or any of the other decorative motifs depicted (Dehejia et al. 2008: 44, fig. 12). An obvious conclusion from this lack of labeling is that these elements of the artists' design vocabulary were too familiar to need to be identified.

The origin or primary stylistic source of Kutch silver has been a key topic of interest since the earliest European and Indian

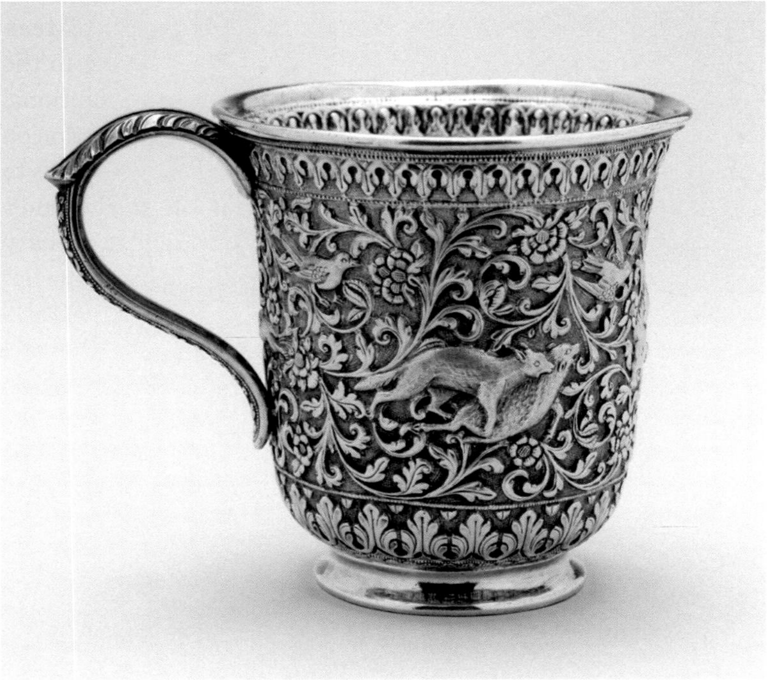

fig. 8.1: Oomersi Mawji and Sons (India, active *c*.1890–1910), Mug with Hunting Scenes, India, Gujarat, Kachchh (Kutch), Bhuj, *c*.1890, *repoussé* silver

fig. 8.2: Detail of *fig* 8.1: maker's mark on base

fig. 8.3: Kṛṣṇa's Ball, India, Gujarat, Kachchh (Kutch), Māṇḍvī, *c.*1875–1900, *repoussé* gold

fig. 8.4: Portal with Tympanum (detail), India, Gujarat, Kachchh (Kutch), dated 1871, wood with copper and iron fittings

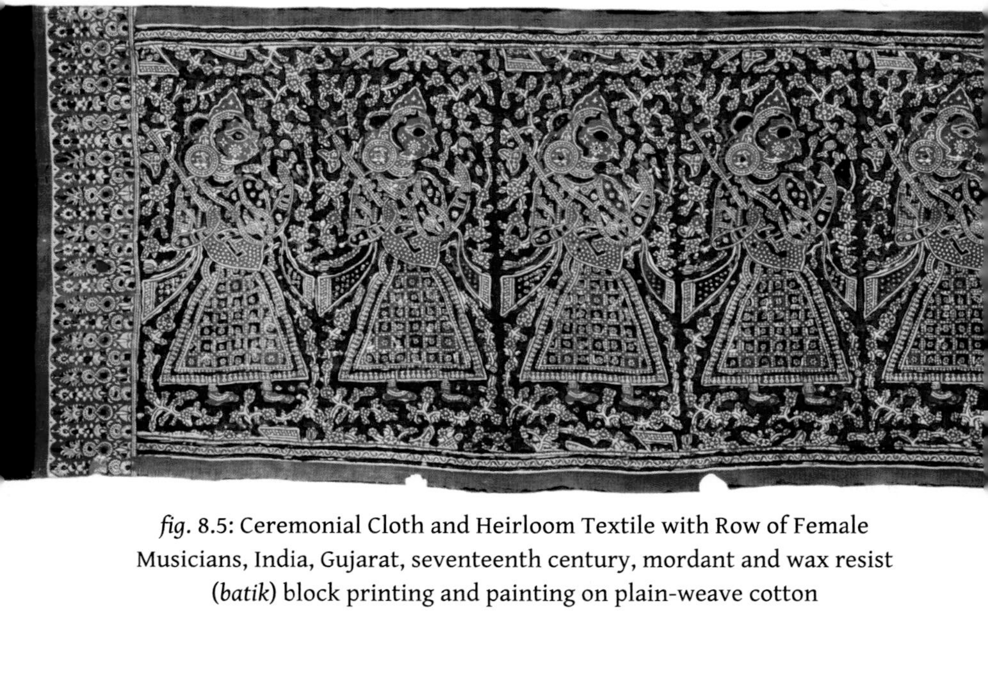

fig. 8.5: Ceremonial Cloth and Heirloom Textile with Row of Female Musicians, India, Gujarat, seventeenth century, mordant and wax resist (*batik*) block printing and painting on plain-weave cotton

curatorial writings on the subject in the late nineteenth century. In the catalogue of the works displayed in the Indian Court of the Paris Universal Exhibition of 1878, which prominently featured Indian gold and silverware from the collection of the Prince of Wales (who later became King Edward VII), Sir George Birdwood (1832–1917) characterized Kutch silver succinctly as being of Dutch origin (Birdwood 1878: 53). This supposition was repeated by subsequent authors such as Mukharji (1883: 39) and Watt (1903: 33). Birdwood further elaborated on his claim for the Dutch origin of Kutch silver in his publication in 1880 of *The Industrial Arts of India*, in which he states that:

> The beautiful silver and gold *repoussé* work of Katch [Kutch] is of Dutch origin, but has been perfectly assimilated to the native style of the province, and is much sought after. —1880: 151

The Dutch origin of Kutch silver is often linked to the well-known account of Ramsingh Malam, a Kutch sailor who had been shipwrecked at sea and rescued by a Dutch vessel that then carried him on to Holland. Ramsingh stayed there for seventeen years and learned a variety of Dutch artistic skills, including metalworking and enameling. Ramsingh then returned to Kutch, where he began a long-term patronage in Bhuj under Rāo Lakhpatjī (r. 1741-60). Ramsingh was instrumental in designing and constructing the Europeanized royal palace of Bhuj, the Āinā Mahal, built *c.*1750. It features Delft-style ceramic floor tiles, European mirrors and prints decorating the walls, and Venetian-style glass chandeliers (Goswamy and Dallapiccola 1983: 19-22; London 2000: 48-75; and Rushbrook Williams 1958: 137-42).

The lasting influence of Ramsingh's introduction of Dutch artistic styles and also direct exposure to Dutch silver itself by means of trade articles form the basis by which Wilkinson (1999) and Wilkinson and Hawkins (2000) identified certain stylistic features of Kutch silver as Dutch in origin:

> The decoration found on early nineteenth-century Kutch silver

> pieces, with their characteristic trailing vines and bunches of grapes, borrows heavily from the decorative motifs adorning Dutch silver work from the late eighteenth and early nineteenth centuries. In addition, the distinctive repousse [*sic*] borders, found on virtually all Kutchi work from the mid to late nineteenth century can be likened to decorative forms embellishing Dutch pieces of a slightly earlier vintage.
> – Wilkinson and Hawkins 2000: 138; see also Wilkinson 1999: 67

Although no illustrations or references for Dutch silver are provided by the authors, a representative Dutch tea caddy dated 1782, now in Leeuwarden, Friesland, does reveal a similar emphasis on exuberant floral imagery (Beeling en Zoon 1980, vol. 2: 260-61).[6] Clearly, however, there are significant differences in the composition density and stylistic treatment of the motifs.

Wilkinson and Hawkins also argue for strong Portuguese stylistic influence on Kutch silver:

> Consider even the most common piece of faience from Coimbra, the great Portuguese-producing center. Immediately in evidence are the same infinite, twisting vines and foliage that constitute the bulk of the decoration found on Kutchi silver. Scattered amid the foliage are animals of all descriptions, from the exotic — mythological birds and beasts, to the mundane — domestic animals and those of the chase. ... A far more direct influence of typical Portuguese silverwork, of the eighteenth and nineteenth centuries, on Kutchi silverwork, is apparent in the cast and applied borders typically found on Portuguese pieces, as these also figure significantly in the nineteenth-century silverwork of Kutch. — 2000: 139; see also Wilkinson 1999: 67

A representative earthenware dish from Coimbra dating from *c.*1650-75, now in the Victoria and Albert Museum, London (C.61-1910), depicts a stylized lion in a landscape thriving with flowers. A representative Portuguese silver ewer and basin dated by hallmarks

[6] For additional studies on Dutch silver, see Frederiks 1952-1961; den Blaauwen 1979; and Victoria & Albert Museum 1953.

to *c*.1768-84, now in the National Museum of Ancient Art, Lisbon (1072, 1073), features the "cast borders" described by the authors (Levenson 1993: 211, no. 26).[7] As was the case with the Dutch tea caddy, however, the similarities of the Portuguese pottery and silver plate decoration to Kutch silver are more of an analogous design conception rather than an exact stylistic and/or iconographic source for the execution of individual motifs.

While the assimilation of Dutch and Portuguese artistic traditions may well have played a role in the development of the distinctive decorative style of Kutch silver, it has long been recognized that important source imagery was readily available in the western Indian stylistic idiom itself. As Baden-Powell declared:

> Cutch [Kutch] ornamentation ... belongs to the same general style which is traceable in the wood carving or stone ornament of Western India.
>
> — 1894: 60

The aforementioned stone *jālī* of the Ahmedabad mosque is likely what Baden-Powell had in mind in referring to the "stone ornament." A wooden tympanum from a Gujarātī portal dated by inscription to 1871, now in the Los Angeles County Museum of Art (M.72.51.1a-h), has deeply cut, exuberant foliage and myriad blossoms that resonate well with the flowering scrolls of Kutch silver (*fig.* 8.4).[8]

There are also general stylistic parallels to be found in the decorative arts of western India. A seventeenth-century Gujarātī textile made for export to Indonesia, now in the Los Angeles County Museum of Art (M.2005.10) (*fig.* 8.5), and an early seventeenth-century inlaid wooden cabinet from Gujarat or Sindh (in present-day Pakistan), now in the Victoria and Albert Museum (885-1905), both feature figures set in a lush field of flowers, which is a common composition used in the decorative arts of western India preceding

---

[7] For additional studies on Portuguese ceramics and silver, see Pereira 1995 and Smith 1968.

[8] See also London 2000: 106-17 and Thakkar 2004.

the development of Kutch silver.

Similarly, some of the major design motifs and even the metalworking technique principally associated with Kutch silver can be found on earlier examples of non-Kutch silver. A mid-seventeenth-century silver antimony flask from a Mughal atelier has decorative borders of stylized acanthus leaves (Markel 1989: 149, fig. 157). This is a common design feature of Kutch silver, where it is generally represented in a smaller scale. An eighteenth-century Rājasthānī silver alloy box, now in the National Museum, New Delhi (61.368), has a *repoussé* flowering scroll that closely parallels those of Kutch silver.

Even the clothing worn by the figures depicted in Kutch silver reveals their western Indian origin. For example, a Kutch beaker attributed to *c.*1880, now in the Virginia Museum of Fine Arts (2011.272), depicts male hunters dressed in Kutch attire, specifically a Gujarātī men's double-breasted garment with a large neck opening held together by a cloth tie (Dehejia et al. 2008: 142, no. 48). It is called a *puṭhiā*, which is a regional form of the well-known *aṅgarakhā* type of upper garment.[9] A nineteenth-century sculpture of a Palace Guardian from Kutch, now in the Los Angeles County Museum of Art (AC1995.151.1), shows him wearing the same style of distinctive garment.

From this small sampling of the polyglot stylistic inspirations and regional artistic traditions, it is evident that the sophisticated vessel forms and exquisite decoration of Kutch silver represent a brilliant amalgamation and ensuing aesthetic expression of the highest order.

---

[9] I would like to thank Dale Carolyn Gluckman for identifying the same *puṭhiā* garment worn by a male rider on a Kutch presentation cup formerly on loan to LACMA from the Collection of Julian Sands (Loan # L.2012.26.6). For technical diagrams of *puṭhiā*, see Bhandari 2005: 204-05.

References

Aitken, M.E., 2004, *When Gold Blossoms: Indian Jewelry from the Susan L. Beningson Collection*, New York: Philip Wilson.

Arts of India, 2001, Auction catalog, London: Christie's, 27 September 2001.

Baden-Powell, B.H., 1894, "The Silver Workers of Cutch (Western India)," *The Journal of Indian Art and Industry*, 5(45): 59-62, pls. 91-103.

Beeling en Zoon, A.C., 1980, *Nederlands Zilver, 1600-1813*, 2 vols., Leeuwarden: By the author.

Bhandari, V., 2005, *Costume, Textiles and Jewellery of India: Traditions in Rajasthan*, London: Mercury Books.

Birdwood, G.C.M., 1878, *Paris Universal Exhibition of 1878: Handbook to the British Indian Section*, London and Paris: Offices of the Royal Commission.

——, 1880, *The Industrial Arts of India*, London: Chapman & Hall; 1st reprint edn., London: The Reprint Press, 1971; 3rd reprint edn., *The Arts of India*, Jersey, CI: The British Book Co., 1986. Republished as B.K. Bhattacharjee, 1998, *Industrial Arts of India*, New Delhi: Indian Publishers Distributors.

den Blaauwen, A.L. (ed.), 1979, *Nederlands Zilver/Dutch Silver: 1580–1830*, The Hague: Staatsuitgeverij.

Busch, J.T., C.L. Futter et al., 2012, *Inventing the Modern World: Decorative Arts at the World's Fairs, 1851–1939*, New York: Skira Rizzoli.

Dehejia, V., Dipti Khera, Yuthika Sharma, and Wynyard R.T. Wilkinson (eds.), 2008, *Delight in Design: Indian Silver for the Raj*, Ahmedabad: Mapin.

Frederiks, J.W., 1952–1961, *Dutch Silver*, 4 vols., The Hague: Martinus Nijhoff.

Goswamy, B.N. and A.L. Dallapiccola, 1983, *A Place Apart: Painting in Kutch, 1720–1820*, Delhi: Oxford University Press; reprint edn., London, 2000.

Gupte, B.A., 1886, "The Baroda Court," *The Journal of Indian Art*, 1(16): 126-33.

Hoey, W., 1880, *A Monograph on Trade and Manufacturers in Northern India*, Lucknow: The American Mission Press.

Kolsky, E., 2009, "Tea, Labor, and Empire in India," in *Steeped in History: The Art of Tea*, ed. B. Hohenegger, pp. 204-15, Los Angeles: Fowler Museum at UCLA.

Levenson, J.A. (ed.), 1993, *The Age of the Baroque in Portugal*, Washington: National Gallery of Art.

London, C.W. (ed.), 2000, *The Arts of Kutch*, Mumbai: Marg Publications.

Markel, S., 1989, "Jades, Jewels, and Objets d'Art," in *Romance of the Taj Mahal*, exh. publication by P. Pal, J. Leoshko, J.M. Dye III, and S. Markel, pp. 128-69, Los Angeles: Los Angeles County Museum of Art; London: Thames & Hudson.

——, 2019 [forthcoming], *Mughal and Early Modern Metalware from South Asia at LACMA: An Online Scholarly Catalogue*, Los Angeles: Los Angeles County Museum of Art.

Mathur, S., 2007, *India by Design: Colonial History and Cultural Display*, Berkeley and Los Angeles: University of California Press.

Mukharji, T.N., 1883, *A Hand-Book of Indian Products (Art-Manufactures and Raw Materials)*, Calcutta: J. Patterson, reprint edn., Charleston, SC: Nabu Press, 2010.

——, 1888, *Art-Manufactures of India*, Calcutta: Superintendent of Government Printing; reprint edns., New Delhi: Navrang, 1974; and New Delhi: Aryan Books International, 2000.

Pereira, J.C.-B., 1995, *Portuguese Tiles from the National Museum of Azulejo, Lisbon*, London: Zwemmer and Lisbon: Instituto Português de Museus.

Rivett-Carnac, J.H., 1902, "On Some Specimens of Indian Metal Work," *The Journal of Indian Art and Industry*, 9(74): 33-39.

Rushbrook Williams, L.F., 1958, *The Black Hills: Kutch in History and Legend*, London: Weidenfeld and Nicolson; reprint edn., 1999, Ahmedabad: Sahitya Mudranalaya.

Sharma, Y., 2008, " 'A House of Wonder:' Silver at the Delhi Durbar Exhibition of 1903," in Dehejia, *Delight in Design: Indian Silver for the Raj*, ed. V. Dahejia et al., pp. 48-64, Ahmedabad: Mapin.

Smith, R.C., 1968, *The Art of Portugal 1500–1800*, London: Weidenfeld and Nicolson.

Thakkar, J., 2004, *Naqsh: The Art of Wood Carving in Traditional Houses of Gujarat; A Focus of Ornamentation*, Ahmedabad: School of Interior Design, Centre for Environmental Planning & Technology.

Victoria & Albert Museum, 1953, *The Golden Age of Dutch Silver*, London: Her Majesty's Stationary Office.

Watt, G., 1903, *Indian Art at Delhi 1903: Being the Official Catalogue of the Delhi Exhibition 1902-1903*, Calcutta: Superintendent of Government Printing, reprint, Delhi: Motilal Banarsidass, 1987.

Wilkinson, W.R.T., 1999, *Indian Silver 1858–1947: Silver from the Indian Sub-continent and Burma Made by Local Craftsman in Western Forms*, London: W.R.T. Wilkinson.

Wilkinson, W.R.T. and M.-L. Hawkins, 2000, "Kutchi Silver: A Meeting of East and West," in *The Arts of Kutch*, ed. C.W. London, pp. 136-45, Mumbai: Marg Publications.

9

Kāśīrāj
The Presentation Album of the Mahārājā of Benares

Tushara Bindu Gude

In 2012 the Los Angeles County Museum of Art (LACMA) acquired the Willard Huyck and Gloria Katz collection of South Asian photography. The 255 works in the collection consist primarily of nineteenth-century views of India and Sri Lanka by various photographers and studios then working in the subcontinent. The collection also includes the complete eight-volume series of *The People of India* (produced between 1868 and 1875) and an album of photographs that is the focus of this essay. Half-bound in leather, with gilt decoration and lettering, the album bears the title, *Views of Benares Presented by the Maharaja of Benares.*[1] Between its covers are forty-one photographs, all but two of which are mounted one to a page. Short descriptive titles are pasted beneath each photograph, and the last page also contains the label, "Madho Prasad Artist to H.H. the Maharajah of Benares."

While photography in colonial India has received much attention in recent years, there has been little discussion of such presentation albums, which were commissioned by royal patrons and executed largely by native photographers, whose

[1] The city is officially known as Vārāṇasī, and popularly as Banāras. For the sake of consistency, throughout this essay I will use the anglicized spelling of "Benares" as it appears in the titles of the LACMA album and other similar works. The term Kāśīrāj, employed in the title of this essay, was synonymous with Benares State.

biographies and bodies of work are otherwise little known.[2] Often, single photographs from albums are discussed in isolation from neighboring images, despite the fact that presentation albums, viewed in their entirety, present a highly selective — and thus, subjective — set of imagery.[3] The presentation album of the Mahārājā of Benares is instructive in this regard. A review of its contents suggests the complex self-positioning of Indian rulers in late nineteenth and early twentieth-century India, as they mediated between their traditional roles and their positions as modern subjects of a colonial state.

The patron of LACMA's album, although not identified by name in its pages, was Mahārājā Prabhu Narayan Singh (r. 1889–1931). A presentation album containing exactly the same series of forty-one photographs, now in the collection of the British Library, is inscribed as having been "Presented to H.E. Lord Reading by Maharaja Benares 1 Dic [*sic*] 1921." A label pasted inside the cover of the Reading album is signed "Prabhu Narayan 1-12-21" (British Library Album 10/6: 1-41). While Prabhu Narayan Singh may have commissioned the majority of the photographs in the LACMA and British Library Reading albums, at least five can be dated to the reign of his predecessor Mahārājā Ishwari Prasad Narayan Singh (r. 1835-89). These earlier photographs may date to *c.*1883 on the basis of their presence in another album, also in the British Library. Stamped with the title: *Views of Benares from the River Side Presented by the Maharaja of Benares*, this album contains a label giving the following information:

---

[2] The major exception is Raja Deen Dayal, whose work has been studied by several scholars.

[3] There has, however, been significant recent research in this area, most notably Deepali Dewan and Deborah Hutton's discussion of Raja Deen Dayal's presentation albums for the Sixth Nizam of Hyderabad, Mahbub Ali Khan, as well as the albums produced for his Prime Minister Asman Jah. Their contents demonstrate the ways in which such photographic compilations could project various statements about governance, social identity, and status (Dewan and Hutton 2013: 82-109, 166-91).

> River-side views of Benares from Ramnagar to Raj Ghat. A continuous set of 37 photos. Taken under special order of H.H. Maharaja, Benares, G.C.S.I. by His Highnesses's [*sic*] Photographer, Babu Jageshwar Prasad. January 1883.
>
> – British Library Album 177: 1–37

An even earlier album in the British Library, similarly titled *Views of Benares from the River Side* indicates that Ishwari Prasad Narayan Singh's patronage of Indian photographers may have begun in the late 1860s, and perhaps even earlier. Each of the twenty-three photographs in this album is accompanied by the label:

> By B.G. Bromochary Photographer to H.H. the Maharaja of Benares — 1869. — British Library Album 985: 1-23

None of Bromochary's photographs are duplicated in the LACMA album, which cannot have been compiled any earlier than 1905 to 1907. The album's last two photographs depict the Aśokan pillar and lion capital at Sārnāth, which were only revealed during Frederic O. Oertel's excavations of 1904 to 1905 (*fig.* 9.5). A photograph of the Bhadaini Pumping Station and Waterworks, which was not fully completed until 1907, is also included (*fig.* 9.3) (London 2005: 134).[4]

Little is known of the three Benares court photographers mentioned above. A scant few additional photographs by Brajo Gopal Bromochary exist, and these include royal portraits in addition to images depicting various manners of teaching in India.[5] The name of Babu Jageshwar Prasad, presumed to be a relative of Madho Prasad, cannot be associated definitively with any photographs beyond those found in the Benares presentation

[4] Detailed analysis of building activities in the city and along the *ghāṭs* will assist in dating and establishing a chronology for the various Benares presentation albums and their photographs, as will a thorough investigation of comparative visual documents and descriptive accounts.

[5] These include the British Library's Photos MSS Eur G38/1(52f) and (52g), and Photos 1000/46(4705)-(4709).

albums.[6] Madho Prasad was a painter as well as photographer to the Benares ruling family, judging from a *c.*1885 portrait, now in the collection of the Asian Art Museum, San Francisco. The painting depicts Mahārājā Ishwari Prasad Narayan Singh with his successors Prabhu Narayan Singh and Aditya Narayan Singh (r. 1931-39) (acc. no. 2005.64.169). The verso side is inscribed with Madho Singh's name and it designates Ramnagar, where the rulers of Benares resided, as its place of production (Bautze 1998: 125-28). That the artist continued to work in the capacity of both a painter and a photographer is suggested by a painted photograph of Prabhu Narayan Singh, signed by Madho Singh and dated 1908, in the British Library (F249).[7]

The presentation albums associated with Madho Singh raise an issue of attribution that has long impacted investigations of Indian photography in the colonial period. As noted above, several of the photographs in the LACMA and Reading albums, as well as other known versions of these Benares presentation albums, can be found in Babu Jageshwar Prasad's album of 1883.[8] In 1929 several of

---

[6] Both Sophie Gordon and Joachim Bautze have suggested that there may have been a relationship between Babu Jageshwar Prasad and Madho Prasad (Gordon 2011: 363 n. 12; Bautze 2006: 220–21).

[7] Although the photographs produced for his urban clientele have not yet been identified, Judith Mara Gutman claims that Madho Prasad, while maintaining a studio in the palace, also operated a shop in the bazaar at Benares. She further claims that Madho Prasad learned photography from Girish Chandra De, a palace engineer in charge of maintenance and repairs. De may have learned photography around 1860, becoming one of the first practitioners of the art at Benares. Gutman credits him with establishing the studio at Ramnagar, and notes a portrait, shot by De in 1877, of the Mahārājā of Benares and Prince Albert (1982: 39, 94, 96).

[8] These additional versions of the album include the British Library's MSS Eur E267/189 (1-41) and Photo 17/3 (1-41). Joachim K. Bautze has also noted corresponding albums in a Christie's sales catalog (London, June 17, 1998, lot 242) and in the collection of H.H. Maharawal Mahipal Singhji of Dungarpur (Bautze 2006: 227 n. 61).

Madho Singh's photographs were included in a presentation album that bears on its last page the label, "Raghunath Prasad Artist and Photographer to H.H. the Maharajah of Benares." The opening photograph in the album is a portrait of Prabhu Narayan Singh, signed and dated by the Mahārājā.[9]

Further complicating investigations into authorship, as well as the relative chronology of photographers working at Benares, is the existence of numerous smaller versions of the Benares presentation albums discussed above. Most of these appear to be titled *Views of Benares from the River Side Presented by the Maharajah of Benares* and contain twenty or twenty-one photographs. Some of these smaller albums, which do not contain the names of photographers, include the same photographs that are attributed to Madho Prasad in the LACMA album.[10] At least one of the albums includes a signed portrait of Mahārājā Aditya Narayan Singh, which demonstrates the persistence of these presentation albums into the 1930s (British Library MSS Eur F138/188: 1-20). A later album, containing a portrait of Mahārājā Vibhuti Narayan Singh (r. 1939–2000) as a young man, appears to have been compiled in the 1940s.[11] Thus, it appears that, from the late nineteenth through the early twentieth century, the work of the various court photographers at Benares constituted a stock, providing images as needed for projects that often combined photographs of different date and authorship into a coherent whole.[12] Some notion of the ways in which these images

---

[9] This album is now in the rare books collection of the Center for Art and Archaeology, American Institute for Indian Studies, Gurugram.

[10] See, for instance, the sales catalog for Bonhams, London, October 2, 2011, lot 378.

[11] I do not know, at present, whether these albums of the 1930s and 1940s included the earlier photographs of *c.*1890–1905.

[12] This is not unlike the manner in which professional studio photographs were selected by travelers for memento albums. It was the practice also at Raja Deen Dayal's studio, where images from the Nizam's 1888 presentation album were repeated in albums compiled several years later (Dewan and Hutton 2013: 104–05).

were joined together to project a carefully crafted image of the state can be gathered from a study of LACMA's *Views of Benares.*

The album begins with an image titled "Fort, Ram-nagar", depicting the river façade of the expansive residence and administrative seat of the Benares rulers (*fig.* 9.1). The fort, which lies on the eastern bank of the Ganges, was founded between 1750 and 1752 by Balwant Singh (r. 1739-70), the first Rājā of Benares. It was the first significant monument to the power of the Bhūmihār clan who were formerly revenue collectors for the Nawabs of Awadh. The majestic image with which the album opens thus serves as a reminder of the Mahārājā's line of descent and his claim to rulership in Benares. Three additional views of Ramnagar are inserted near the middle of the album, immediately after a series of *ghāṭ* photographs, and include a courtyard scene as well as two prominent gateways, one of which serves as a backdrop to the silver state carriage. These are followed by a photograph showing the nearby Rambagh garden with the pleasure pavilion constructed by Balwant Singh's successor, Chet Singh (r. 1770-81), and an image of the adjacent Sumeru Devī Temple, founded by the latter in the 1770s. The temple, with its prominent spire, was an ambitious statement of piety and status, and later came to play an integral role in the annual Rāmalīlā pageants sponsored by the Benares rulers (Freitag 1989: 42).

The photographs of Ramnagar and Rambagh interpose, at the center of the album, a sense of their royal patron's dynastic prominence. Thus, the photos parallel their place at the center of the built environment that came to define Benares in the late nineteenth and early twentieth centuries. Royal legitimacy was not just linked to patronage; it also had roots in the religious identity of the royal lineage. The Mahārājās of Benares considered themselves the earthly representatives of Lord Viśvanātha. Accordingly, the Viśvanātha Temple erected by Ahilyābāī of Indore in 1877, which was built near an earlier temple partially destroyed by Aurangzeb, is the most important Śaiva structure in Benares. It defines the center of the *antargṛha* (innermost sanctum) of the city itself (Eck 1982: 96, 354-55). The domes of the Viśvanātha Temple and those of the adjacent Jñānavāpī Mosque — which incorporates a wall of the earlier temple — appear in the presentation album, in a photograph entitled "Golden Temple and Aurangzeb's Mosque" (*fig.* 9.2).

The nineteen photographs between the first image of Ramnagar and the middle group of views discussed above depict various *ghāṭ*s that line the western bank of the Ganges River from the south to north. Since many *ghāṭ*s have since been renamed, or have been divided into several units, the labels on the photographs do not always reflect present-day designations. The second photograph in LACMA's album, for instance, is labeled "Assisangam-ghat," and as such is intended to mark the confluence of the Asi and Ganges rivers, a place of great spiritual potency and the first of Benares' *pañcatīrtha*s (literally, "five crossings"). The structures depicted in the photograph today correspond to the Gaṅgā Mahal and Rewā Ghāṭs (the latter known formerly as Lālā Miśrā Ghāṭ).

Two labels attached to the third photograph in the album point out the "Bhadaini Water-works" and "Rani Sursar Ghat," in a view encompassing what are today the Bhadainī, Jānakī, and Chedī Lāl Ghāṭs (*fig.* 9.3).[13] Of particular interest is the attention drawn to the Bhadainī Water-works, a pumping plant that delivered water from the Ganges to a filtering and distribution station at Bhelupura (Greaves 2003: 36). Upon the completion of these buildings, which were begun in the late 1890s, Benares was said to have become the first city in India to be supplied with water piped from the sacred river (Parker 1895: 41). Bhadainī was designed in the Indo-Saracenic style familiar from many civic buildings in nineteenth-century India. Its inclusion in the Benares presentation album suggests that it was seen as a marker of progress and — along with several other civic monuments pictured — as emblematic particularly of Prabhu

13 The Rānī of Sursand, to whom the label refers, built a temple above the *ghāṭ* from which it derives its present name (Gutschow 2006: 206).

Narayan Singh's benevolent leadership and cordial relationship with the colonial government.

The British had assumed administrative control over Benares in 1795, but in 1911 invested Prabhu Narayan Singh with full ruling powers over a newly recognized princely state.[14] Although the British retained direct rule in Benares city, they allowed the Mahārājā's capital to remain at Ramnagar (Singh 2009: 80-83, 95; Freitag 1989: 10-11). Scholars have noted Prabhu Narayan Singh's considerable support of public works and civic structures in Benares, and photographs 29 through 32 in the presentation album are suggestive of this, despite the fact that the Mahārājā's direct involvement in some of them is unclear. These photographs depict "The Town Hall," "Prince of Wales Hospital," "Ishwari Memorial Hospital," and "Queen's College." The Gothic Revival-style Queen's College — now Sampurnanand Sanskrit University — was designed and partially funded by the British and completed in 1853. The Town Hall was erected between 1873 and 1875 by the Mahārājā of Vizianagaram in the Indo-Saracenic style, which also describes the architecture of the two hospitals (London 2005: 131, 135). Following the photographs of these four buildings is an image of the neo-classical "Nadesar House," a late-eighteenth-century East India Company guesthouse that was purchased by Ishwari Prasad Narayan Singh to function in a state capacity (London 2005: 127-28). As the photograph does not show any of Ishwari Prasad Narayan Singh's refurbishment of the building, it may belong among the earlier works in the presentation album. As a group, these images of secular monuments in recognizably European hybrid styles convey the Mahārājā's progressive leadership and self-positioning among a colonial elite.

Returning to the photographs of *ghāṭs*, many of these feature

---

[14] They had previously recognized the allegiance of Ishwari Prasad Narayan Singh by conferring on him a knighthood in the Star of India, one of the chivalric orders invented for colonial subjects. Subsequent rulers were awarded similar honors.

monumental palaces and other structures built by South Asian rulers, which also attest to the Māharājā of Benares' role as a steward of history and tradition in India's holiest city. Chet Singh's late eighteenth-century palace, for instance, dominates a view titled "Shivala-ghat."[15] The *c.*1830 palace of King Digpatiya of Champaran (in Bihar) is seen in a photograph labeled "Dhunrao Panth-ghat," and the *c.*1670 palace of Rana Jagat Singh of Udaipur appears in a photograph of "Rana-mahal Ghat" (*fig.* 9.4). Other impressive edifices include the Indore State Palace Complex of 1778 to 1785 at "Ahilya Bai's-ghat", the "Observatory of Manmandir", erected in 1710 atop the *c.*1586 palace constructed by Raja Man Singh of Amber, the 1843 Samrājeśvara Temple and associated complex, identified in the album as "Lalta-ghat and Napalees Temple," and the 1795 Bhonsle Palace at "Ghosla-ghat." The activities of royal patrons from throughout India and Nepal, over several centuries, contributed to the remarkable riverscape attested in the album's pages. Certainly, one intention of gathering these images together was to suggest the mahārājā's presiding role over a vast network of elite patronage and pilgrimage, and his maintenance of Benares as a sacred center. The inclusion of several of Benares' most important pilgrimage *ghāṭ*s, such as Daśāśvamedha Ghāṭ, Maṇikarṇikā Ghāṭ, and Pañcagaṅgā Ghāṭ — all three of which are among the *pañcatīrtha*s — underscore this point.

The Pañcagaṅgā Ghāṭ is depicted in a photograph labeled "Minaret and Panch-ganga Ghat," which draws attention to the Dharahara, or Ālamgīrī, Mosque that has dominated this view of the riverbank since 1699. The aforementioned photograph of the Viśvanātha Temple, in which the domes of the Jñānavāpī Mosque are visible, and a photograph of a Sufi tomb some distance from Benares, are the only other testaments to Muslim presence in the region.[16] Eight photographs at the end of the album, all

15 The name of Śivālā is today attached to a *ghāṭ* slightly north of the one depicted in the photograph.

16 The Sufi tomb, which figures in a photograph titled "Latif Shah Waterfall,"

titled "Buddhists [*sic*] remains (Sarnath)," depict a much earlier religious history, however. The photographs include three views of the Dhamekh *stūpa* at Sārnāth and three photographs of sculptures recovered from archaeological excavations. The final two photographs in the album, both pasted on one page, show the broken upper portion of the Aśokan column at Sārnāth. In one, it appears at close view; in the other, it appears from a distance, revealing the presence of the famous lion capital that was also unearthed at this site (*fig.* 9.5).

The album closes, then, with an evocation of the Mauryan emperor whose reign was, by the early twentieth century, considered a pinnacle in Indian history, and whose ethical and tolerant behavior was increasingly upheld as a model of kingship.[17] Two images of rule — one, contemporary, and the other, historical and symbolic — thus frame the contents of the presentation album. Surely, this was an intentional statement about the domain of the illustrious Kāśīrāj presented in the various photographs that appear between these two "bookends" and which conceptually link the Mahārājā of Benares with the glorious Indian past.[18]

References

Bautze, Joachim K., 1998, *Interaction of Cultures: Indian and Western Painting 1780–1910*, Alexandria, VA: Art Services International.

——, 2006, "Examples of Unlicensed Copies and Versions of Views from Benares: Their Authorship and Identification," in *Visualizing Space in Banaras: Images, Maps, and the Practice of Representation*, ed. Martin Gaenszle and Jörg Gengnagel, pp. 213-32, Wiesbaden: Harrassowitz Verlag.

---

appears after the Ramnagar series.

17 A notable recent study that examines the legacy of Aśoka is Olivelle, Leoshko, and Ray 2012.

18 There are a number of additional ways, beyond the scope of this short essay, in which the Benares presentation album engages with historical referents, pictorial antecedents, and colonial and nationalist ideologies and rhetoric. These are the focus of a more detailed forthcoming analysis.

fig. 9.1: "Fort, Ram-nagar"

fig. 9.2: "Golden Temple and Aurangzeb's Mosque"

fig. 9.3: "Bhadaini Water-works" and "Rani Sursar Ghat"

fig. 9.4: "Rana-mahal Ghat"

fig. 9.5: "Buddhists [*sic*] remains (Sarnath)"

Dewan, Deepali and Deborah Hutton, 2013, *Raja Deen Dayal: Artist-Photographer in 19th-Century India*, New Delhi: Alkazi Collection of Photography and Ahmedabad: Mapin.

Eck, Diana, 1982, *Banaras: City of Light*, Princeton: Princeton University Press.

Freitag, Sandra B. (ed.), 1989, *Culture and Power in Banaras: Community, Performance, and Environment, 1800–1980*, Berkeley: University of California Press.

Gaenszle, Martin and Jörg Gengnagel (eds.), 2006, *Visualizing Space in Banaras: Images, Maps, and the Practice of Representation*, Wiesbaden: Harrassowitz Verlag.

Gengnagel, Jörg, 2011, *Visualized Texts: Sacred Spaces, Spatial Texts and the Religious Cartography of Banaras*, Wiesbaden: Harrassowitz Verlag.

Gordon, Sophie, 2011 [unpublished], *Monumental Visions: Architectural Photography in India, 1840–1901*. Doctoral dissertation: SOAS.

Greaves, Edwin, 2003 [first published 1909], *Kashi, The City Illustrious, or Benares*, Allahabad: The Indian Press and New Delhi: Asian Educational Services.

Gutman, Judith Mara, 1982, *Through Indian Eyes*, New York: Oxford University Press and International Center for Photography.

Gutschow, Niels, 2006, "Panoramas of Banaras," in *Visualizing Space in Banaras: Images, Maps, and the Practice of Representation*, ed. Martin Gaenszle and Jörg Gengnagel, pp. 191-212, Wiesbaden: Harrassowitz Verlag.

London, Christopher W., 2005, "Churches and Civic Monuments: The British Contribution," in *Banaras: The City Revealed*, ed. George Michell and Rana P.B. Singh, pp. 126-37, Mumbai: Marg.

Michell, George and Rana P.B. Singh (eds.), 2005, *Banaras: The City Revealed*, Mumbai: Marg.

Olivelle, Patrick, Janice Leoshko and Himanshu Prabha Ray, (eds.), 2012, *Reimagining Aśoka: Memory and History*, New Delhi: Oxford University Press.

Parker, Arthur, 1895, *A Hand-Book of Benares*, Benares: E.J. Lazarus.

Singh, Rana P.B., 2009, *Banaras: Making of India's Heritage City*, Newcastle upon Tyne: Cambridge Scholars Publishing.

10

Circuits of Exchange

Muraqqās and Illustrated Gift Books in the Early Twentieth Century[1]

Saleema Waraich

The decorative patterns and illustrated manuscripts associated with Muslim patrons inspired innovations in British and French design, influencing the Arts and Crafts and Art Nouveau movements as well as the Golden Age of Illustration in the late nineteenth and early twentieth century. In turn, these innovations in European art provided a means by which artists under colonial rule could reclaim traditional artistic practices derided by European colonialists, thereby challenging European colonial rhetoric and policies at the turn of the twentieth century. This essay explores a key aspect of these circuits of exchange through an examination of the artistic, philosophical, and commercial strategies of M.A.R. Chughtai (1899–1975), one of the first South Asian artists to consciously position

---

[1] I am delighted to present this essay in honor of Prof. Robert L. Brown because I first began researching M.A.R. Chughtai's work under his guidance during my graduate career. Years prior to that, taking an undergraduate course with Prof. Brown inspired me to pursue art history and to apply to graduate school, and his enormously kind, supportive, and thoughtful mentorship has guided me through all of graduate school and my career to date. As a mentor and a role model, Prof. Brown is truly exemplary, and I am tremendously thankful to him.

I would also like to express my appreciation to Rob DeCaroli, Paul Lavy, and Bindu Gude for all that they have done to make this festschrift for Prof. Brown materialize. Their dedication, commitment, time, and effort are immensely appreciated.

himself as a Muslim artist. Chughtai drew upon his Muslim identity and his vision of a Muslim and Mughal past to promote his art as an authentic commodity and to assert the place of Muslims on an international stage as well as in Indian history. Chughtai's artistic projects endeavored to rescue Islamic art from various forms of cultural appropriation by Europeans and Americans. Furthermore, in contrast to prominent contemporaries who claimed that Muslim artistic practices should be dismissed as foreign influences on "pure" Indian art, Chughtai's early work championed Islamic art with its far-reaching connections to promote an Indian national identity that was diverse, porous, and inclusive.

Chughtai's artistic career began as the struggle for India's independence from British rule was escalating. As part of an artistic movement that openly rejected colonial influence, Chughtai turned away from the European academic painting styles that were associated with British authority and had helped displace local artistic practices. In the process, Chughtai and like-minded South Asian artists embarked upon a new path; no longer anonymous members of a collective workshop, they emerged as individual artists striving to assert their originality and to promote their art as a marketable commodity. At the nexus of colonialism, nationalism, and modernity in South Asia, concepts of originality and artistic authenticity were seen in this period as being dependent upon one's ethnic origins and religious affiliations. While Chughtai and fellow artists sought to align their work with lofty ideals (whether Eastern spirituality, nascent nationalism, or artistic originality), the role of consumer demand in shaping these ideals must also be examined, in part since the value of a given work of art was determined by its perceived authenticity based upon an artist's religious and cultural identity. Operating in the shadow of an international market for Islamic and modern South Asian art, Chughtai's actions at times engaged in resistance to colonial practices and at other times appear to be the practical product of commercial opportunism. As this essay argues, he drew upon his Muslim identity and Persian roots to carve a niche in an international art market, and this enabled him to contribute to a Western dominated discourse involving Islamic art as well as emerging Indian nationalist narratives that marginalized Muslims.

Even though Chughtai's essays and paintings assert an artistic vision that was purportedly based on an authentic religious experience and cultural identity, he was not limited or restricted by his identity politics but rather drew upon them to demonstrate the potential for self-empowerment. To understand Chughtai's motivations for establishing himself as a Muslim artist, the first section of this essay will discuss the relationship between Muslim artistic practices and European art movements in the late nineteenth and early twentieth centuries, especially the Arts and Crafts movement, the Art Nouveau movement — and the Golden Age of Illustration — with a focus on the illustrations of the French artist Edmund Dulac. Equally important to understanding Chughtai's formation as an artist is his relationship to Hindu modern artists, particularly Abanindranath Tagore. This topic is considered in this essay's second section. These discussions shed light on why themes of competitiveness and claims of ownership and authenticity appear in Chughtai's writings. In the third section, I focus on a specific publication by Chughtai, *Muraqqā-ī-Chughtai, Dīwān-ī-Ghālib* (1928), to discuss the ways in which his political, social, and cultural concerns are made manifest in visual and literary forms.

The Construction and Collection of Islamic Art in the "West"[2]

It is generally agreed that the category "Islamic art" is a

[2] In utilizing the designations of "East/Eastern" and "West/Western" it is not my intention to reify a conceptual divide between "East" and "West." Rather the use of these terms in this essay refers to the essentialist ideas about these imagined geographical constructs that informed the perspectives and practices of European colonialists and artists. Given the pervasiveness of colonial discourse, it was inevitable that such ideological constructions would permeate the language of the colonized, even when they resisted the embedded pejorative assumptions.

nineteenth-century European colonial construction (Blair and Bloom 2003; Flood 2007; Labrusse 2017; Shaw 2012). That is, the artisans, artists, architects, and patrons from the seventh century onwards who hailed from the various regions from which "Islamic art" objects were later collected did not see themselves as producing and contributing to a unified homogeneous visual culture but rather to a wide variety of dynastic, regional, and temporal identities. Later Western constructions of "Islamic art" were the result of the preferences, desires, and perceived needs of European and American collectors, manufacturers, artists, and writers (Labrusse 2017). Like the broad category of "Islamic art," the resulting collections of Islamic art found throughout Europe and America are largely the result of European imperialism in various Muslim-majority regions. While signaling the authority to amass large numbers of objects, the decorative patterned work and the illustrated manuscripts associated with Muslim patrons also provided inspiration for innovations in British, French, and American design in the late nineteenth and early twentieth centuries. Chughtai's formation as an artist must be seen within the context of the emerging discourse surrounding "Islamic art" and the formation of Islamic art collections. Chughtai, one of the first artists to consciously position himself as a Muslim artist, expressed distress over European collections of exemplary art from various parts of the world, including albums of paintings (*muraqqās*) produced for Muslim patrons. As he stated, it "seemed to me [Chughtai] that it all truly belonged to the West, because it is in their possession" (Chughtai quoted in Dadi 2010: 85 n. 151).

Inspired by essentialist ideas regarding the artistic practices of "Eastern" cultures, European architects, artists, and designers of the mid-to-late nineteenth century such as Owen Jones and William Morris & Co. admired the art and architecture associated with Muslim-majority regions for their sophisticated and intricate decorations (Labrusse 2017: 1206-11). They sought to remedy the perceived deterioration of craftsmanship at the hand of the

Industrial Revolution and free themselves from what Jan Bowman has called the "stifling restrictions of high Victorian aesthetics" (2007). By privileging the decorative elements of a body of material that came to be categorized as Islamic art, Europeans found, as David Tresilian has described, "a model for a 'renaissance' of Western applied arts" (2007: 8-14; see also Labrusse 2017: 1209-11). Likewise, the interest in and attention to ornamentation by Art Nouveau artists resulted in the exaltation of Arabic and Persian calligraphy and design (Brenner 2000: 7; Bruns 1979). The "arabesque," a term used by Europeans to refer to what they hailed as a distinctive trait of Islamic art, influenced the long, sinuous, curvilinear lines of Art Nouveau, perhaps most popularly associated with the work of Aubrey Beardsley (*fig.* 10.1; Brenner 2000: 7; Bruns 1979; see also Jackson 2000: 100-13 and Vanke 2000: 114-25). The Arts and Crafts and Art Nouveau movements also looked to European medieval manuscripts and the exquisitely produced books and albums made for Muslim patrons. These works were extolled for the dexterity displayed by the various vocations involved in the production of a single book (Bruns 1979). Although assisted by modern machines and new printing technologies, the European books produced in the Golden Age of Illustration (*c.*1890–1930) took their cue from these models of meticulous craftsmanship.

In the work of Edmund Dulac (1882–1953), one of Europe's most celebrated illustrators, one sees the apex of the influence of Persian illustrated manuscripts and design on European Art Nouveau book illustration. Dulac's first illustrated *Arabian Nights*, published in 1907, was a huge success and became one of the most popular editions of these stories (Felmingham 1988: 58).[3] Dulac, who became known as "the Arabian Nights man," is important not only because his illustrations of the *Stories from the Arabian Nights* and the *Rubaiyat* of Omar Khayyam dominated the European market, but also because they shaped the European imagination of the Muslim world (White

[3] Dulac's illustrations of *The Arabian Nights* (1907) and subsequent editions were published by Hodder and Stoughton.

1976: 53).[4] While one of the hallmarks of Islamic influence on Art Nouveau is the sleek, curving line, Dulac meticulously researched the colour and design of Persian miniature paintings (Felmingham 1988: 58).[5] Consequently, his paintings were deliberately diminutive, decorative, and rich in details, patterns, and bright colors (Bruns 1979: 2-11). Persian painting also enabled Dulac to move away from his era's conventions of perspective to produce a distinctive, "flatter, almost two-dimensional quality," thereby differentiating his oeuvre from the work of his contemporaries and creating a niche for himself in a competitive market (Felmingham 1988: 58).[6] It also imbued his images with a sense of credibility and authenticity; by painting in a style associated with the regions being represented in his illustrations, Dulac attempted to provide his audiences a more authentic experience of the "East" (White 1976: 61, 65).[7] Dulac's illustrated editions further heightened the sensual pleasure, romantic exoticism, fantasy, and caricature of the "East" and its people, already established by distorted translations of the text (Haddawy 1990).

Nevertheless, it is significant that Dulac and his contemporaries found in Islamic art, and Eastern art more generally, an alternative to dominant Western modes of production. This turn eastwards carried with it a critique of modern, industrialized British society, a critique that was shared by European Orientalist scholars working

---

[4] His fame as "the Arabian Nights man" was in place by 1912.

[5] His appreciation of Eastern art had been ignited at an early age by a collection of "Oriental" art owned by his uncle, an importer of goods from East Asia.

[6] His reputation for invoking the decorative styles of the "East" was affirmed repeatedly through his illustrations of subsequent editions of the *Arabian Nights* (1907), *The Rubaiyat of Omar Khayyam* (1909), *Ali Baba* (1911), *Princess Badoura* (1913), and *Sinbad the Sailor* (1914), all published by Hodder and Stoughton and issued in numerous editions and bindings.

[7] Indeed, Dulac took pride in his belief that his illustrations mirrored the *souks* of Tunis.

in India (Davis 1997: 177-78; also, Guha-Thakurta 1992: chap. 5). At the same time this encounter prompted anxieties about being influenced by a "culturally inferior other," especially since the birth of modern avant-garde art was reliant upon "non-Western" influences, including Islamic, Japanese, and Chinese art. The associated discourse relegated such artistic influences to a stagnant past that in the hands of European and American artists sparked creativity and originality. As is frequently the case, such influence did not travel on a one-way street. While Art Nouveau artists were influenced by illustrated manuscripts associated with Muslim patrons, their work in turn helped mobilize Muslim and Hindu artists in South Asia in their endeavors to resist European cultural hegemony. Chughtai was well aware of Western adaptations of literary and artistic landmarks associated with Muslim culture and, while building upon their international appeal, he sought to rescue these practices from Western fantasies of an exotic "East." More generally speaking, Chughtai did not want them to become the exclusive property of the "West" and endeavored to reclaim them from Europe's possession. These border crossings are intriguing not only for the exchange of artistic practices and styles — however unbalanced — but also for what they tell us about forms of colonial resistance alongside the effects of global markets, and their opportunities, on artistic production.

Linking Ethnic and Religious Affiliation to Claims of Artistic Authenticity

In addition to addressing interactions between the "East" and "West," Chughtai was also engaged with issues pertaining to the divisions developing between Hindus and Muslims at the time. In this context, it is important to consider the work of one of his contemporaries, Abanindranath Tagore, to identify the reasons why Chughtai drew upon his Muslim beliefs and his vision of a Muslim heritage to establish his own artistic identity. Although Chughtai's claims of authenticity may presuppose an allegiance to a belief in a "pure" religious or cultural identity that seemingly reified difference, in fact, Chughtai's discussion of an authentic Muslim artistic practice ironically draws attention to its fluid and porous qualities. Moreover, it is used as a means of protesting the exoticization and/or romanticizing of Islamic landmarks and asserting the legitimacy of his vision over others.

It is perhaps not surprising that artistic movements like Art Nouveau and the Golden Age of Illustration appealed to modern artists in South Asia who were looking for alternatives to the imposition of European academic art. Cultivating European art forms was an aspect of imperial policy beginning in the second half of the nineteenth century that reflected the British commitment to helping the Indian colony "develop" and to "guide good taste." The pre-eminent Indian artist painting in this European-influenced academic style was Ravi Varma (1848–1906), who was known for his attempts to valorize Indian themes — historical and mythological — in keeping with the style and standards of European academic painting (Guha-Thakurta 1995: 11). By the early twentieth century, the escalating numbers of Indians agitating for independence led to outcry against British imperial practices — including academic art which was closely identified with British colonial policy — as being antithetical to establishing a sovereign national identity. In contrast, Indian nationalists hoped to identify a unique Indian essence, one that was resilient enough to withstand foreign influences.

Indian nationalists found sympathetic allies in a group of British Orientalist scholars who sought to locate an alternative to modern, industrialized British society in Indian culture (Hoskote 2001: 27). They typically located this essence in India's ancient Buddhist and Hindu past, before the arrival of Muslims. The questionable position of Muslims as seen from a nationalist point of view was also related to a tendency of British colonial writers in the nineteenth century to claim that the British shared a "foreign" identity with Muslim rulers as a means of bolstering support for their own outsider regime, while simultaneously positioning themselves as superior (Hasan 1996: 186). Moreover, in the late 1800s the British adopted a type of rule they described as enlightened or benevolent despotism that actively invoked Mughal symbols and rituals to justify their reign of India (Metcalf 2001: 25-27; Parchami 2009: 100).[8] British colonial discourse sustained a Hindu nationalist narrative (as opposed to an Indian secular one) wherein Islam, India's Muslim rulers, and the Muslim population all were seen as a distinct and extrinsic community. This interpretation pointed to Islam's origins in the Arabian Peninsula and the Central Asian or Persian origins of the founders of several Indo-Islamic empires, despite the fact that the majority of the Muslim population in India consisted of local converts to Islam. Indian Muslims were thus posited as a separate, distinct minority community with questionable standing and rights.

Such European Orientalist and Hindu nationalist attitudes would come to bear on artistic production and reception. As Partha Mitter has noted, Margaret Noble — a prominent British colonial voice about Indian art and a figure involved in the promotion of an Indian nationalist art — based her 1910 review of an exhibition of modern art in part on the criteria of religious authenticity. Noble praised the beauty of Asit Haldar's *Moazzim* (The Call to Prayer), but lamented that the Muslim subject of the painting, created by a Hindu artist, lacked "genuine Islamic feeling." In contrast, she praised a Mughal style portrait by a Muslim artist, Hakim Mohammed Khan, "for its Muslim serenity, so unlike the 'mental intensity' of the Hindu artists" (Mitter 1994: 321). In other words, artists like Haldar, who depicted subjects outside their own religious sphere, in this case a Hindu depicting a Muslim subject,

[8] The term "Mughal" refers to a dynasty that ruled from the sixteenth through the mid-nineteenth centuries. The Mughals were Muslim rulers of Central Asia and, by the fourth emperor, South Asian ancestry who consolidated an empire that covered a large part of the Indian subcontinent. The Mughal period is generally considered the height of Muslim rule in South Asia.

were susceptible to critique. By contrast, Khan's example suggests an artist who depicted elements of his or her own religious heritage had more opportunity to garner praise and success. It is worth noting that European reviews based on "authenticity" — as opposed to creativity or originality, which was viewed as the domain of European and American artists — upheld the British classification system used to define and categorize Indian colonial subjects based on religion, caste, and ethnicity. In addition to maintaining British colonialists' self-perceived sense of superiority as the harbingers of modernity, their standard of authenticity upheld essentialist constructions of Indians and simultaneously fulfilled European desires for the exotic.

Some Indians adopted a similar position: for example, Sikh scholar, Sardar Puran Singh, wrote a letter in 1921 to Chughtai describing the limitations of non-Muslims, for example the Hindu artist Abanindranath Tagore, in portraying Muslim subjects. He writes:

> I do not think ... Abanindranath Tagore or any of the Bengal school can do justice to [Omar Khayyam] and of course all Western painters have so far failed to render him. ... Your Omar Khayyam I have no doubt would come as a revelation to all lovers of spirituality. — Singh 1921: 31

Although religious affiliation and artistic evaluation became linked in public perception, this did not prevent Abanindranath Tagore from looking beyond his religious identity for inspiration. He stands as one of the few Hindu artists of the era who explored Muslim themes at a time when they were becoming marginalized in the effort to promote Indian nationalist art. A foundational figure in the development of modern painting in India, Tagore had a tremendous influence on Chughtai as a source of inspiration, competition, and differentiation.

It was during the Delhi Durbar of 1902-03 — a British coronation ceremony during which Edward VII (r. 1901-10) was proclaimed emperor of India — that Tagore first gained national exposure. Lord Curzon, the British Viceroy, presided over this event, which was loosely based on ceremonial gatherings associated with Mughal rulers. The British demonstrated their ascension to the Mughal throne by placing themselves in settings that utilized domes and arches evocative of Mughal architecture and incorporated Mughal-inspired ceremonies. Curzon also attempted to draw connections to the Mughal capital by holding the Durbar in Delhi rather than in Calcutta, the British capital. The Durbar became an occasion to promote Indian arts to showcase the role of the Raj as patrons. A few contemporary works were shown, including, from Tagore's "Mughal" series, *The Construction of the Taj* and *The Final Moments of Shah Jahan*. The series encapsulated romantic episodes in the British colonial imagination of India's history (Guha-Thakurta 1995: 22-23; Mitter 1994: 285). In British eyes, they could not have asked for more relevant thematic works since this series commemorated the rule of the predecessors of the British Empire (because the British fashioned themselves as the heir to the Mughal throne) while simultaneously marking the demise of Mughal power.

Tagore's painting *The Final Moments of Shah Jahan* (1902) shows the imprisoned and ailing Shah Jahan, attended by his daughter, forlornly gazing upon the Taj Mahal, the mausoleum he built for his wife Mumtaz Mahal. While the painting was seen by British audiences as affirming British succession, intriguingly, this painting would come to represent a milestone in *swadeshi* (self-rule) art. Partha Mitter writes, Tagore "blended in a true Victorian fashion the passing grandeur of the Mughal Empire with the pathos of Shah Jahan's dying moments" (Mitter 1994: 288). For Tagore, this painting of Shah Jahan was a nostalgic evocation of pre-British rule. "Why is the picture so moving?", he wrote, "I put in it all the pain and sorrow I felt for the daughter I lost [to the Calcutta plague of 1902]" (Guha-Thakurta 1992: 245). The grief depicted over Shah Jahan's death and for the lost glory of the Mughal dynasty was literally his own. This painting did not represent affirmation of British rule;

instead, it reflects a personal tragedy.

Yet, it is worth noting that Tagore's success in conveying *bhāva* (emotion) in this painting marked his accomplishment as an artist. As much as he admired the technique and design of Mughal painting, he believed the emotional element was lacking; by conveying *bhāva* Tagore felt he fulfilled the destiny of Mughal painting (Guha-Thakurta 1992: 243; 1995: 23). His beliefs and efforts seem to have been shared and recognized. Percy Brown, who wrote the catalog for the exhibition that accompanied the Delhi Durbar, commented that the Bengali painter's works were infused with a feeling of life that was rarely attained by Mughal artists. Without casting doubt on Tagore, it is worth considering how his statements about reinvesting Muslim painting with emotion could be viewed within the context of "the great Indian synthesis," an influential theory of the time. Articulated by E.B. Havell, an arts administrator who became an ally of Tagore, this theory proposed that Hindu religion and culture subsumed everything else. Thus, the "Indianness" of Mughal art was emphasized by showing how the foreign elements within it were transformed by the force of "pre-existing Hindu traditions" (Guha-Thakurta 1994: 51).

Throughout his career, Tagore diversified his subject matter and style, remaining committed to a pan-Asian ideal as laid out by the Japanese artist-activist Okakura Kakuzo as well as to his local Kolkatan identity, and by never turning away from Mughal and Muslim themes (Appasamy 1968: 17). Tagore also produced illustrations of some non-Indian "Islamic" texts. Between 1906 and 1911, he finished twelve paintings that were published (1910) in London in an illustrated version of Omar Khayyam's *Rubaiyat*, which was translated by Edward Fitzgerald. Like Edward Lane's and Richard Burton's translations of the *Arabian Nights*, Fitzgerald's translation took liberties with the Persian text and promoted a romanticized image of the Orient (Banerji 2010: 44). In 1930 Tagore illustrated another Orientalist favorite, the *Arabian Nights* but situated "the exoticism and fantasy of the world of the 'Arabian

Nights' " within the environs of Calcutta (Guha-Thakurta 1992: 267; 1995: 28). Although one may question Tagore's choice of texts (as Orientalist favorites), it is significant that he selected texts that worked against the nationalist definitions of his time by refusing to limit his artistic production to Hindu and Buddhist themes. Moreover, as Debashish Banerji proposes, Tagore interrupted Orientalist clichés by infusing these images with a local Kolkatan and spiritual sensibility (Banerji 2010: 24).

In summary, two trends are important for understanding Chughtai's work: first, the exoticization and/or romanticizing of Islamic landmarks, and second, the discourse surrounding the "foreign" roots of the Mughals and Muslims. This latter sentiment was projected onto Muslim communities and, as a result, their affiliation with Islam was seen as calling into question their standing as Indians. Chughtai articulated a deep unease with the exoticization and romanticizing of Islamic architectural and literary landmarks and was also concerned with the growing tension surrounding South Asian Muslims' standing as Indians. Chughtai's response was to articulate and emphasize a space where foreign influence was not considered exotic or alien but rather an active and natural aspect of cultural identity. It must also be noted that Dulac and Tagore's popular success with paintings of Muslim and/or Mughal subjects seems to have functioned as both a source of inspiration and aggravation for Chughtai. It is worthwhile to distinguish here between Chughtai's interest in Mughal painting as compared to Mughal heritage: Chughtai was not reclaiming Mughal painting (specifically the "miniature" practice), but rather a Mughal past. That is, he was not trying to revitalize a traditional practice per se but rather to repair a misjudged and misconstrued history of Muslim presence in the subcontinent.

Between Mughal History and Modern Markets

M.A.R. Chughtai was born in 1899 to a family that traced its lineage to Persia. Growing up in Lahore (now in Pakistan but then the capital of the Punjab province under British colonial rule), Chughtai first learned calligraphy and *naqsh* (popularly known as arabesque in the West) from his uncle Baba Mira Baksh, who had a studio in the Wazir Khan Mosque, a mosque built in the seventeenth century by a Mughal official. In 1911 he enrolled in the Mayo School of Art, formerly directed by Lockwood Kipling. Chughtai became increasingly concerned with finding, expressing, and asserting what he proposed was a legitimate or authentic Muslim voice. This impulse is evident in the way Chughtai positioned himself with respect to the esteemed philosopher-poet Muhammad Iqbal as well as with a group of progressive literary figures in Lahore and a circle of like-minded artists whom he identified as the Punjab School. Much like Tagore's Bengal School was associated with a Hindu artistic revival, even if Tagore himself was not, members of the Punjab School were Muslim and it consequently became associated with a Muslim Revival. By the 1920s, Chughtai consciously aligned his work with an "Islamic" and Mughal aesthetic and promoted himself as a Muslim artist (Dadi 2006: 52).

It would seem that consumer expectations and demands played a role in Chughtai's turn in this direction. Chughtai used his Muslim identity to assert the authenticity and the superiority of his own rendering of Muslim themes, which gave him a competitive edge in an international market. This also enabled him to assert a voice on behalf of the larger Muslim community based on claims of allegiance and ownership. Chughtai's Muslim identity thus served as a source of artistic exploration, as a marketable commodity, and a political position. To understand how this manifested, it is useful to reflect upon his artistic relationship with Tagore.

Chughtai was aware of Tagore's Mughal series of 1903 and other Muslim subjects to the extent that he once complained that some of his most cherished Islamic subjects had already been depicted by Tagore. Indeed, Tagore had earned international fame with his Taj Series, and the continuing popularity of his painting, *The Passing of Shah Jahan*, was evidenced by the fact that it was the cover of

fig. 10.1: Drawing by Aubrey Beardsley, design for a headpiece to the preface of Thomas Malory's *Le Morte D'Arthur*, vol. I

fig. 10.2: M.A.R. Chughtai, *The Passing of Shah Jahan*, 1919

fig. 10.3: M.A.R. Chughtai, Illustration of the first couplet of *Dīwān-ī-Ghālib* in *Muraqqā-ī Chughtai*, 1928

the journal *Modern Review* (1918) and featured in the first edition of *Chatterjee's Picture Album* (1919), some fifteen years after it was first exhibited (Nesom 1984: 234). Chughtai decided to paint his own depiction of Shah Jahan's last days, drawing upon photos he took during a trip to Agra and Delhi in 1916. Stirring his decision to paint this subject was Chughtai's belief that the Emperor Shah Jahan's patronage epitomized Muslim contributions to the national landscape. Moreover, he traced his own family ancestry to Shah Jahan's chief architect, Ahmad Mimar Shahjahani, who was involved in building architectural feats such as the Taj Mahal and the Red Fort at Delhi (Chughtai 2005: 23). *The Passing of Shah Jahan* (1919) (*fig.* 10.2) emphasizes the grief and piety demonstrated by Shah Jahan's daughters over their father's imminent death instead of showing Shah Jahan gazing longingly at the Taj Mahal, which would have invoked the Taj as a romanticized symbol of Shah Jahan's love for his wife. In Chughtai's rendition, the inclusion of the Taj in the distance serves instead as a reminder of Shah Jahan's architectural accomplishments, not of personal, romanticized longing. *The Passing of Shah Jahan* won first prize in the Simla exhibition of 1922 and was purchased by Shamsher Jung Bahadur, chief minister of Nepal. Interestingly, although Chughtai imbued the painting with emotion — a quality believed by Tagore and Brown to be lacking in Mughal painting — Tagore criticized it as "a veritable riot of color and movement" in what should have been a "quiet solemnity of a death scene" (Tagore 1922: 64).

The Taj Mahal continued to engage Chughtai: he painted at least three versions of an image of the Taj Mahal in the distance framed by a white peacock depicted on a tree branch in the foreground. First called *Symbols* and later *Storyteller*, the first version was accompanied by a poem expressing a romantic lament, "The spirit of the peacock throne broods in the magic of the Taj," which connected his depiction of a large peacock to Shah Jahan's legendary peacock throne. The Taj Mahal had become India's pre-eminent tourist site amongst European visitors, largely because of the British emphasis on the immortalization of a king's love for his wife. In contrast, for Chughtai, the Taj Mahal was the symbol of the golden era of Muslim history and simultaneously its loss (Nesom 1984: 254). Chughtai was distressed by European romanticization of the Taj Mahal and the illustrated versions of the *Arabian Nights* and Omar Khayyam's poetry, which he viewed as flights of fantasy that trivialized Muslim contributions to the world. Recalling the comments of European responses to Hindu and Muslim artists and their subjects, Chughtai also critiqued Tagore's incorporation of Muslim subjects on the premise that, as he put it, they "lacked a genuine Muslim experience" (Mitter 1994: 336). Yet, he observed that "I painted from the *Rubayyat* but Bengal had already put its stamp on it." In order to differentiate and validate his own work, I propose that Chughtai asserted the "authenticity" of his art to increase its value. For example, Chughtai claimed that his own paintings:

> not only paint Omar Khayyam's thoughts but embody the Islamic values which were part of me. ... On account of their background, the emphasis [of the Bengal School] was different. Therefore, my work confirms our values as does [the] Rubayyat.
>
> — Mitter 1994: 336

Undoubtedly, such claims of genuine expression and artistic authenticity were inflected with a competitive edge that asserted his position in an international art world. Yet, it is critical to note that his intention was to reclaim the political and cultural significance of subjects associated with an Islamic heritage and also to salvage architectural and literary masterpieces associated with a Muslim past from being reduced to romanticized visions of the exotic "East," a project made more evocative by the increasing marginalization of Muslims in the present. Chughtai's claims to genuine expression or artistic authenticity also signified protests against the act of being represented by outsiders or by members of the dominant community and to assert the right to self-representation. Thus, inherent to these criticisms is Chughtai's resistance to acts of cultural appropriation and a larger struggle over the right to access images associated with a particular history, as well as the rightful place of Muslims and their history in India.

Of *Muraqqās* and European Illustrated Books: The Two Faces of *Muraqqā-ī-Chughtai, Dīwān-ī-Ghālib* (1928)

Muraqqā-ī-Chughtai, Dīwān-ī-Ghālib (Chughtai's Album, Ghalib's Collected Verses) established Chughtai's reputation as a modern, cosmopolitan, Muslim artist and brought him international acclaim. Chughtai sent copies of his illustrated book, published through his own press, to art historians, art patrons, artists, and art journals in Europe, the United States, and India. In the same year of its publication, the work was reviewed in journals published from Paris, London, and New York (Nesom 1984: 49). The *Muraqqā* brought Chughtai recognition from Europe and firmly consolidated his career in South Asia (Nesom 1984: 49). *Muraqqa-i-Chughtai, Dīwān-ī-Ghālib* features illustrations of the Urdu poetry (*dīwān*) of the Mughal poet, Mirza Ghalib (1797–1869). Associated with the twilight of the Mughal Empire, Ghalib has since been seen as a key figure in the Persian and Urdu poetic tradition, his work marking one of the great achievements of Indo-Muslim culture. At the same time, as Iftikhar Dadi observes, "Ghalib wrote his works during the dissolution of Muslim political power, [and] the inwardness, difficulty, and philosophical character of his poetry can be understood as an internal, formal response to the widespread crisis of Muslim life in nineteenth century India," a crisis that continued to haunt the Muslim communities of India in the early twentieth century (2010: 67).

In keeping with Ghalib's poetry, some paintings in *Muraqqa-i-Chughtai* illustrate a sense of separation, loss, and despair. In several instances, a woman is shown waiting for her beloved to return. Presumably because of the endless waiting, these figures have become weak, reaching the extremes of desperation (Sirhandi 1988: 3). These illustrations in particular can be tied to established themes of *soz o sauz* (passion and pathos) in *ghazal*s specifically and Sufi literature more broadly. *Ghazal*s include metaphors involving the lamp (beloved) and moth (lover), in which the moths are consumed by the flames of their passion, or the woman waits through the night for her beloved and is overcome with feelings of weariness, longing and despair (Nesom 1984: 171). Chughtai's own pain over the loss of an esteemed past cleverly intersected with the "mood of disease and degeneration" associated with the *fin de siècle* of the Decadents (Mitter 1994: 338, 342). Here, though, Chughtai laments the deterioration of Muslim culture and standing. By presenting his paintings as a reflection of Muslim experience in the contemporary social and political world, Chughtai implies the current plight of Muslims demands action and advocates internal reform — a position articulated by his essay in the *muraqqā*. Although Chughtai had talked about producing an illustrated book based on Omar Khayyam's poetry, it is significant that Chughtai chose to illustrate Ghalib's work for this project, thus distinguishing it from European illustrations of the *Arabian Nights* and Omar Khayyam, and the work of Abanindranath Tagore. Moreover, by affiliating himself with Ghalib, whose Dewan "would sit in [a] place of honour in an alcove in every Urdu-speaking Muslim household," Chughtai imagined that "he would be seen as an artist of Muslim India, representing the Indo-Persian cultural synthesis which the Mughals had pulled off so brilliantly and successfully" (Naqvi 1998: 75-76, 78).

As the title suggests, Chughtai aligned his publication of *Muraqqa-i-Chughtai, Dīwān-ī-Ghālib* with the *muraqqā* (album) that in earlier Ottoman, Persian, and Mughal contexts contained an assemblage of exceptional painting, calligraphy, and illumination. Chughtai, however, "reinvented the *muraqqa* in the age of mechanical reproduction, enacting numerous technical and aesthetic transformations" (Dadi 2010: 67). To do so, Chughtai relied on Western "techniques of production and reproduction demonstrat[ing] the difficulty and considerable labour needed to transform a manuscript form into a modern, mechanically produced book" as well as "the impossibility in modernity of disengaging Europe from its others" (Dadi 2010: 73). Chughtai seems to acknowledge this impossibility of disengagement in the structure of the book itself but also suggests how such engagements could become strategic, creative opportunities for self-representation and empowerment. One of the innovative and intriguing features of Chughtai's publication is that it was constructed to be read in both directions and thereby invoked both earlier *muraqqā*s and the illustrated books of Europe. Following the custom of Persian and Urdu manuscripts, it could be read from right to left as it begins with an introduction written by Chughtai in Urdu. The first two-thirds of the book (from the right) contains Ghalib's poetry; these pages are all filled with calligraphy and decorative designs, which are interspersed with a handful of line drawings that intentionally blurred the lines (literally and figuratively) associated with Islamic design and Art Nouveau.

Chughtai also linked his *muraqqā* to the European tradition, *c.*1890–1930, of publishing illustrated books beginning with Beardsley and culminating with Dulac. These illustrated gift books, as described by Rebecca Bruns, were "bound in calf-skin, with gold embossed covers, heavy vellum pages, and illustration tucked like little masterpieces behind sheets of tissue," and Chughtai's *muraqqā* closely followed this format (Bruns 1979: 2-11). If the book is read from left to right, in the European tradition, it begins with an introduction by the Irish Theosophist, James Cousins, followed by another essay in English by the philosopher Iqbal. The twenty-six images that follow Cousins and Iqbal's essays are mostly colored illustrations paired with couplets from Ghalib's poetry. The illustrations are Chughtai's visual translations of Ghalib's couplets into his synthesis of Mughal, Punjab Hills, Bengal School, and Art Nouveau painting styles.

Thus, *Muraqqā-ī-Chughtai* worked as two books in one, as both a *muraqqā* and a European illustrated book, such as the English editions of Omar Khayyam's *Rubaiyat* and the *Arabian Nights*.

Chughtai's decorative borders and arabesque motifs provide a sense of uniformity and a purposeful comment on the *source* of Art Nouveau's decorative elements, especially the curvilinear sinuous lines (*fig*. 10.3). He clearly displays the influence of a European style as well, but one cannot dismiss his attraction to Art Nouveau for its ties to Asian art in general and Islamic art in particular. Chughtai appreciated Art Nouveau's rejection of Victorian ideals and its utilization of Islamic decoration as a response to the mechanical nature of the Industrial Age. At the same time, Chughtai's *muraqqā* may be seen as an act of preservation and resistance to European avant-garde artists' "final goal ... to obliterate it [Islamic art] by founding a global modern (i.e. Western-dominated) visual culture" (Labrusse 2017: 1210). Moreover, Chughtai points out the cyclic nature of artistic influence, citing the European artists and designers who were inspired by his Muslim forefathers. By reclaiming this style and to increase the value of his work, he also sought to demonstrate his own technical superiority and argue for his artistic authenticity in comparison to artists of the Art Nouveau movement and leading Indian artists, especially Abanindranath Tagore. Correspondence between Chughtai and the various European museums and libraries to which he sent copies of his book suggest that he met his goal. Expressing admiration for the book, Frederick Wagner from Berlin informed Chughtai,

> I have shown your book already to a good number of people and I shall continue to do so. Many enjoyed it very much. ... The State Library, reluctant to buy Dulac's Omar Khayyam is ready to receive your book. — Berlin 1931: 36

Aligning himself with a Mughal prototype as well as with the poetry of Ghalib, Chughtai firmly roots this publication in historical precedent as a means of commenting upon the place of Muslims in India. Furthermore, by tying his work with Iqbal, who was asked to write an essay for *Muraqqā-ī-Chughtai, Dīwān-ī-Ghālib,* Chughtai invested his own artistic project with a type of spirituality with which Muslims could identify. Iqbal and Chughtai looked to a spiritually superior "East" but not one derived exclusively from Hinduism, and thereby participated in a vision of a spiritually superior India that was available to Muslims too. This inclusiveness is emphasized in Chughtai's introduction where he extols the contributions of Muslims to Indian art and culture, including the significance of Mughal patronage and, very significantly, their synthesis of various styles. In Mughal workshops, as emphasized by Chughtai in the introduction to the *muraqqā*, Persian and Indian artists collaborated to paint Hindu epics and romances, such as the *Rāmāyaṇa* and *Mahābhārata*, and Persian literary classics (Chughtai 1928). Chughtai aimed to fulfill the desires and expectations of his varied audiences by advancing claims of authenticity even as he challenged and complicated such notions. That is, he articulated and affirmed the belief that Muslims are a distinctive community — one that had been characterized by fruitful interactions between different groups — while at the same time arguing against the notion of a homogeneous religious/cultural identity. In this way, Chughtai's art emphasized that there has always been fluidity across cultures.

Chughtai attempted to establish himself as a legitimate heir to Mughal and Islamic traditions and proclaimed his standing to European audiences. By positioning himself as a Muslim artist and using his religious identity to validate his own work, he contributed to the development of a new discourse about Islamic art. When Chughtai invoked religion to herald artistic difference he did so with three goals in mind. First, by asking who possesses the right to represent whom, it is apparent that behind his claims of artistic authenticity lay a sensitivity to and a reaction against the process of being represented by others. Second, his religious identity became a means of carving a niche for himself in an increasingly competitive global market, predicated upon consumer expectations and the quest for an authentic experience, a market that was dominated by Tagore and the Bengal School in India as well as by illustrators such as Dulac in the West. For Chughtai, his training in decorative design and calligraphy provided a fitting and purposeful means for asserting a Muslim style, because Arts and Crafts, Art Nouveau and the Golden Age of Illustration had been deeply influenced by Islamic arts. Third, and a point that exists in tension with the first, this approach to religion was simultaneously a means of calling for inclusiveness; that is, while Chughtai was enforcing notions of cultural purity through his claims of religious authenticity, he was also in his way protesting against it. Chughtai's work complicates and expands contemporary notions of an Indian national identity, as well as Islamic art, by accounting for Hindu/Muslim collaboration and "East/West" exchange.[9] In doing so, Chughtai highlights a fluid, layered, multivalent cultural identity where Muslims were important contributors to Indian and European culture, and so-called "foreign" influence was not alien but a pervasive, active, and natural part of a cultural identity. His work implodes notions of authenticity even as his marketing angle reaffirmed them.

References

Appasamy, Jaya, 1968, *Abanindranath Tagore and the Art of His Times*, New Delhi: Lalit Kala Akademi.

Banerji, Debashish, 2010, *The Alternate Nation of Abanindranath Tagore*, New Delhi: Sage.

Berlin, Frederick Wagner, 1931, cited in Chughtai 1997.

Blair, Sheila S. and Jonathan M. Bloom, 2003, "The Mirage of Islamic Art: Reflections on the Study of an Unwieldy Field," *The Art Bulletin*, 85(1): 152-84.

Bowman, Jan, 2007, "The Age of Enchantment: Beardsley, Dulac and Their Contemporaries, 1890-1930," London: Institute of Ideas, http://www.culturewars.org.uk/2007-12/enchantment.htm.

Brenner, Carla McKinney, 2000, *Teaching Art Nouveau, 1890–1914*, Washington: National Gallery of Art.

Bruns, Rebecca, 1979, "Arabian Nights and Art Nouveau," *Saudi Aramco World*,

[9] Chughtai's initial response to the conflation of an Indian and Hindu national identity was not to call for a separate national identity for Muslims, although this did occur later.

30(4): 2–11, http://archive.aramcoworld.com/issue/197904/arabian.nights.-.and.art.nouveau.htm.

Chughtai, Arif, 1997, "The Story Teller," *A Century of Commentary on the Art of M.A.R. Chughtai*, Lahore: Chughtai Museum.

——, 2005, *The Challenge of M.A.R. Chughtai to the Bengal School of Art*, Lahore: Chughtai Museum.

Chughtai, M.A.R., 1928, "Preface," *Muraqqā-ī-Chughtai, Dīwān-ī-Ghālib*, Lahore: Jahangir Book Club [pages unnumbered].

Dadi, Iftikhar, 2006, "Miniature Painting as Muslim Cosmopolitanism," *ISIM Review*, 18 (Autumn): 52-53.

——, 2010, *Modernism and the Art of Muslim South Asia*, Chapel Hill: University of North Carolina Press.

Davis, Richard, 1997, *Lives of Indian Images*, Princeton: Princeton University Press, 1997.

Felmingham, Michael, 1988, *The Illustrated Gift Book, 1880-1930: With a Checklist of 2500 Titles*, Aldershot, England: Scholars' Press.

Flood, Finbarr Barry, 2007, "From Prophet to Postmodernism?: New World Orders and the End of Islamic Art," in *Making Art History: A Changing Discipline and Its Institutions*, ed. Elizabeth Mansfield, pp. 31-53, London: Routledge.

Guha-Thakurta, Tapati, 1992, *The Making of a New 'Indian' Art: Artists, Aesthetics and Nationalism in Bengal, c.1850–1920*, Cambridge: Cambridge University Press.

——, 1994, "Orientalism, Nationalism, and the Reconstruction of Indian Art in Calcutta," in *Perceptions of South Asia's Visual Past*, ed. Catherine B. Asher and Thomas R. Metcalf, pp. 47-66, New Delhi: American Institute of Indian Studies.

——, 1995, "Visualizing the Nation: The Iconography of a 'National Art' in Modern India," *Journal of Arts and Ideas*, 27-28: 7-40.

Haddawy, Husain, 1990, "Introduction," *The Arabian Nights: Based on the Text of the Fourteenth-Century Syrian Manuscript*, ed. Muhsin Madhi, pp. xi-xxxvi, New York: Norton.

Hasan, Mushirul, 1996 [repr. 2005], "The Myth of Unity: Colonial and National Narratives," in *Making India Hindu: Religion, Community, and the Politics of Democracy in India*, ed. David Ludden, pp. 185-210, Delhi: Oxford University Press.

Hoskote, Ranjit, 2001, "E.B. Havell and A.K. Coomaraswamy," *Art India*, 6(2): 26-27.

Jackson, Anna, 2000, "Orient and Occident," in *Art Nouveau 1890–1914*, ed. Paul Greenhalgh, pp. 100-13, London: V&A Publications.

Labrusse, Remi, 2017, "Islamic Arts and the Crisis of Representation in Modern Europe," in *A Companion to Islamic Art and Architecture*, ed. Gülru Necipoğlu and Finbarr Barry Flood, pp. 1196-1217, London: Wiley Blackwell.

Metcalf, Thomas, 2001 [first published 1994], *Ideologies of the Raj*, Cambridge: Cambridge University Press.

Mitter, Partha, 1994, *Art and Nationalism in Colonial India 1850-1922: Occidental Orientations*, Cambridge: Cambridge University Press.

Naqvi, Akbar, 1998, *Image and Identity: Fifty Years of Painting and Sculpture in Pakistan*, Karachi: Oxford University Press.

Nesom (now Sirhandi), Marcella, 1984 [unpublished], "*A.R. Chughtai: A Modern* South Asian Artist", doctoral dissertation, Ohio State University.

Parchami, Ali, 2009, *Hegemonic Peace and Empire: The Pax Romana, Britannica and Americana*, London: Routledge.

Shaw, Wendy, 2012, "The Islam in Islamic Art History," *Journal of Art Historiography*, 6: 1-34.

Sirhandi, Marcella Nesom, 1988, *Paintings from Pakistan*, Islamabad: Idara Saqafat-e Pakistan, Pakistan National Commission for UNESCO.

Singh, Sardar Puran, 1921, *Gwalior* cited in Chughtai 1997.

Tagore, Abanindranath, 1922, "Priyadarshika, or the Amiable Critic: Being Discursive Notes on the 13th Exhibition of the Indian Society of Oriental Art, Calcutta," *Rupam: An Illustrated Quarterly Journal of Oriental Art*, 10: 61-65.

Tresilian, David, 2007, "Paris: Capital of Design," *Al-Alhram*, no. 870, http://weekly.ahram.org.eg/Archive/2007/870/cu2.htm.

Vanke, Francesca, 2000, "Arabesques: North Africa, Arabia, and Europe," in *Art Nouveau 1890-1914*, ed. Paul Greenhalgh, pp. 114-125, London: V&A Publications.

White, Colin, 1976, *Edmund Dulac*, New York: Charles Scribner's Sons.

Part III
Southeast Asia

11

Early Vaiṣṇava Sculpture in Southeast Asia and the Question of Pallava Influence

Paul A. Lavy

Introduction: Rethinking Pallava Influence

Among Prof. Robert L. Brown's important scholarly contributions have been his careful considerations of the nature, degree, and mechanisms of South Asian artistic influence in Southeast Asia, particularly during the period from approximately the sixth through the eighth centuries CE. In numerous studies, he has argued that

1. South Asian influences, first stemming from perhaps "random" sources, were "filtered" through a relatively small number of Southeast Asian centers;
2. early Southeast Asian art developed primarily through the selective and "internal" sharing of a few Southeast Asian styles associated with these centers, rather than emerging out of the passive "amalgamation" of a "heterogeneous splattering of Indian styles" arriving in a sequence of distinct artistic waves; and
3. initial South Asian artistic models were likely few in number and modified so quickly that "specific moments of connection" are difficult to find and the identification of prototypes is challenging, perhaps even unproductive (Brown 1992: 49-50; 1994: 10-13; 1996: 183-88; 2000: 2; 2014: 19-20).

While recognizing the important roles that South Asian art and culture have often played in Southeast Asia, he has also argued that Southeast Asian art followed a distinct line of development and should not be seen as simply a derivation or extension of — nor as either parallel or convergent with — what was occurring in South Asia (Brown 1994: 19-20; 2017: 48).

In this essay, I return to these issues in order to re-examine the artistic relationships between the Pallava period art of southern India and early Southeast Asian Vaiṣṇava sculpture, *circa* sixth to eighth centuries. The cultural milieu of the Pallava dynasty (early fourth to late ninth century CE) — more specifically the *circa* early seventh to late ninth century Pallava art of Tamil Nadu — has long been argued to have exerted decisive influences in Southeast Asia.[1] Scholars have perceived various degrees of Pallava influence, for example, in aspects of early Khmer, Cham, and Javanese architecture (Chihara 1996: 8-11, 79, 97-99, 161; Dumarçay 1993: 13, 35-36, 57; Dumarçay and Royère 2001: 42; Parmentier 1927: 345, 347, 352, 365-67; 1931: 143); the composition and ornament of some pre-Angkorian lintels in Khmer art of the seventh century (Coral Rémusat 1934a: 113; 1934b: 242-50); the style of Southeast Asian Avalokiteśvara images of the seventh-eighth centuries (Guy 2004: 163-73; 2014: 36-37; Nandana Chutiwongs 2002: 61-62, 177, 252, 254, 263, 310-11); Khmer dynastic legends and genealogical traditions (Cœdès 1911: 391-93; 1968: 37-38, 66; Goloubew 1924: 501-10), as well as use of the suffix *-varman* in the names of ruling elites (Briggs 1951: 26); the origins of the "*devarāja* cult" at Angkor (Poundurai 2005: 25-40); and either specifically Pallava, or more general south Indian, influence on the preference in Khmer art for portraying Durgā Mahiṣāsuramardinī standing on a pedestal adorned with a buffalo head (Bhattacharya 1961: 92; Boisselier 1990: 42; Guy 2014: 138).

[1] For an up-to-date historical and historiographical discussion, see Francis 2013: 17-57, 306-07.

Numerous scholars have also commented on what they perceive to be similarities between Pallava sculpture and the treatment of headdresses on Southeast Asian images of Viṣṇu and other Brāhmanical deities, or what Henri Parmentier characterized as the "same strange cylindrical mitre" (1927: 307, 347).[2] Some claims have been rather extravagant. L.P. Briggs, for instance, stated that:

> The Pallavas were people of India who seem to have exerted the greatest influence on the Indianized colonies of Indonesia and Indo-China. —1951: 24-26

Hermann Goetz emphasized Pallava stylistic influence on Khmer art to such a degree that he used the term "Pallava sculpture" to refer to several notable pre-Angkorian Viṣṇu and Harihara statues (1959: 122).[3] Also worth mentioning are the largely discarded theories of H.G. Quaritch Wales regarding the "Four Main Waves of Indian Cultural Expansion" in Southeast Asia with the second of the "waves" and "peak periods of mediaeval Indian civilization" being "the Pallava (*ca.* A.D. 550 to 750)" (1974: 29-30). More recent statements regarding supposed Pallava artistic influence tend to be more tempered, but unsubstantiated statements commonly persist regarding supposed Pallava "contacts with Southeast Asia ... reflected in many of the early Hindu remains ... " (Christie 1998: 241; also Kulke 2009: 10), the "influence of Pallava sculptural idiom" (Shanmugam 2009: 210), and the "resemblance" of "the early sculptures of Cambodia" to Pallava sculptures at Māmallapuram (Sundaresh and Gaur 2011: 237; citing R. Nagaswamy).

Few of these assertions regarding the supposedly decisive, pivotal and, in some cases, sweeping role of Pallava artistic influences in Southeast Asia have been subjected to thorough critique. Although some scholars have raised brief challenges, to

---

2 See also, for example, Guy 2014: 170.

3 For example, in his discussion of the "Spread of Pallava Art," he discusses Funan, "where Pallava sculpture (at Prasat Andet, Van Pan Morai, Trepan Phon, Kompon Cham, etc.) competed with sculpture in the Gupta style."

my knowledge the only studies that have seriously engaged with the question of Pallava artistic influence in a sustained manner are those by Stanley J. O'Connor involving early Viṣṇu sculptures from peninsular Thailand and Julie Romain's balanced reassessment of south Indian stylistic influences on the temples of the Dieng Plateau in Java, Indonesia (Romain 2011: 299-316).

O'Connor, whose influential work is of immediate relevance to this essay, convincingly refuted Pierre Dupont's arguments that the impressive Viṣṇu from Takua Pa, Thailand (*fig.* 11.1), "is an almost pure reflection of Pallava style" and instead argued that it represents "a fully developed product of an isthmian workshop" or, in other words, "the culmination of a local school" (1972: 41-51). On the other hand, in his discussion of a group of three Hindu sculptures from the hill of Phra Narai (also in Takua Pa district), O'Connor advocated, probably correctly, a late Pallava date due to the fact their "style and costume are almost classic statements of later Pallava art" (1972: 52-55, figs. 28-31) (*fig.* 11.2 depicts the Viṣṇu and central image from this triad).[4] However, he was quick to point out, also quite correctly, that

> [t]here is nothing that leads up to the Pra Narâi group, and no other Hindu image in the Peninsula which would appear to be even remotely related to it. — O'Connor 1972: 55

While this essay largely corroborates O'Connor's work and argues that vaguely defined Pallava artistic influence in Southeast Asia has often been overestimated by scholars, I also seek to highlight several specific, albeit rather limited, cases in which Pallava style did influence Southeast Asian sculpture.

Early Inscriptions and the Supposed Pallava Connection

One of the reasons for according such a pivotal role to Pallava sculpture in the early development of Southeast Asian art has been

[4] For discussion of the history of these images with more recent photographs that depict their present state, see Jacq-Hergoualc'h 2002: 329, figs. 151-54.

the belief that many of the early (pre-mid-eighth century) stone inscriptions in Southeast Asia were written in Pallava script.[5] The most influential proponents of Pallava connections were Vogel (1918) and Chhabra (1965 [1935]), both of whom produced important studies on the pillar (*yūpa*) inscriptions from the Kutei or Kutai region of eastern Kalimantan (Borneo) issued by a king/chief named Mūlavarman and the inscriptions from western Java associated with the polity of Tārumā and another king/chief named Pūrṇavarman.[6] Primarily on the basis of epigraphic analysis by Vogel (1918: 218-32) and Chhabra (1965 [1935]: 50) that stressed Pallava relationships, the Mūlavarman inscriptions are typically dated to *c.*400 CE. The Pūrṇavarman inscriptions are generally believed to date slightly later, *circa* the mid-fifth century CE (Sarkar 1959: 135-36; Vogel 1925: 33-34). Through comparison to both Pallava epigraphy and the Pūrṇavarman inscriptions, a similar date (second half of the fifth century) has been assigned to one of the few inscriptions associable with the early polity of Funan, the inscription of Guṇavarman (K.5), which was found at Prasat Pram Loven (Gò Tháp) in what is today Đồng Tháp Province, southern Vietnam (Cœdès 1931: 4).

Other and more recent scholarship, however, has raised questions about the dates attributed to these inscriptions as well as their supposed Pallava affiliation.[7] J.G. de Casparis questioned whether the "earliest scripts of Southeast Asia" can be seen "as mere overseas branches of south Indian Pallava script" (1979: 382-87). According to K.A. Nilakanta Sastri,

[5] I am leaving aside here the complicated and contested arguments surrounding the Võ Cạnh inscription, typically advanced as the earliest locally produced stone inscription in Southeast Asia. For a useful critical discussion, see Zakharov 2010: 17-21.

[6] For recent discussions of Tārumā and Pūrṇavarman, see Santiko 2001 and Wessing 2011.

[7] Already in 1959, H.B. Sarkar (p. 135) warned that "we must remember that there was not much change in Pallava-Grantha characters between A.D. 400 and 750."

> ... we should give up the emphasis laid by Vogel in 1918 on Pallava influence when he edited the Yūpa inscriptions of East Borneo and rather speak of the script prevalent in the East Coast of the Madras Presidency, as the Telugu Country has furnished many early records of this type of writing which do not belong to the Pallavas but to other lines like the Śālankāyanas. — 1949a: 17

Arlo Griffiths, who has suggested a fifth century date for the Kutei inscriptions and a sixth century date for those from Tārumā, puts the matter succinctly:

> ... there is virtually no direct evidence of any Pallava involvement, certainly not for the earliest centuries, and the Pallavas were by no means the only southern Indian kings to use this script during the early first millennium. Moreover, the inscriptions of other dynasties show a form of writing that looks just as much like the script used in Southeast Asia as does the script seen in Pallava inscriptions. — 2014: 53-54[8]

Rather than the designations "Pallava Script" or "Pallava-Grantha" used by previous scholars, Griffiths advocates greater precision and more "neutral" terminology (2014: 53-54). Following an early phase characterized by a "box-headed" form of script (*circa* fourth-fifth centuries, including the Kutei inscriptions), he distinguishes a subsequent "Late Southern Brāhmī" period (*circa* sixth-eighth centuries, including the Tārumā inscriptions). Given the level of uncertainty surrounding these inscriptions, their supposed Pallava affiliation should not be used a priori as evidence of Pallava artistic influences in Southeast Asia.

South Indian Immigrant Communities and Imported Art

Decoupling early Southeast Asian inscriptions from the Pallavas as a working hypothesis is not intended to dismiss south Indian,

---

[8] Griffiths and Emmanuel Francis have promised a forthcoming monograph on the inscriptions of Mūlavarman and Pūrṇavarman. Pollock emphasizes early Cāḷukya (Karnataka, India), rather than Pallava, relationships with Southeast Asian epigraphy (2006: 123-24).

and particularly Tamil, relationships with Southeast Asia. There is much archaeological, epigraphical, and literary evidence to indicate an ancient and relatively sustained role played by Tamil merchants along the maritime trading routes of coastal Southeast Asia as far as Quanzhou in southern China's Fujian Province (Guy 2011: 248-59). For example, portable Tamil-inscribed objects, including a *circa* second-century CE pottery fragment and a third or fourth-century goldsmith's touchstone, have been recovered from peninsular Thailand (Boonyarit Chaisuwan 2011: 84-94). Likely imported from India, such artifacts may provide interesting clues about the presence of Tamil-speaking merchants and artisans, the circulation of prestige objects, and the possible diffusion of some Indian technologies, but they provide little insight about the development of stone sculpture in Southeast Asia.

Tamil mercantile activity seems to have intensified during the late Pallava and Coḷa periods as a result of several interconnected factors: (1) the influence of south Indian merchant guilds, (2) Coḷa (tenth–thirteenth centuries CE) expansionism and engagement with Song dynasty China (960–1279 CE), and (3) competition for maritime trade and prestige culminating in Coḷa naval raids of Śrīvijaya (Palembang) and neighboring port cities on Sumatra and the Malay Peninsula (in 1017[?], 1025, and 1067-68 CE) (Abraham 1988: 127–56; Karashima 2009: 149-53; Kulke 2009: 1-19; Sen 2009: 61-75). Seven Tamil inscriptions from peninsular Thailand, Pagan (Myanmar), Sumatra, and Quanzhou — ranging in date from the mid-ninth to thirteenth century — provide testimony of this expansive Tamil trading network.[9]

The earliest of these inscriptions, found in Takua Pa near the aforementioned Phra Narai Hindu triad, places a tank under the protection of the Maṇikkirāmam, a merchant guild known from ninth to fourteenth-century inscriptions in Tamil Nadu and Kerala

[9] Francis provides a recent list with discussion and critique of earlier scholarship (2008/2009: 412).

(Karashima 2002: 11-12). The precise relationship between the sculptures, the inscription, and the nearby remains of what may have been a small square shrine is poorly understood, but the *circa* ninth century date of the inscription (Nilakanta Sastri 1949b: 26-29) makes it approximately contemporary with, or slightly later than, the likely date of the three sculptures, *c.*750–850 CE, as determined through comparisons with late Pallava sculpture (Jacq-Hergoualc'h 2002: 330, figs. 156-57; O'Connor 1972: 53-54).[10] The triad consists of a 2.42 m Viṣṇu image (*fig.* 11.2) perhaps flanked by his consort Bhūdevī and Sage (*ṛṣi*) Mārkaṇḍeya.[11] Unusual among Southeast Asian stone sculptures, they correspond closely to the late Pallava style and, conversely, exhibit little to associate them with the sculpture of peninsular Thailand. It is, therefore, typically argued that they were either imported from southern India or made locally by Indian artists to serve the resident Tamil community (Jacq-Hergoualc'h 2002: 330; O'Connor 1972: 55).

While it may seem unlikely that such large sculptures could be imports, it is worth pointing out that there are other large stone sculptures that may have been transported considerable distances in the remote past, for example, a *circa* seventh or eighth-century Gaṇeśa (H. 1.75 m) found in Palembang, South Sumatra, but possibly imported from the Cāḷukyan realm in south India (Brown 1987: 98-100; Hardiati 2009: fig. 5.4), and a *circa* eighth-century Buddha (H. 1.72 m) in the Dvāravatī style of central Thailand but found in Tingkip, South Sumatra (Hardiati 2009: fig. 5.5). A number of *circa*

---

[10] Due to a possible reference to the Pallava king Nandivarman III in the Takua Pa inscription, Nilakanta Sastri associated it with this reign, initially dated by him to 826-50, and therefore suggested a date for the inscription in the second quarter of the ninth century (1949b: 29). He later revised his dating of Nandivarman III's reign to 846-69 (1975: 159-60). Lefèvre dates his reign to 829-53 (2006: 319). According to Francis, he ruled for as many as twenty-three years *c.*850-60 (2013: 256).

[11] For discussion of the complicated circumstances of these sculptures, see Jacq-Hergoualc'h 2002: 329-30, figs. 151-55 and Piriya Krairiksh 2012: 174, figs. 2.82-2.83. The Mārkaṇḍeya image measures 1.11 m in height.

tenth or eleventh-century Coḷa images — likewise either imports or locally crafted in Southeast Asia by Indian artists — have been found in peninsular Thailand (Jacq-Hergoualc'h 2002: 382-86, figs. 183-88; O'Connor 1972: 60-63, figs. 32-34) and at Kota Cina in North Sumatra (Hardiati 2009: 82-83, fig. 5.17).[12] All of them probably correspond to the period of Coḷa intervention in Southeast Asia and are associated with regions that appear to have been frequented by Tamil merchants and perhaps inhabited by Indian immigrant communities. They provide testimony of a dynamic period of trans-regional interactions, but these Coḷa-related images, as well as the Pallava-related Phra Narai triad, stand outside Southeast Asian artistic traditions and seem to have played a rather minimal and indirect role in local artistic developments.[13] Like the early inscriptions discussed above, they should not be construed as indicative of long-standing patterns of Pallava influence in Southeast Asia.[14]

Pallava Metal and Stone Sculpture

Scholars have long debated the role of south Indian metal images in the dissemination of Buddhism and Buddhist art to Sri Lanka and Southeast Asia (Barrett 1954; Brown 2014; Guy 2004; Lunsingh Scheurleer and Klokke 1988; Schastok 1994). A *bodhisattva* image, perhaps Avalokiteśvara, reportedly found in an irrigation canal

---

[12] Note also the architectural elements from Nakhon Si Thammarat, Thailand, rendered in what appears to be Coḷa style (one example in Lee 2012: 16, fig. 0.2).

[13] However, note (among other possible examples) several south India-related bronzes in the Nakhon Si Thammarat National Museum dating to *circa* the sixteenth-eighteenth centuries (Natthapatra Chandavij and Saengchan Traikasem 2000: 89-96), as well as the extraordinary sixteenth-century bronze Hindu goddess in the Bangkok National Museum (969KH) (Gude 2005: 134-37, cat. no. 38 with references to related images from both Thailand and India).

[14] Shanmugam provides a rather vague and incomplete survey of Pallava and Coḷa artistic influences in Indonesia (2009: 212-26).

of the Kr̥ṣṇā River in Andhra Pradesh and now in the Victoria and Albert Museum (IM.300-1914), has been emphasized as a pivotal image in the dissemination of south Indian artistic style. Variably dated to the fifth (Srinivasan 2008: 388-89; 2013: 172), sixth (Guy 2014: 36-37, cat. no. 7), second half of the seventh (Irwin 1948: 105-06, pl. I), and late seventh–eighth century CE (Guy 2004: 70, pl. 15.14), it has been described as "early Andhra Pallava" (Srinivasan 2013: 172), "early Pallava" (Sivaramamurti 1963: 45, pl. 2b), and "Pallava" (Irwin 1948: 105-06), yet there is little evidence to link it definitely with the Pallavas or with Pallava art. Rather it represents a style of uncertain date that was broadly shared between multiple regions of India, Sri Lanka, and parts of Southeast Asia. Like the bronzes of the so-called "Late Amarāvatī School," it is not presently possible to determine production sites or specific paths of influence with any degree of certainty (Brown 2014: 14-18). The same is generally true of a number of Buddhist bronzes from various sites in Indonesia that have been associated with the Pallava style (Srinivasan 2013: 176).[15]

There is also the question of a potential role for bronzes of Hindu, or Brāhmanical, subject matter in the dissemination of the Pallava style. It has been suggested, for example, that Pallava bronzes of Viṣṇu have "affinities" with Javanese Buddhist bronze and stone sculpture (Srinivasan 2013: 175). In order to assess this idea, some discussion of Pallava style Viṣṇu images in both stone and metal is necessary. The validity of the term "Pallava bronzes" and the very existence of Pallava-period Brāhmanical bronzes have been the subjects of much debate (Barrett 1965: 42). Although most scholars now seem to agree that there was a distinct Pallava-period bronze style, they differ widely in the dates they assign to its inception and development.[16] It must also be recognized that

[15] See Lunsingh Scheurleer and Klokke 1988: 26-27, 58 [cat. 6], 61 [cat. 9], 63 [cat. 11], 65 [cat. 13], 111 [cat. 59].

[16] See Sivaramamurti 1963: 47-52, pls. 6-15a; Srinivasan 1994 [1963]: 29-57, figs. 15-31; Khandalavala 1969: 27-30; Nagaswamy 1988: 142-57; Nagaswamy 1995: 102-08; Srinivasan 2004: 220-23, 236-42.

there is no clear evidence to link any bronze sculpture directly to the patronage of the Pallava dynasty (Francis 2013: 120-22; Lefèvre 2006: 221-28).

The Brāhmanical bronzes associated with the Pallava period (for example, *fig.* 11.3) predominantly represent standing (*sthānaka*) images of Viṣṇu with rigid bodies (*samabhaṅga*) and evenly placed feet (*samapādasthānaka*). They all have four arms (*caturbhuja*). A discus (*cakra*) and conch (*śaṅkha*), both usually adorned with flames, are held in the upper proper right and left hands respectively. The lower right hand holds a lotus (*padma*) or a gem (*ratna*) and displays either *abhaya-mudrā* or *varada-mudrā*, while the lower left hand rests either on the hip (*kaṭihasta-mudrā* or *kaṭyāvalambitahasta-mudrā*) or on the pommel of a downturned mace (*gadā*).

Among the stylistic elements that distinguish these bronze Viṣṇus are the following: relatively small size, conical crowns, or mitres (*kirīṭamukuṭa*), a bejeweled or pearl stomach-band (*udarabandha*), an ankle-length lower garment with numerous narrow parallel folds or stripes, a waistband (*kaṭisūtra*) fixed by a large looped knot that sometimes exhibits a pronounced "oblique twist," one or more semi-circular looping sashes of variable length over the thighs, tassels hanging vertically down the thighs from an additional waistband or from the sashes, a thick wedge-like bunching of the fabric near the ankles, and, on some examples, large bows at each hip with long fabric pendant along the outside of the thighs (Khandalavala 1969: 29-34; Srinivasan 1994 [1963]: 32-48). One of the most distinctive features, and one often used by scholars as a diagnostic trait of the period, is the treatment of the sacred thread (*yajñopavīta*) (Craven 1970: 262; Khandalavala 1969: 29; Narasimhan 1960: 22; Pal 1969/70: 25).[17] On many, but not all, of

[17] This feature is not, however, unique to Pallava sculpture; a similar arrangement of the *yajñopavīta* also occurs, for example, on images in the cave and structural temples of Bādāmī (Karnataka, India) dating to the Early Western Cāḷukya period (*circa* mid-sixth to mid-eighth centuries CE). See Tartakov 1997: pls. 82-83.

the bronzes associated with the Pallava period, it drapes over the lower proper right forearm in a configuration that similarly appears on some Pallava stone images (Narasimhan 1960: figs. 8-11).[18]

Indeed, while the style of stone and metal images of a given period often differ due to the specific properties of each media and their respective techniques of production, scholars often highlight the close relationship between Pallava stone and bronze sculpture. Khandalavala, for example, has suggested that Pallava artists "merely copied the stone images" and in so doing transferred elements from stone sculpture that were "not suitable" for bronze casting, for example, the *yajñopavīta* over the forearm and the large looping knots of the waistband (1969: 29). Similarly, Craven argued that "the unique treatment of the triangular cloth area above and between the ankles, at the hem-line, appears distinctively solid and unclothlike to suggest that we are still witnessing here in metal, the lingering presence of stone-carving techniques" (1970: 262). Given how poorly the precise chronology of Pallava art is understood, such judgments are difficult to gauge, but numerous stylistic features are shared by Pallava stone and bronze Viṣṇu images. In addition to those already mentioned, these include: the prominent stomach-band, a similar (yet variable) system of sashes with bows at the hip and pendant fabric along the outside of the legs, the large looping knot of the waistband, and on some images the folds or striations of fabric cascading down the front of the garment (*figs.* 11.2 and 11.4).[19] Only a few of these traits occur in Southeast Asian sculpture, either individually or jointly; those that do are discussed below.

---

18 It does not, for example, appear on the Pallava Viṣṇus pictured here (*figs.* 11.2-11.4).

19 See also Jacq-Hergoualc'h 2002: fig. 156 (from Tirrukaravayil/Tirukkaraivasal) and fig. 157 (from Kottur), both late Pallava Viṣṇu images (*c.* eighth or ninth century) in the Thanjavur Art Gallery; a *circa* ninth or tenth-century Viṣṇu in the Ashmolean Museum (Harle and Topsfield 1987: 54, no. 65, acc. no. 1981.10); and the *circa* tenth-century Sathyamangalam (Śāttamaṅgalam) Viṣṇu in the Government Museum, Chennai.

The Pallava Style and Early Southeast Asian Viṣṇu Images

The earliest Vaiṣṇava image from Southeast Asia is probably the well-known Vāsudeva-Kṛṣṇa (Viṣṇu) image, from Chaiya, Surat Thani province in peninsular Thailand, probably dating to *c.*500 CE. Although the possibility of pre-Pallava stylistic influences from Andhra Pradesh cannot be completely dismissed, its closest stylistic and iconographic relationships are probably with late fifth- early sixth-century northern Indian sculpture from sites including Bhinmāl, Mandsaur, and Bhumara (Brown 1992: 46-47; Lavy 2014: 158-64). It belongs to a group of Southeast Asian images distinguished by the conch shell held akimbo by the proper left hand against the hip. In Southeast Asia, conch-on-hip images appear — according to current evidence and confirmed through stylistic analysis — to have been exclusively early in date, or, in other words, confined to the sixth and perhaps early seventh centuries CE (Lavy 2014: 154-55).

During the late sixth and early seventh centuries, the conch-on-hip iconography was replaced by, or evolved into, a new iconographical type (Brown 2000: 10). The conch was no longer placed on the left hip, but was instead elevated in the raised left hand with the *cakra* mirroring it in the raised proper right hand. Thus, the new arrangement of the attributes became, clockwise from the lower proper right hand, the orb (likely representing the earth), *cakra*, conch, and mace or club (*fig.* 11.5).[20] This new iconography became standard for most Viṣṇu images in much of what are today Thailand, Cambodia, Laos, and southern Vietnam, and appeared to a more limited degree in Indonesia and Myanmar. It persisted for many centuries in Khmer art, perhaps as late as the sixteenth century. The same iconography occurs, for example, in several late twelfth- or early thirteenth-century relief sculptures from the Bayon,

[20] With a lotus (*padma*), rather than — or synonymous with — the orb, this configuration is identified in the Indian iconographical texts that enumerate the twenty-four forms of Viṣṇu as either Janārdana or Vāsudeva (Bidyabinod 1920: 23-33).

including depictions of enshrined standing four-armed Viṣṇu statues equipped with the same configuration of four attributes.

A related arrangement also occurs in Pallava bronze sculptures of Viṣṇu with the seventh century being the earliest date so far suggested for some of these images (Narasimhan 1960: 20) (*fig.* 11.3).[21] However, while the *cakra* and conch may be similarly held in the upper proper right and left hands respectively, the club is often absent, with the lower proper left hand instead held in *kaṭihasta-mudrā*.[22] In the instances in which an object is held in the lower proper right hand of Pallava bronzes, it is a lotus or gem and never the earth-orb that characterizes Southeast Asian Viṣṇu images (Lavy 2014: 165-66).[23] Furthermore Pallava bronze Viṣṇus typically hold *cakra*s and conches adorned with flames, but such flames are absent from Southeast Asian Viṣṇu images, save for the rare aforementioned examples that were likely Coḷa-style imports (Jacq-Hergoualc'h 2002: 383-84, fig. 185; O'Connor 1972: 61, fig. 32a-b; Piriya Krairiksh 2012: 175, fig. 2.84). Thus the rise of this

---

[21] *Figure* 11.3 has been variably dated to the seventh century (Srinivasan 2013: 174-75, fig. 13.5), the eighth or ninth century (Sivaramamurti 1963: 49-50, pl. 10b and 10d), the second quarter of the ninth century (Srinivasan 1994 [1963]: 46-47, figs. 25 and 26) and *c.*940 (Barrett 1968: 127). See also Gravely and Ramachandran, 2002 [1932]: 63-64, pl. ii, fig. 1.

[22] With the lower proper left hand in *kaṭihasta-mudrā*, see Srinivasan 1994 [1963]: figs. 15 and 21; Sivaramamurti 1963: pls. 12a (also published in Srinivasan 1994 [1963]: fig. 23) and 14a; Singh and Singh 2016: 49, cat no. 4; 108, cat. no. 90 (also published in Sivaramamurti 1963: pl. 10a). With the lower proper left hand holding a club and the corresponding right hand extended and holding what is probably a lotus or lotus bud, see Narasimhan 1960: pl. VII, fig. 1(c); pl. VIII, fig. 3; Sivaramamurti 1963: pl. 11a. With a club in the lower left hand but the corresponding right hand in *abhaya-mudrā* while also holding a lotus, see Sivaramamurti 1963: pl. 14b and *fig.* 11.3, a configuration that does not seem to exist in Southeast Asian art.

[23] For other examples with a lotus held in the lower proper right hand, see Srinivasan 1994 [1963]: figs. 15 and 17. With a gem in this hand, see Srinivasan 1994 [1963]: fig. 21.

new standardized Viṣṇu iconography in Southeast Asia could not have been the result of a direct unmediated link to Pallava stylistic or iconographic developments. Rather, it appears to have been a local innovation that pre-dated the possibility of Pallava influence (Brown 2000: 10; Lavy 2014: 165-70). The most that can be said is that Pallava bronzes may have reinforced this iconography in Southeast Asia, however, it is important to note that, thus far, no imported Pallava bronze images of Viṣṇu have been found in Southeast Asia.

Because Southeast Asian Viṣṇu images typically include the *gadā*, they are even more removed from Pallava stone Viṣṇus, which consistently *omit* the *gadā* altogether (*figs.* 11.2 and 11.4).[24] With such a fundamental iconographic difference, Pallava stone Viṣṇu images are an unlikely source for Southeast Asian art. Decorative elements, carving technique, and the approach to anatomy also cast the influence of Pallava stone sculpture into doubt. As O'Connor observed, Pallava stone figures tend to be more heavily ornamented with sacred thread and elaborate necklaces, they are generally quite flat (particularly the torso) with little muscle definition, and they rarely have their upper arms cut free from the body; when they do, the arms are not separated above the elbow (1972: 43-44) (compare *figs.* 11.1 and 11.2).[25] In contrast, after the initial sixth-century group of conch-on-hip images from peninsular Thailand, most early Southeast Asian sculpture was, compared to Pallava sculpture, more simply adorned, more fully modelled, and carved more completely in-the-round. This tendency is particularly evident in the late sixth to eighth-century Viṣṇus of pre-Angkorian Khmer art and in those

[24] Additional examples include the Viṣṇus at Māmallapuram's Ādivarāha Cave (Krishna 1980: pl. 17), the Tiruccirāppaḷḷi lower cave temple (Pattabiramin 1975: 34-35, pl. XC, 1), and Kīḷmāvilaṅgai (Krishna 1980: pl. 22).

[25] Examples of Pallava stone Viṣṇus that, to varying degrees, cut the arms free from the body include an image from Kāñcīpuram now in the National Museum, New Delhi (acc. no. 6501), and one from Vaḍakkalathur (Nagaswamy 1971: 56, fig. 1). See also the tenth-century Sathyamangalam Viṣṇu in the Government Museum, Chennai.

from peninsular Thailand, most spectacularly the aforementioned Viṣṇu from Takua Pa (*fig.* 11.1) which, as O'Connor notes, "would look out of place in the family of Pallava images" (1972: 44).

In an early study, however, Pierre Dupont argued that Pallava stone statuary was the "prototype" for the *circa* sixth to eighth century mitred Viṣṇu images of Southeast Asia, including those of Thailand, Cambodia, and southern Vietnam (1941: 248-53). His argument was based primarily on the work of M. Jouveau-Dubreuil, who associated the elevated *cakra* and conch exclusively with Pallava innovations and who incorrectly believed that the cylindrical and united shape of the mitre first occurred in the Pallava art of the seventh century (1914: 60–65).[26] First, the same hand position for *cakra* and conch can also be found in the sculpture of the Cāḷukyas (for example, the sixth-century Viṣṇu images in Bādāmī Cave 3) and Pāṇḍyas (for example, the *circa* eighth-century Viṣṇus in the Sevilipaṭṭi and Tirumālapuram cave temples); in other words, it is not at all exclusive to Pallava art.[27] Second, it is now increasingly clear that the origins of the cylindrical mitre (*kirīṭamukuṭa*) are best sought in earlier northern Indian art, namely the fifth or sixth century Śiva Temple at Bhumara in Madhya Pradesh (Lavy 2014: 161, fig. 17; Quaritch Wales 1948: 4; Woodward 1973: 211).[28]

---

[26] Dupont also drew some brief, and quite vague, comparisons between the garments of Southeast Asian Viṣṇus and those worn in reliefs at Ellorā and by the Pallava image of Viṣṇu-Anantaśayana in the Mahiṣāsuramardinī Cave, Māmallapuram. He approached these comparisons to Indian art with caution, however, and remarked that it was not possible to trace the specific details of the Southeast Asian Viṣṇus back to India due to the fact that Pallava art is not adequately understood and because the Southeast Asian Viṣṇus were a distinct tradition (Dupont 1941: 249-50).

[27] For the Viṣṇu images in Bādāmī Cave 3, see Tarr 1970: figs. 28-29. For the Sevilipaṭṭi and Tirumālapuram Viṣṇus, see Pattabiramin 1975: 41, 60, pls. CXIV, 1 and CLXXVII, 1. For the chronology of early Pāṇḍyan cave temples, see Soundara Rajan 1998: 46-59.

[28] My thanks to Hiram Woodward for bringing Quaritch Wales' Bhumara comparison to my attention.

Pallava mitres in stone sculpture of the seventh through eighth centuries vary and change over time, but they are typically taller, narrower, and more tapering than their Southeast Asian counterparts. Representative examples of these tall Pallava mitres can be seen at Māmallapuram (or Mahābalipuram), for example, on the Trivikrama in the Varāha Cave, the Viṣṇu-Anantaśayana in the Mahiṣāsuramardinī Cave, and on images of Viṣṇu and the portrait of King Narasiṁhavarman I at the Dharmarāja Ratha (Beck 2006: 103, 132-33, 143, 196, 204). They are often capped by a disc, or diminishing series of discs, culminating in a convex crowning protuberance (*kudmala*) with what appear, at least in some cases, to be floral decorative forms. A squatter variation consists of a truncated cylinder or cone surmounted by a steep conical crowning peak; these occur most notably on the portraits of two kings in the Ādivarāha Cave, also at Māmallapuram (Beck 2006: 154-57) (one of these portraits is depicted in *fig*. 11.6).[29] Bronze images that may be assignable to the Pallava period (*fig*. 11.3), are topped by a multi-tiered cone-like element or, alternately, by a finial-like knob that resembles a floral element or bud.[30]

Perhaps originally inspired by the Pallava sculpture of south-eastern India, a convex protuberance, or small button, on the top of the mitre is encountered on a number of seventh to eighth-century sculptures from early Cambodia and Thailand. The few examples from Cambodia include a goddess from Kampong Khleang in Siem Reap Province (Dupont 1955: 135, 165-66, pl. XXXVIIA).[31] A flatter

[29] For a useful summary of the various dates and identities that have been suggested for the Ādivarāha cave temple royal portraits inscribed as "Siṁhaviṇṇapottrāḍhirājan" and "Mahendrapottrāḍhirājan," see Lefèvre 2006: 260-63, figs. 27-28; 2011: 172-74, figs. 55-56. For recent discussion of the inscriptions (IR 51 and 52) and bibliography pertaining to them, see Francis 2013: 284-85; 2017: 538, 563-64.

[30] For further examples, see Sivaramamurti 1963: pls. 10a-d, 11a, 11c, 12a, 14a-b; Srinivasan 1994 [1963]: figs. 15-26, 30-31.

[31] The Kampong Khleang goddess (sandstone, H. 62.5 cm) is in the National Museum of Cambodia, Phnom Penh (acc. no. Ka. 887).

disc-like protuberance tops the mitre of a head, probably Viṣṇu and reportedly from Cambodia, in the Boston Museum of Fine Arts (acc. no. 26.206; Coomaraswamy 1928: 16). A lintel from Tuol Ang (Kampong Speu Province) portrays a Viṣṇu-Anantaśayana wearing a very tall, slender mitre with a crowning disc and small protuberant button (Dupont 1955: pl. XXVIB; Boisselier 1955: 105).

Thailand has also yielded a similar example on a Viṣṇu from Ratchaburi Province (*fig.* 11.7).[32] It wears a mitre that terminates in two diminishing discs that swell outward like flat cushions but are otherwise unadorned. This feature is comparable to the mitres worn by the two outermost attendant maidens in the seventh-century Gajalakṣmī scene in the Ādivarāha cave temple (*fig.* 11.8), as well as by the royal portraits in the same cave (*fig.* 11.6). In Southeast Asia, similar crowning discs are more commonly encountered on images from, or associated with, the site of Si Thep in Phetchabun Province, Thailand. These include, for example, a Kr̥ṣṇa-Govardhana in the Bangkok National Museum (Piriya Krairiksh 2012: 108, fig. 1.107) and a fragmentary goddess in the Linden-Museum Stuttgart (Thomsen 1982: 160, fig. E46; Kreisel 1987: 104-05, fig. 115) (*fig.* 11.9), the latter of which wears a mitre and ear adornments that closely resemble the aforementioned Gajalakṣmī attendants in the Ādivarāha cave (*fig.* 11.8).[33]

It is also possible to isolate particular sartorial elements of

---

[32] The image was reportedly found at Wat Tho in Ratchaburi Province and is now in the Bangkok National Museum (inv. no. KKH 7, stone, H. 1.52 m). Boisselier (1959: 216-17, fig. 4), Dupont (1941: 235-37, pl. XXVIIIB), and O'Connor (1972: 47-48, fig. 19) mistakenly, it seems, identified the image as having come from Phetchaburi. Opinions on the date of the Ratchaburi Viṣṇu differ. Dupont and O'Connor do not explicitly advance a date, but imply seventh century or later. Boisselier (1959) and Piriya Krairiksh (2012: 107, fig. 1.105a-b) consider it to be a relatively late example of the mitred Viṣṇu tradition, *circa* second half of the seventh century. In contrast, Lavy has emphasized features that suggest the possibility of an earlier date, *circa* late sixth-early seventh century (2004: 312-15).

[33] Linden-Museum goddess: acc. no. SA 34 180L, sandstone, H. 1.35 cm.

some Viṣṇus from peninsular Thailand and Cambodia and relate them to Pallava art. These include, for example, the median fold that bifurcates into a large wedge-like horizontal hem at the ankles (compare *fig*. 11.4 with *fig*. 11.5), the slender belt tied at the waist with a looping knot (for example, Viṣṇus from Khao Si Vichai and Mueang Si Mahasot, Thailand), and the large hip-level bow with pendant swag of cloth along the thigh (for example, Viṣṇu from Tuol Chuk, Kandal Province, Cambodia; another from Si Mahasot; a variation with a less pronounced bow can be seen on *fig*. 11.7).[34] O'Connor suggested that the presence of some of these features in Southeast Asian sculpture might "reflect a response to Pallava art of the 7th century, assimilated into an earlier [local Southeast Asian] tradition" (1972: 48). However, he also noted the "danger in isolating a single feature ... without reference to the stylistic context of the whole work of art, and drawing chronological and cultural conclusions on the basis of a similar feature on an image thousands of miles away, existing in a different social, political, and ethnic context" (1972: 45).

With this warning in mind, it is important to note that all of the aforementioned sartorial features rarely occur in unison on either Pallava or Southeast Asian stone images. One Southeast Asian image that exhibits many of them is the *circa* eighth-ninth century Viṣṇu from Candi Banon in central Java.[35] It combines elaborate

---

[34] The Khao Si Vichai (or Khao Śrīvijaya) Viṣṇus (H. 1.70 m and 43 cm) are in the Bangkok National Museum and the Nakhon Si Thammarat Museum (O'Connor 1972: figs. 17, 23; Jacq-Hergoualc'h 2002: figs. 10-11). The Mueang Si Mahasot Viṣṇus (H. 1.48 m, 1.25 m, 1.70 m) are in the Prachin Buri National Museum (acc. nos. 129/24 [587/2519] and 134/24) and the Musée national des Arts asiatiques Guimet (acc. no. MA 6341) (Phiset Chiachanphong, Saranya Suriyarattanakon, and Sakchai Photchananwanit 1999: 62-64; Baptiste and Zéphir 2009: 126 no. 38). The Tuol Chuk Viṣṇu (H. 94 cm) is in the Phnom Penh National Museum (acc. no. Ka.1610) (Dupont 1955: pl. XVIIb).

[35] Now in the National Museum, Jakarta, acc. no. 4847/18e (H. 2.0 m). See Kempers 1959: 36-37, pl. 42. Unfortunately, all four hands and associated

ornamentation, a sacred thread, a stomach-band, a complex system of sashes, and, at each hip, large bows with trailing fabric pendant alongside the legs, all of which invite Pallava comparisons (Tōkyō Kokuritsu Hakubutsukan 1997: 25, cat. no. 14). However, its subtle modelling, swelling musculature, and the fact that it is carved fully in-the-round closely align this image with a broadly shared Southeast Asian aesthetic and separate it quite dramatically from the Pallava style.

When all the sartorial elements occur together in Pallava stone sculpture, as with a Viṣṇu relief on the second level of the Dharmarāja Ratha (Srinivasan 1975: pl. XIX[b]), it can be argued that the differences from Southeast Asian sculpture outweigh the similarities. The iconography (*abhaya-mudrā* and *kaṭihasta-mudrā* with no *gadā*), the more complex arrangement of sashes, the cascading parallel folds down the front of the garment, and the higher degree of ornamentation all suggest that whatever stylistic relationships might have existed between Pallava and Southeast Asian art, they were neither particularly close nor direct. They perhaps ultimately amounted to "a last and very weak wave" as phrased by Jean Boisselier (1955: 264) in a discussion of seventh-century Khmer art.

Concluding Remarks

The intention of this discussion has not been to replace the Pallava style with another Indian style as the model for Southeast Asian art. On the contrary, the point is to suggest, following Prof. Brown, that Indian art is often of limited utility in seeking to understand the development of art in Southeast Asia. Southeast Asian art was of course closely related to Indian art and, at times, it developed along similar, sometimes connected, and perhaps occasionally parallel pathways, but direct Indian models and prototypes are exceedingly rare. Instead, Southeast Asian artists seemed to have rapidly

---

attributes are missing and, with them, other potential stylistic and iconographic comparisons.

fig. 11.1: Viṣṇu, found at Khao Phra Noe, Takua Pa district, Phang Nga Province, Thailand, *circa* mid-to-late seventh century CE, stone

fig. 11.2: Viṣṇu, found near Khao Phra Narai, Takua Pa district, Phang Nga Province, Thailand, *circa* ninth century CE, stone

fig. 11.3: Viṣṇu, Pallava period, *circa* eighth-ninth century CE, bronze

fig. 11.4: Viṣṇu, Trimūrti Cave Temple, Māmallapuram (Mahābalipuram), Tamil Nadu, India, seventh century CE, granite

fig. 11.5: Viṣṇu, first observed in Ayutthaya, Thailand, but probably from Surat Thani Province, Thailand, *circa* late sixth-early seventh century CE, stone

fig. 11.6: Mahendrapottrādhirājan and queens, south wall, Ādivarāha Cave Temple, Māmallapuram (Mahābalipuram), Tamil Nadu, India, seventh century CE, granite

fig. 11.7: Viṣṇu, found at Wat Tho, Ratchaburi Province, Thailand, *circa* seventh century CE, stone

fig. 11.8: Gajalakṣmī with attendants, east wall, Ādivarāha Cave Temple, Māmallapuram (Mahābalipuram), Tamil Nadu, India, Pallava period, seventh century CE, granite

fig. 11.9: Goddess, Si Thep, Phetchabun Province, Thailand, *circa* seventh-eighth century CE, greenish ferruginous sandstone

selected, assimilated, and synthesized Indian influences from a variety of sources and adapted them to already well-established local sensibilities. As stated by Mireille Bénisti in reference to "Indo-Khmer relations" in pre-Angkorian art, "if numerous connections exist ... there [was] no transmission of a coherent whole from India to Khmer country" (1970: 101).[36]

While particular elements of Southeast Asian art taken in isolation may have Pallava counterparts, no suite of stylistic characteristics exists in Southeast Asia to conclusively prove that there was significant Pallava influence per se, let alone direct Pallava artistic relationships. Imported Pallava stone sculpture was rare and perhaps consisted only of the Phra Narai triad (main image shown in *fig.* 11.2), which is stylistically isolated in Southeast Asia, too late to have influenced the mitred Viṣṇu tradition (*figs.* 11.1, 11.5, and 11.7) and had very little impact on local artistic developments. Pallava Brāhmanical bronze images (*fig.* 11.3) may have served as a "vehicle" for the limited dissemination of style, but their relationship to Southeast Asian sculpture is far from clear-cut or one-to-one (and it must be remembered that none has come to light in Southeast Asia). Too often, furthermore, scholars suppose that Indian material, including Pallava art, is more precisely dated than it really is (Brown 1992: 45). Rarely does a presumed Pallava association provide greater chronological precision or illuminate Southeast Asian art in a meaningful way. Unless and until more conclusive evidence is forthcoming, the rather privileged and exceptional status that has been accorded Pallava art in Southeast Asian art history should be abandoned.

References

Abraham, Meera, 1988, *Two Medieval Merchant Guilds of South India*, New Delhi: Manohar.

Baptiste, Pierre and Thierry Zéphir (eds.), 2009, *Dvāravatī: aux sources du bouddhisme en Thaïlande*, Paris: Réunion des musées nationaux and Musée national des Arts asiatiques-Guimet.

---

[36] Author's translation.

Barrett, Douglas, 1954, "The Later School of Amaravati and Its Influences," *Art and Letters*, 28(2): 41–53.

——, 1965, *Early Cola Bronzes*, Bombay: Bhulabhai Memorial Institute.

——, 1968, "A Bronze Srinivasa Group," *The British Museum Quarterly* (Spring), 32(3/4): 126-32.

Beck, Elisabeth, 2006, *Pallava Rock Architecture and Sculpture*, Pondicherry: Sri Aurobindo Society.

Bénisti, Mireille, 1970, *Rapports entre le premier art khmer et l'art indien*, vol. 1, Paris: École française d'Extrême-Orient.

Bhattacharya, Kamaleswar, 1961, *Les Religions brahmaniques dans l'ancien Cambodge: d'après l'épigraphie et l'iconographie*, Paris: École française d'Extrême-Orient.

Bidyabinod, Pandit B.B., 1920, "Varieties of the Vishnu Image," *Memoirs of the Archaeological Survey of India*, 2: 23-33.

Boisselier, Jean, 1955, *La statuaire khmère et son évolution*, Saigon: École française d'Extrême-Orient.

——, 1959, "Le Visnu de Tjibuaja (Java Occidental) et la Statuaire du Sud-Est Asiatique," *Artibus Asiae*, 22(3): 210-26.

——, 1990, "Mahisasuramardini," *Orientations*, 21(2): 40-42.

Boonyarit Chaisuwan, 2011, "Early Contacts between India and the Andaman Coast in Thailand from the Second Century BCE to Eleventh Century CE," in *Early Interactions between South and Southeast Asia: Reflections on Cross-Cultural Exchange*, ed. Pierre-Yves Manguin, A. Mani, and Geoff Wade, pp. 83–111, Singapore: Institute of Southeast Asian Studies.

Briggs, Lawrence Palmer, 1951, *The Ancient Khmer Empire*, Transactions of the American Philosophical Society, n.s. 41(1), Philadelphia.

Brown, Robert L., 1987, "A Note on the Recently Discovered Gaṇeśa Image from Palembang, Sumatra," *Indonesia*, 43: 95-100.

——, 1992, "Indian Art Transformed: The Earliest Sculptural Styles of Southeast Asia," in *Panels of the VIIth World Sanskrit Conference*, ed. Johannes Bronkhorst, pp. 40-53, Leiden: E.J. Brill.

——, 1994, "'Rules' for Change in the Transfer of Indian Art to Southeast Asia," in *Ancient Indonesian Sculpture*, ed. Marijke J. Klokke and Pauline Lunsingh Scheurleer, pp. 10-32, Leiden: KITLV Press.

——, 1996, *The Dvāravatī Wheels of the Law and the Indianization of South East Asia*, Leiden: E.J. Brill.

——, 2000 [unpublished], "The Early Viṣṇu Images from Southeast Asia and their Indian Relationships," paper presented at *Crossroads and Commodification: A Symposium on Southeast Asian Art History*, University of Michigan, Ann Arbor, MI, March 25-26, 2000.

——, 2014, *Carrying Buddhism: The Role of Metal Icons in the Spread and Development of Buddhism*, Amsterdam: J. Gonda Fund Foundation of the KNAW.

——, 2017, "The Trouble with Convergence," in *India and Southeast Asia: Cultural Discourses*, ed. Anna L. Dallapiccola and Anila Verghese, pp. 37-50, Mumbai: The KR Cama Oriental Institute.

Casparis, J.G. de, 1979, "Palaeography as an Auxiliary Discipline in Research on Early South East Asia," in *Early South East Asia: Essays in Archaeology, History, and Historical Geography*, ed. R.B. Smith and W. Watson, pp. 380-94, New York: Oxford University Press.

——, 1986, "Some Notes on the Oldest Inscriptions of Indonesia," in *A Man of Indonesian Letters: Essays in Honour of Professor A. Teeuw*, ed. C.M.S. Hellwig and S.O. Robson, pp. 242-56, Dordrecht: Foris Publications.

Chhabra, Bahadur Chand, 1965 [first published in 1935], *Expansion of Indo-Aryan Culture during Pallava Rule (as Evidenced by Inscriptions)*, 2nd edn., Delhi: Munshiram Manoharlal.

Chihara, Daigoro, 1996, *Hindu-Buddhist Architecture in Southeast Asia*, tr. Rolf W. Giebel, Leiden: E.J. Brill.

Christie, Jan Wisseman, 1998, "The Medieval Tamil-Language Inscriptions in Southeast Asia and China," *Journal of Southeast Asian Studies*, 29(2): 239-68.

Cœdès, George, 1911, "Études cambodgiennes: I. La légende de la nāgī," *Bulletin de l'École française d'Extrême-Orient*, 11(3/4): 391-93.

——, 1931, "Études cambodgiennes: XXV. Deux inscriptions sanskrites du Fou-nan," *Bulletin de l'École française d'Extrême-Orient*, 31(1): 1-12.

——, 1968, *The Indianized States of Southeast Asia*, 3rd edn., ed. Walter F. Vella, tr. Sue Brown Cowing, Honolulu: University of Hawai'i Press.

Coomaraswamy, Ananda, 1928, "An Early Khmer Head of Vishnu," *Bulletin of the Museum of Fine Arts*, 26(153): 16-17.

Coral Rémusat, Gilberte de, 1934a, "Concerning Some Indian Influences in Khmer Art as Exemplified in the Borders of Pediments," *Indian Art and Letters*, n.s. 7(2): 110-21.

——, 1934b, "De l'origine commune des linteaux de l'Inde Pallava et des linteaux khmers préangkoriens," *Revue des Arts Asiatiques*, 8(4): 242-50.

Craven, Roy C., Jr., 1970, "An Early 'Pallava Type' Vishnu Icon," *Oriental Art*, n.s. 16(3): 262-64.

Dumarçay, Jacques, 1993, *Histoire de l'architecture de Java*, Paris: École française d'Extrême-Orient.

Dumarçay, Jacques and Pacal Royère, 2001, *Cambodian Architecture Eighth to Thirteenth Centuries*, tr. Michael Smithies, Leiden: Brill.

Dupont, Pierre, 1941, "Viṣṇu mitrés de l'Indochine occidentale," *Bulletin de l'École Française d'Extrême-Orient*, 41: 233-54.

——, 1955, *La statuaire préangkorienne*, Ascona: Artibus Asiae Supplementum.

Francis, Emmanuel, 2008/2009, "Une inscription tamoule inédite au musée d'Histoire du Vietnam de Hô Chi Minh-Ville," *Bulletin de l'École française d'Extrême-Orient*, 95/96: 409-24.

——, 2013, *Le discours royal dans l'Inde du Sud ancienne. Inscriptions et monuments pallava (IVème–IXème siècles)*, vol. 1: *Introduction et sources*, Publications de l'Institut orientaliste de Louvain 64, Louvain-la-Neuve: Institut orientaliste, Université catholique de Louvain.

——, 2017, *Le discours royal dans l'Inde du Sud ancienne. Inscriptions et monuments pallava (IVème–IXème siècles)*, vol. 2: *Mythes dynastiques et panégyriques*, Publications de l'Institut orientaliste de Louvain, 65, Louvain-la-Neuve: Institut orientaliste, Université catholique de Louvain.

Goetz, Hermann, 1959, *India: Five Thousand Years of Indian Art*, New York: McGraw-Hill.

Goloubew, Victor, 1924, "Mélanges sur le Cambodge ancient: I. Les legends de la Nagi et de l'Apsaras," *Bulletin de l'École française d'Extrême-Orient*, 24(3/4): 501-10.

Gravely, F.H. and T.N. Ramachandran, 2002 [first published in 1932], *Catalogue of the South Indian Hindu Metal Images in the Madras Government Museum*, Chennai: Commissioner of Museums and Government of Tamil Nadu. [Originally published in *Bulletin of the Madras Government Museum*, n.s. 1(2).]

Griffiths, Arlo, 2014, "Early Indic Inscriptions of Southeast Asia," in *Lost Kingdoms: Hindu-Buddhist Sculpture of Early Southeast Asia*, ed. John Guy, pp. 53-57, New York: The Metropolitan Museum of Art.

Gude, Tushara Bindu, 2005, Cat. no. 38 ("A Hindu Deity, Probably Uma"), in *The Kingdom of Siam: The Art of Central Thailand, 1350–1800*, ed. Forrest McGill, pp. 134-37, San Francisco: Asian Art Museum.

Guy, John, 2004, "South Indian Buddhism and Its Southeast Asian Legacy," in *Cultural Interface of India with Asia: Religion, Art and Architecture*, ed. Anupa

Pande and Parul Pandya Dhar, pp. 155-75, New Delhi: D.K. Printworld.

——, 2011, "Tamil Merchants and the Hindu-Buddhist Diaspora in Early Southeast Asia," in *Early Interactions between South and Southeast Asia: Reflections on Cross-Cultural Exchange*, ed. Pierre-Yves Manguin, A. Mani, and Geoff Wade, pp. 243-62, Singapore: Institute of Southeast Asian Studies.

—— (ed.), 2014, *Lost Kingdoms: Hindu-Buddhist Sculpture of Early Southeast Asia*, New York: The Metropolitan Museum of Art.

Hardiati, Endang Sri, 2009, "Hindu-Buddhist Sculptures from Sumatra II: Treasures from Bumiayu and Provincial Museums," in *Sumatra: Crossroads of Cultures*, ed. Francine Brinkgreve and Retno Sulistianingsih, pp. 70-83, Leiden: KITLV Press.

Harle, J.C. and Andrew Topsfield, 1987, *Indian Art in the Ashmolean Museum*, Oxford: Ashmolean Museum.

Irwin, John, 1948, "Masterpieces of Oriental Art, 11: South Indian Figure Sculpture, 7th to 10th century A.D.," *The Journal of the Royal Asiatic Society of Great Britain and Ireland*, 2: 105-07.

Jacq-Hergoualc'h, Michel, 2002, *The Malay Peninsula: Crossroads of the Maritime Silk Road*, tr. Victoria Hobson, Leiden: Brill.

Jouveau-Dubreuil, Gabriel, 1914, *Archeologie du sud de l'Inde*, vol. 2: *Iconographie*, Paris: Librairie Paul Geuthner.

Karashima, Noboru, 2002, "Tamil Inscriptions in Southeast Asia and China," in *Ancient and Medieval Commercial Activities in the Indian Ocean: Testimony of Inscriptions and Ceramic-sherds*, pp. 10-18, Tokyo: Taisho University.

——, 2009, "South Indian Merchant Guilds in the Indian Ocean and Southeast Asia," in *Nagapattinam to Suvarnadwipa: Reflections on the Chola Naval Expeditions to Southeast Asia*, ed. Hermann Kulke, K. Kesavapany, and Vijay Sakhuja, pp. 135-57, Singapore: Institute of Southeast Asian Studies.

Kempers, A.J. Bernet, 1959, *Ancient Indonesian Art*, Cambridge: Harvard University Press.

Khandalavala, K., 1969, "The Chronology of South Indian Bronzes," *Lalit Kalā*, 14: 26-37.

Kreisel, Gerd, 1987, *Linden-Museum Stuttgart, Südasien-Abteilung*, Stuttgart: Linden-Museum.

Krishna, Nanditha, 1980, *The Art and Iconography of Vishnu-Narayana*, Bombay: Taraporevala.

Kulke, Hermann, 2009, "The Naval Expeditions of the Cholas in the Context of Asian History," in *Nagapattinam to Suvarnadwipa: Reflections on the Chola*

Naval Expeditions to Southeast Asia, ed. Hermann Kulke, K. Kesavapany, and Vijay Sakhuja, pp. 1-19, Singapore: Institute of Southeast Asian Studies.

Lavy, Paul A., 2004 [unpublished], "Viṣṇu and Harihara in the Art and Politics of Early Historic Southeast Asia", Doctoral Dissertation, University of California, Los Angeles.

——, 2014, "Conch-on-hip Images in Peninsular Thailand and Early Vaiṣṇava Sculpture in Southeast Asia," in *Before Siam: Essays in Art and Archaeology*, ed. Nicolas Revire and Stephen A. Murphy, pp. 152-73, Bangkok: River Books.

Lee, Risha, 2012 [unpublished], "Constructing Community: Tamil Merchant Temples in India and China, 850–1281", Doctoral Dissertation, Columbia University.

Lefèvre, Vincent, 2006, *Commanditaires & artistes en Inde du Sud: Des Pallava aux Nāyak (VIe–XVIIIe siècle)*, Paris: Presses Sorbonne Nouvelle.

——, 2011, *Portraiture in Early India: Between Transience and Eternity*, Leiden: Brill.

Lunsingh Scheurleer, Pauline and Marijke J. Klokke, 1988, *Ancient Indonesian Bronzes: A Catalogue of the Exhibition in the Rijksmuseum Amsterdam with a General Introduction*, Leiden: Brill.

Nagaswamy, R., 1971, "Pallava Bronzes from Vadakkalathur," *Oriental Art*, n.s. 17(1): 55-59.

——, 1988, "South Indian Bronzes," in *The Great Tradition: Indian Bronze Masterpieces*, pp. 142–79, New Delhi: Brijbasi Printers.

——, 1995, "On Dating South Indian Bronzes," in *Indian Art & Connoisseurship: Essays in Honour of Douglas Barrett*, ed. John Guy, pp. 100-29, New Delhi: Indira Gandhi National Centre for the Arts.

Nandana Chutiwongs, 2002, *The Iconography of Avalokiteśvara in Mainland Southeast Asia*, New Delhi: Aryan Books International.

Narasimhan, V.M., 1960, "Some Pallava Icons," *Lalit Kalā*, 7: 19-28.

Natthapatra Chandavij and Saengchan Traikasem (eds.), 2000, *Visitors Guide to the Nakhon Si Thammarat National Museum*, 2nd edn., Bangkok: Fine Arts Department.

Nilakanta Sastri, K.A., 1949a, *History of Sri Vijaya (Sir William Meyer Lectures, 1946–47)*, Madras: University of Madras.

——, 1949b, "Takuapa and Its Tamil Inscription," *Journal of the Malayan Branch of the Royal Asiatic Society*, 22(1): 25-30.

——, 1975, *A History of South India*, 4th edn., Delhi: Oxford University Press.

O'Connor, Stanley J., Jr., 1972, *Hindu Gods of Peninsular Siam*, Ascona, Switzerland: Artibus Asiae Publishers.

Pal, Pratapaditya, 1969/1970, "Some Interesting South Indian Bronzes," *Archives of Asian Art*, 23: 24-30.

Parmentier, Henri, 1927, *L'Art khmèr primitif*, vol. 1, Paris: École française d'Extrême-Orient.

——, 1931, "The History of Khmer Architecture," *Eastern Art*, 3: 141-79.

Pattabiramin, P.Z., 1975, *Sanctuaires rupestres de l'Inde du sud: II. Tamilnāḍu et Kerala*, Pondichéry: Institut Français d'Indologie.

Phiset Chiachanphong, Saranya Suriyarattanakon, and Sakchai Photchananwanit, 1999, *Namchom Phiphitthaphanthasathan hæng Chat Prachin Buri* [*Guide to the Prachin Buri National Museum*], 2nd edn., Bangkok: Samnak Borannakhadi læ Phiphitthaphanthasathan hæng Chat, Krom Sinlapakon. [In Thai]

Piriya Krairiksh, 2012 [first published in Thai in 2010], *The Roots of Thai Art*, Bangkok: River Books.

Pollock, Sheldon, 2006, *The Language of the Gods in the World of Men: Sanskrit, Culture, and Power in Premodern India*, Berkeley: University of California Press.

Poundurai, Raju, 2005, "Cultural Contacts of South India and South-East and Far-East Asia: An Exploration of the Phenomenon of the Devaraja Cult," in *God and King: The Devarāja Cult in South Asian Art and Architecture*, ed. Arputha Rani Sengupta, pp. 25-40, New Delhi: Regency Publications.

Quaritch Wales, Horace Geoffrey, 1948, "Culture Change in Greater India," *Journal of the Royal Asiatic Society of Great Britain and Ireland* (April), 1: 2-32.

——, 1974 [first published in 1951], *The Making of Greater India*, 3rd edn., London: Bernard Quaritch.

Romain, Julie, 2011, "Indian Architecture in the 'Sanskrit Cosmopolis': The Temples of the Dieng Plateau," in *Early Interactions between South and Southeast Asia: Reflections on Cross-Cultural Exchange*, ed. Pierre-Yves Manguin, A. Mani, and Geoff Wade, pp. 299-316, Singapore: Institute of Southeast Asian Studies.

Santiko, Hariani, 2001, "The Religion of King Pūrṇawarman of Tārumānagara," in *Fruits of Inspiration: Studies in Honour of Prof. J.G. de Casparis*, ed. Marijke J. Klokke and Karel R. Van Kooij, pp. 423-33, Groningen: Egbert Forsten.

Sarkar, Himansu Bhusan, 1959, "Four Rock Inscriptions of Batavia," *Journal of the Asiatic Society*, 1(2): 135-41.

Schastok, Sara, 1994, "Bronzes in the Amarāvatī Style: Their Role in the Writing of Southeast Asian History," in *Ancient Indonesian Sculpture*, ed. Marijke J. Klokke and Pauline Lunsingh-Scheurleer, pp. 33-56, Leiden: KITLV Press.

Sen, Tansen, 2009, "The Military Campaigns of Rajendra Chola and the Chola–Srivijaya–China Triangle," in *Nagapattinam to Suvarnadwipa: Reflections on the Chola Naval Expeditions to Southeast Asia*, ed. Hermann Kulke, K. Kesavapany, and Vijay Sakhuja, pp. 61-75, Singapore: Institute of Southeast Asian Studies.

Shanmugam, P., 2009, "India and Southeast Asia: South Indian Cultural Links with Indonesia," in *Nagapattinam to Suvarnadwipa: Reflections on the Chola Naval Expeditions to Southeast Asia*, ed. Hermann Kulke, K. Kesavapany, and Vijay Sakhuja, pp. 208-26, Singapore: Institute of Southeast Asian Studies.

Singh, Tejpal and Sanjib Kumar Singh, 2016, *Ecstasy of Classical Art, Indian Bronze: National Museum Collection*, New Delhi: National Museum.

Sivaramamurti, C., 1963, *South Indian Bronzes*, New Delhi: Lalit Kala Akademi.

Soundara Rajan, K.V., 1998, *Rock-cut Temple Styles: Early Pandyan Art and the Ellora Shrines*, Mumbai: Somaiya Publications.

Srinivasan, K.R., 1964, *Cave-Temples of the Pallavas*, New Delhi: Archaeological Survey of India.

——, 1975, *The Dharmarāja Ratha and Its Sculptures, Mahābalipuram*, New Delhi: Abhinav Publications.

Srinivasan, P.R., 1994 [first published in 1963], *Bronzes of South India*, Madras: Commissioner of Museums.

Srinivasan, Sharada, 2004, "Chronology and Metal Sources of South Indian Images: Some Insights and Scientific Analysis," in *Archaeology as History in Early South Asia*, ed. Himanshu Prabha Ray and Carla M. Sinopoli, pp. 219-56, New Delhi: Indian Council of Historical Research.

——, 2008, "Megalithic and Early Historic Metalwork in Southern India," in *Archaeology of Early Historic South Asia*, ed. Gautam Sengupta and Sharmi Chakraborty, pp. 375-92, New Delhi: Pragati Publications.

——, 2013, "Techno-cultural Perspectives on Medieval Southeast Asia and Southern India: Pallava Bronzes and Beyond," in *Materializing Southeast Asia's Past*, selected papers from the 12th International Conference of the European Association of Southeast Asian Archaeologists, vol. 2, ed. Marijke J. Klokke and Véronique Degroot, pp. 167-78, Singapore: National University of Singapore Press.

Sundaresh and A.S. Gaur, 2011, "Marine Archaeological Investigations along the Tamil Nadu Coast and Their Implications for Understanding Cultural Expansion to Southeast Asian Countries," in *Early Interactions between South and Southeast Asia: Reflections on Cross-Cultural Exchange*, ed. Pierre-Yves Manguin, A. Mani, and Geoff Wade, pp. 221-39, Singapore: Institute of Southeast Asian Studies.

Tarr, Gary, 1970, "Chronology and Development of the Chāḷukya Cave Temples," *Ars Orientalis*, 8: 155-84.

Tartakov, Gary Michael, 1997, *The Durga Temple at Aihole: A Historiographical Study*, Delhi: Oxford University Press.

Thomsen, Margrit, 1982, "Südasien," in *Ferne Völker, frühe Zeiten: Kunstwerke aus dem Linden-Museum Stuttgart, Staatliches Museum für Völkerkunde*, vol. 2: *Orient, Südasien, Ostasien*, pp. 105-86, Recklinghausen: Verlag Aurel Bongers.

Tōkyō Kokuritsu Hakubutsukan [Tokyo National Museum], 1997, *Indoneshia kodai ōkoku no shihō/Treasures of ancient Indonesian kingdoms*, Tokyo: Tokyo National Museum. [In Japanese and English]

Vogel, J.Ph., 1918, "The Yūpa Inscriptions of King Mulavarman from Koetei (East Borneo)," *Bijdragen tot de Taal-, Land- en Volkenkunde van Nederlandsch-Indië*, 74: 167-232.

——, 1925, "The Earliest Sanskrit Inscriptions of Java," *Publicaties van den Oudheidkundigen Dienst in Nederlandsch-Indië*, 1: 15-35.

Wessing, Robert, 2011, "Tarumanagara: What's in a Name?," *Journal of Southeast Asian Studies*, 42(2): 325-37.

Woodward, Hiram W., Jr., 1973, "Review of *Hindu Gods of Peninsular Siam* by Stanley J. O'Connor, Jr.," *Journal of the Siam Society*, 61(2): 210-13.

Zakharov, Anton O., 2010, "A Note on the Date of the Vo-Canh Stele," *The South East Asian Review*, 35(1-2): 17-21.

12

Central Javanese Statues of Hindu Deities and Their Anthropomorphic Vehicles

Bokyung Kim

THE three Javanese statues examined in this essay collectively depict the *trimūrti*. This term encompasses Brahmā the creator, Viṣṇu the preserver, and Śiva the destroyer (*figs.* 12.2-12.4).[1] These three deities exemplify some of the popular types of Hindu icons worshiped in Java during the Central Javanese period, *circa* eighth to the tenth centuries CE. These particular statues, reportedly discovered on the Dieng Plateau in Central Java (*fig.* 12.1), are housed at Museum Dieng Kailāsa. Although it is unclear whether or not they were made as a set, it is highly likely that a group of three statues such as these would have been installed for worship in a temple complex located in the region.

Worshiping these three deities in a temple was not new in eighth-century Central Java, but the iconographic features of these statues are unique. The deities appear with their animal mounts (*vāhana*), a goose (*haṁsa*), a bird of prey (Garuḍa), and a bull (Nandī),

---

[1] The identification of these statues is based on the characteristics of their mounts, since all of the statues have lost either their entire upper bodies (*fig.* 12.4) or heads (*figs.* 12.2 and 12.3). While the bull and a bird of prey are evident, the *haṁsa* mount of Brahmā (*fig.* 12.4) is only identifiable by its elongated ears and the trace of a goose's head that are consistent with other Central Javanese Brahmā statues that include his anthropomorphic mount (Tōkyō Kokuritsu Hakubutsukan 1997: no. 10; Girard-Geslan et al. 1998: fig. 165).

respectively.[2] Here they are not represented as animals, but rather as partially anthropomorphic figures sitting in a crossed-leg position, supporting the deities on their shoulders and holding the deities' feet in their palms, which serve as pedestals. The unusual sizes and static postures of these animal mounts are particularly conspicuous. Although the upper parts of these sculptures are now damaged, it appears that animal mounts (*vāhana*) were almost as large as the deities on their shoulders. In these examples, the *vāhana*s are depicted not merely as mounts to transport their deities, but as powerful deities with robust muscles, and yet, at the same time, they are depicted in peaceful postures. This group of statues suggests a new type of Hindu iconography that was developed in Central Java and quickly became popular across the region.

This paper will examine the meaning and usage of this unique Hindu iconography, which was possibly created and developed in the Dieng Plateau during the Central Javanese period. A closer look at sculptural examples from the region will suggest that the Dieng Plateau functioned as the center of distinctive, and sometimes idiosyncratic, artistic innovation for a longer period of time than is typically acknowledged, thus providing us with the opportunity to redefine the region's role in the development of Central Javanese art and architecture.

The Iconography: Its Origin and Changes

Two of the aforementioned statues were photographed together on the Dieng Plateau in the 1860s (*figs.* 12.2 and 12.4) along with other Hindu statues discovered in the region, and they have remained

[2] The bull, Śiva's mount, is often called Nandī or Nandin, but it has been suggested that Nandī or Nandin was originally a *gaṇa* (attendant), whose entirely anthropomorphic appearance was different from the bull who was Śiva's mount. That vehicle was simply called the bull (*vṛṣa* or *vṛṣabha*) (Bhattacharya 1977; Pal 2009). I will use "Nandī" as a term to identify Śiva's mount in this paper, however, I would like to note that further research is needed on how the Javanese used and understood these terms and concepts, especially during the Central Javanese period.

there ever since.[3] The plateau lies at an altitude of approximately 2,000 m above sea level at the foot of two major volcanic mountains: Mt. Prahu and Mt. Ungaran. To date, eight small Śaivite temples in fairly good condition, as well as a number of loose sculptures, have been discovered in the region. These rich artistic and architectural materials from the plateau represent crucial sources for us to evaluate the earliest development of art and architecture during the Central Javanese period.

Interestingly, the artistic and architectural materials from the Dieng Plateau show several eccentric features that are prevalent across the entire plateau. Representations of Hindu deities appearing with their mounts (*vāhanas*) are not uncommon either in India or in peninsular Southeast Asia, but the examples shown in these three Dieng statues, as well as others discovered in the region, exhibit several distinctive features. Their vehicles

---

3 This photograph is part of the Isidore Van Kinsbergen (1821–1905) collection, now in the Kern Institute, Leiden (inv. no. P-044117; see http://hdl.handle.net/1887.1/item:83635), in the Museum Volkenkunde, Leiden (inv. no. RV-1404-3791-20; see https://hdl.handle.net/20.500.11840/706169), and was published in Theuns-de Boer and Asser 2005: 238, fig. 108. Two of the images from the photograph remain in the Dieng museum (*figs.* 12.2 and 12.4), but the current location of a Viṣṇu image in the photograph is unknown. Van Kinsbergen, a self-taught photographer, was asked by the Batavia Society to photograph the ancient Javanese sites and statues in 1862 under the direction of J.F.G. Brumund (1814-63) and he continued to work on his own after Brumund's sudden death in 1863 (Paul 1978: 323; Scheuleer 1991: 37-38). At the annual meetings of the Batavian Society of Arts and Science held in 1864, his photographs were reviewed and the condition of the Dieng Plateau was also discussed at the meeting based on his visit (Scheurleer 1991: 37-38; Theuns-de Boer 2002: 32). Therefore, his photographs of the Dieng Plateau, including the one mentioned above, were most likely taken during his journey to the site between 1862 and 1864. Afterwards, the prints of his photographs were made and assembled as portfolios titled *Antiquities of Java* (Scheurleer 1991: 38), and a list of his photograph collection was published in 1914 (Kinsbergen 1914: 21).

are anthropomorphic with heads that are partially or entirely zoomorphic. Each sits with its legs crossed in front of the body and supports a deity on its shoulders. In addition, the size of these mounts matches that of the main deities, giving the impression that they were not inferior to the gods. The mounts appear similar to the deities with confidence and strength in their own right. What do these new iconographic features tell us about religious and artistic activities in the region? Do they signify any changes in the use of icons in a particular architectural setting? How and why did these unique iconographic features become popular in the region?

The concept of a Hindu statue with a partially anthropomorphic mount was first seen in India as early as the fifth or sixth century CE, and it is likely that this idea was transmitted to Central Java and other parts of Southeast Asia in the following centuries. However, the original Indian concept of a partially anthropomorphic mount changed as it spread to Central Java. In India, the use of a partially anthropomorphic vehicle was limited to the image of Viṣṇu's mount Garuḍa and was not applied to other Hindu deities. In India prior to the sixth century, Garuḍa was typically represented as an eagle or hawk, with an emphasis on physical features such as wings and a large curved beak.[4] During the sixth century, Garuḍa began to

---

[4] Examples of the *garuḍa* as a bird include the guardians on the eastern gateway of Bharhut, which carry lotus standards surmounted by a *garuḍa*, and the inner side of the middle architrave of the eastern gateway of Sāñcī where a *garuḍa* is shown with other animals worshiping the Buddha (Banerjea 1956: 530-31; Krishna 1980: 78). In Gandhāra, by contrast, the images of *garuḍas* appeared as realistic depictions of an eagle or hawk, as seen in two examples of the *Kākatī Jātaka* in which a *garuḍa* attacks snakes or abducts Queen Kākatī (The Metropolitan Museum of Art, inv. no. 1980.325; the Victoria and Albert Museum, inv. no. IS 5-1973). Later, the reverse side of several of Candragupta II's (375–414 CE) copper coins depict a *garuḍa* with outspread wings and long human arms adorned with bracelets. This is known as the first example of a *garuḍa* with human features, before it was used as Viṣṇu's mount in the next century (Banerjea 1956: 531-32).

acquire human characteristics while retaining some of his original animal features such as wings, a beak, and bird legs.[5] Examples of a partially anthropomorphic Garuḍa in Indian art include Viṣṇu images at the Daśāvatāra Temple at Deogaṛh (*c.*500-25 CE), Caves No. 2 and No. 3 at Bādāmī (*c.*550 CE), Cave No. 15 at Ellorā (eighth century), the Virūpākṣa Temple in south India, Svacchandabhairavī in Chamba, Utpala (ninth century), Gajendramokṣa or Karivarada in the Virūpākṣa Temple in south India, the Galaganātha Temple in Aihoḷe,.and many more.[6] It is unclear whether this transformation resulted from changes in the role of the deity and/or *vāhana,* but it has been suggested that Garuḍa's role in the *Mahābhārata* as a heroic rescuer of his mother might have influenced changes in his visual representation (Krishna 1980: 106-07).

The later form of Viṣṇu with an anthropomorphized Garuḍa

---

[5] Garuḍa's humanized form became a common way of depicting him as Viṣṇu's mount in eastern Indian statues after the sixth century. F.M. Asher has dated one Viṣṇu relief with a flying Garuḍa found in the Lower Son Bhandar Cave to the fifth century, slightly earlier than the other examples from Bengal and Bihar mentioned here (Asher 1980: 52 and pl. 82).

[6] There are a number of scholarly works about the Indian iconography of Viṣṇu riding on Garuḍa, including Krishna (1980: 72-82) and Banerji (1998: 106-07). In these Indian examples, Garuḍa was presented either as a fully zoomorphic figure that was in a static and fully frontal position (Banerji 1998: pl. XLVIII (c); Asher 1980: pls. 189 and 107) or as an anthropomorphic Garuḍa with two humanized legs portrayed in a gesture of "flying" (Asher 1980: pl. 237). During the eleventh and twelfth centuries in north Bengal, these stylistic characteristics continued from earlier depictions of Viṣṇu on Garuḍa (Bautze-Picron 2002: 3-13; Maitra 1920: 2-7; Marcus 1967: 240-62). Unlike the Javanese examples, Garuḍa appears as a "flying" deity indicated by the position of his legs, the left foot on the ground and the right leg folded. These later Indian examples from north Bengal are often compared to the controversial eleventh or thirteenth-century East Javanese depictions of Viṣṇu riding on Garuḍa based on the shared use of this unique posture (Scheurleer 2009: 189-218). However, only one Viṣṇu statue from north Bengal has a posture similar to the Central Javanese examples, and it is dated much later than them, i.e. the eleventh and twelfth century (Banerji 1998: Plate XLVIII (a)).

in India was likely transmitted into Java during the early stage of the Central Javanese period at the same time that Garuḍa's heroic character in the epic also became known among the Javanese. Scheurleer (2009: 214) mentions that a late tenth-century Old Javanese text contains the story of Garuḍa, who courageously rescued his mother and became Viṣṇu's mount; yet it is probable that the story was already known to the Javanese as early as the eighth century when the Dieng Plateau began to be used by the locals as a Hindu religious site.

Nonetheless, even in these earliest examples from the Dieng Plateau, the Javanese adoption and adaptation of the Indian ideas are evident. The use of an anthropomorphic vehicle was not limited to the mount of Viṣṇu but became expanded to the mounts of Śiva and Brahmā as well, thus completing the *trimūrti.* These images were possibly meant to be worshiped in a small temple complex in the region where they met popular demands. Although the exact placements of these statues are unknown, it is likely that three small temple structures were built as a set. Temple complexes of this type usually place a shrine dedicated to Śiva at the center as a major god with Brahmā and Viṣṇu on each side, as subordinates. The ninth-century temple of Lara Jonggrang in the Prambanan plain is probably the best-known example dedicated to these three deities in this configuration.

The Javanese examples of *trimūrti* sculptures lack narrative and emphasize the deities' static, peaceful, yet powerful characters. They were probably meant to be placed in three separate temple buildings, either in the form of steles or as three-dimensional sculptures carved in the round. This particular mode of depicting the gods and their *vāhana*s never appeared in a narrative context. Interestingly, this tendency continued throughout the Central Javanese period even when narrative reliefs became popular in the Kedu and Prambanan plains in Central Java.

The adaptation of these ideas into a form of major iconic image suggests that the Javanese artists in the region were clearly

fig. 12.1: View of Arjuna Group, Dieng Plateau

fig. 12.2: Śiva riding Nandī, *circa* eighth century, volcanic stone

fig. 12.3: Viṣṇu riding Garuḍa, *circa* eighth century, volcanic stone

fig. 12.4: Brahmā riding a Haṁsa, *circa* eighth century, volcanic stone

fig. 12.5: Śiva riding Nandī, *circa* ninth century, volcanic stone

conscious of their roles as creative artists. A similar iconographic type, depicting Viṣṇu riding Garuḍa with human characteristics, was present in mainland Southeast Asia such as appeared in later Khmer art, but the earliest Khmer example of this kind appeared in the mid-ninth century, much later than the Dieng examples.[7] Only one statue from the mainland, a Central Vietnamese sculpture, can be discussed in connection to the Javanese examples, because it shares the same fundamental iconography.

This image, a Viṣṇu-Garuḍāsana now in the Guimet Museum in Paris, was reportedly discovered in the so-called "Marble Mountains" near Da Nang city in Quảng Nam Province, where the famous Cham sites of Mỹ Sơn, Đồng Dương, and Trà Kiệu are located (Baptiste and Zéphir 2005: 198-99; no. 12). The Cham image depicts Viṣṇu, riding his mount Garuḍa; although the God is missing two arms, the two remaining arms hold a conch shell and a ball of earth. The missing two hands likely held a discus (*cakra*) and a club. All these attributes follow the typical iconography for Viṣṇu in this period and region. What is peculiar is how the Viṣṇu-Garuḍāsana is represented. In this figure, Garuḍa is enlarged, almost to the size of the deity, and is depicted as an anthropomorphized figure rather than in the shape of a bird. He kneels and supports Viṣṇu with his hands holding the deity's legs, thereby giving the viewers a sense of security. Like much Cham art, this Viṣṇu sculpture was discovered without an archaeological context, making it difficult to date. However, its stylistic and iconographic characteristics suggest that it should be dated to the early ninth century, roughly

[7] Khmer examples of Garuḍa as Viṣṇu's *vāhana* first appeared in the mid-ninth century as a part of lintel reliefs (Stern 1938: pls. XLVII, B, C, and XLVIII; Jessup and Zéphir 1997: fig. 32), and later in the tenth century as three-dimensional sculptures, for example, from Banteay Srei (Boisselier 1951: 17; Jessup and Zéphir 1997: 228-30, no. 53). The anthropomorphic Garuḍa from Banteay Srei has a human torso and limbs as well as wings, tail, feathered legs, and clawed feet. Its seated posture, with one leg raised, and animal features are very similar to the one Cham example discussed here (Baptiste and Zéphir 2005: no. 12; Girard-Geslan et al. 1998: fig. 131).

coinciding with the late Mỹ Sơn E1 style and prior to the Đồng Dương style. It is therefore clearly later than the earliest Javanese examples (Baptiste and Zéphir 2005: 198).[8] Although it suggests a possible link between the artists of Java and Champa in the eighth and ninth centuries, it seems evident that the concept of an anthropomorphic mount was limited to the image of Viṣṇu in mainland Southeast Asia.[9]

Central Javanese Examples

The concept of depicting three Hindu deities with their enormous but peaceful anthropomorphic mounts was a dramatic departure from the Indian prototypes and appears to have been limited to Central Java. During my research, I found approximately fourteen images of this type that have been discovered around Central Java.[10] Based on stylistic characteristics and information about

---

[8] This statue has been discussed in relation to the statues discovered at Mỹ Sơn temple E1 and specifically in terms of the stylistic relationships with two half-humanized *garuḍas* on each side of the lintel portraying Viṣṇu-Anantaśayana, which depicts Brahmā's birth from Viṣṇu's navel. This lintel was reportedly discovered at temple E1 at Mỹ Sơn and is now kept in the Da Nang Museum of Cham Sculpture (Le Bonheur 1998: 260).

[9] Although artistic interchange between Champa and Java requires further research, the development of this iconography in Cham and Khmer art shows a slightly different process than in Java. It is only associated with Viṣṇu statues and the humanized Garuḍa's posture is used to express his flying moment as in the Indian examples. Even an early example like the Guimet Viṣṇu-Garuḍāsana shows the "flying" movement of Garuḍa, and his "bird-like" character is indicated by the position of his legs, the left foot on the ground and the right leg folded. Additionally, this image displays the feathers on his lower body, which is typical of many Indian examples.

[10] These fourteen images include six sculptures of Śiva with his mount, four sculptures of Viṣṇu with his mount, three sculptures of Brahmā with his mount, and one small relief showing both Śiva and Viṣṇu together. For more information, see fns. 12-15.

their discoveries, all can be dated to the Central Javanese period.[11]

Regardless of their different sizes, all these examples represent a major Hindu deity riding an animal mount that is depicted with human characteristics. The artists intentionally removed narratives and any exaggerated gestures in order to display the deities in a static and peaceful mode. Although slight stylistic variations are evident, these statues share the same iconographic elements, suggesting to us that the artists clearly recognized this newly introduced and modified iconography and actively incorporated it into the temples of several different regions in Central Java. All these Central Javanese examples were carved in the round or as steles with flat backs, and not as narrative reliefs or architectural motifs. In other words, the majority of these statues must have been installed in central shrines as major icons or in narrow rectangular niches in exterior temple walls. Such niches contain images of minor gods who are subordinate to a major one installed in an interior shrine. These fourteen statues are approximately 100 cm in height, enough to be a major icon in any Hindu temple discovered in Central Java.[12] Slight stylistic variations are present among them such as the shape of the lotus pedestal, the sitting posture of the deities' mounts, the positions of the deities' bodies and the existence of carvings on the back. But these variations should

---

11 As I briefly mentioned above, in East Java, there is one statue of this type, Garuḍa carrying Viṣṇu in the Trowulan Museum. This has been known as the portrait image of King Airlangga (1016-49), yet Pauline Lunsingh Scheurleer has argued that this might have been the main image installed in Candi Kidal (dated *c.*1260) (Scheurleer 2009: 189-218). In my opinion, this East Javanese statue should be considered to be a Javanese version of Indian Viṣṇu statues mainly sculpted in north Bengal in the eleventh-twelfth century, not as part of the tradition continued from the Dieng examples.

12 Only one of the statues, Viṣṇu and Śiva on their vehicles, measures approximately 50 cm in height, which is half of the size of the other statues in the group. This small relief depicts Viṣṇu and Śiva side by side on their mounts (National Museum of Indonesia, Jakarta, inv. no. 22).

be understood as attempts by the artists to adjust the statues to different architectural settings in Central Java, and not as different understandings of what was essentially consistent iconography.

It is intriguing that the majority of these fourteen sculptures, including the three examples mentioned at the beginning of this paper, were all discovered on or in the vicinity of the Dieng Plateau. In particular, two statues show striking similarities; one is a Viṣṇu-Garuḍāsana statue that was photographed by Van Kinsbergen in the 1860s (around the same time as the aforementioned three statues);[13] the other is a Brahmā statue from Central Java (Girard-Geslan et al. 1998: fig. 165).[14] The four-armed Viṣṇu statue, whose head is missing, holds a club in his lower right hand and an earth ball in his lower left hand. His upper right hand is partially broken, but it is likely that it holds a disc, and presumably a conch shell was held in the now missing upper left hand. These attributes are consistent with other Viṣṇu images discovered in the region. The Brahmā statue at the Museum Volkenkunde also has four arms. A rosary is held in his upper proper left hand, a water jar in his lower left hand, and a lotus and a fly whisk in his right hands. Viṣṇu's anthropomorphic mount, Garuḍa, is only identifiable by his beak as in the abovementioned Viṣṇu statue from the Dieng Plateau (*fig.* 12.3) and Brahmā's mount, the *haṁsa*, is depicted as a human figure with a goose's head added on top of his anthropomorphized head.

Some of the stylistic affinities shared by these two statues

---

[13] The inventory number of the photograph of this statue in the Kern Institute Photography collection is P-044173; see http://hdl.handle.net/1887.1/item:77861. Theuns-de Boer and Asser (2005: 244, fig. 156) also include the same photograph. According to Van Kinsbergen's description, this statue was transported from the Dieng Plateau to Bandjarnegara and then to the Batavia Museum, present-day Jakarta National Museum (Kinsbergen 1914: 22).

[14] The exact location of its discovery is unknown, but the statue is now at the Museum Volkenkunde in Leiden (inv. no. RV-1403-1858, see https://hdl.handle.net/20.500.11840/703849).

include the crossed-leg postures (*padmāsana*) of the animal mounts, the shape of the lotus pedestals, the two thick lines above the upper bellies of the *vāhana*, the comparable size of the mount to the main deity, and the style of the main deities' accessories which include an armband, a waistband, and a jeweled band crossing the upper body. All these iconographic and stylistic affinities support the idea that the Viṣṇu and Brahmā were either made as a set and enshrined in the same temple structure or produced in the same workshop, possibly located on the Dieng Plateau.

There are other statues discovered in the vicinity of the Dieng Plateau that display similar characteristics. This suggests that this iconography might have lasted for an extended period of time. First, an image of Śiva riding on his bull mount, now at Museum Radya Pustaka in Solo, Central Java (*fig.* 12.5), exhibits a combination of a repetitive square pattern in the ornament around the torso and an unadorned snake-shaped ornament that crosses the chest (*upavītaulara*). Both are typical for sculptures discovered on the Dieng Plateau and, like many Dieng sculptures, the Śiva image is fully carved in the round and three-dimensional. However, the sitting posture of the mount, the way in which Śiva places his feet, and the way his mount holds them are similar to the ninth-century examples discovered in the Kedu Plain.[15] Such variations in the depiction of Hindu deities with their partially anthropomorphic vehicles point to the expansion of this particular artistic feature to other regions of Central Java, such as the Kedu Plain, after it was first created on the Dieng Plateau.

---

15 One additional Śiva statue at the National Museum of Indonesia also shows slightly different features as compared to the Dieng statues, as seen in *figs.* 12.2-12.4 (see Tōkyō Kokuritsu Hakubutsukan 1997: no. 12; inv. no. 23). Lacking a double lotus pedestal, it is seated in a crosed-leg position on a simply raised pedestal and the back of statue is not carved, suggesting that it was likely made in the Kedu Plain and can be approximately dated to the early ninth century. This late dating suggests that the tradition of making Hindu deities with anthropomorphic vehicles continued beyond the Dieng Plateau.

Second, two statues, one Brahmā and one Viṣṇu — discovered at Wonosobo, only 30 km from the Dieng Plateau, and now kept in the National Museum of Indonesia — also appear with their anthropomorphic mounts (Tōkyō Kokuritsu Hakubutsukan 1997: nos. 10 and 11). These statues were made on the basis of the same understanding of iconography, including an anthropomorphic mount, but they show slight stylistic variations. They were made as steles that fit into long rectangular niches. The plumpness of both the main deities and their vehicles is also noticeable in these two examples; the round contour of their faces and bodies, the proportion of the bodies, and the form of the steles all show stylistic affinities with the examples from the Prambanan Plain. This further suggests that the sculpture of the Dieng Plateau has a clear connection with those that are dated to the ninth century in the Prambanan Plain. Thus, the stylistic diversities of the examples from the Dieng Plateau or in the vicinity of the Dieng show that this particular type was made for an extended period of time during the Central Javanese period, at least until the mid-ninth century CE.

Other architectural and artistic sources from the Dieng Plateau suggest that this unique type of Hindu statue might have been one of the most popular trends in the Dieng Plateau and was related to the artists' interests in original, sometimes idiosyncratic, elements. This trend seemingly lasted through the Central Javanese period. Among the eight extant Dieng temples, Candi Bima has always been at the center of scholarly discussion because of its peculiar architecture, which differentiates it from the other Dieng temples. Located on a southern hill overlooking the Arjuna group, Candi Bima represents an architectural type that deviates from the typical Javanese *candi* styles as seen in the remaining Dieng temples. Unlike the other Dieng temples, this temple stands on a thick square base with a projecting roof on each side, giving the impression that it is laid out on an octagonal plan. The upper structure of the temple is also dissimilar from the other temples at the Dieng Plateau. Rather than emphasizing horizontality, Candi Bima follows the north

Indian architectural type by having an Indian spire (*śikhara*). In fact, several scholars have argued that the unusual architectural appearance of Candi Bima indicates its slightly later date than the rest of the temple structures in the area — perhaps dating to around the late eighth century — and even define it as the "New" or "Later" Dieng style.[16]

In any case, I would like to consider the peculiar style of Candi Bima from a different perspective. Aside from its unusual architecture, Candi Bima includes architectural details that deviate stylistically from the Javanese norm. The *kāla-makara* motif, for example, is rendered differently from other Central Javanese *kāla-makaras*. Only the eastern and western sides of the temple still retain the *kāla-makara* niches. What makes the *kāla-makara* motif at Candi Bima unusual is the presence of a coiled snake below each of the *makara* heads on either side of the base of the niche.[17] In addition to these two flanking snakes, the shape of the *makara* head also differs from other Dieng temples. The peculiarities of its overemphasized elephant trunk and its partially open mouth are certainly not comparable to those found in the other temples of the Dieng Plateau or to any other Javanese temple for that matter. In addition, the protruding tongue of the *kāla* is a feature rarely found in Java. More importantly, the *makaras*' bodies, constituting

---

16 The dating of Candi Bima has been discussed by several scholars, and it should be noted that these studies are mainly based on the architectural elements. J. Williams (1981: 35) argues that Candi Bima dates to the early ninth century based on its use of round moldings that became prevalent in the ninth century in the southern part of the Dieng Plateau. Chihara (1996: 107, 112), on the other hand, classifies Candi Bima as "the Later Dieng style" or period (*c*.730-80).

17 While the *kāla-makara* image on the eastern side of the temple is partially damaged (Vogler 1949: pl. X 105a), the western side niche provides an excellent example of the unique appearance of the *kāla-makara*. The western side of the temple can be seen in one of the photographs in the Kern Institute (inv. no. KITLV 114769; see https://hdl.handle.net/1887.1/item:775309).

the frame of the niche, are decorated with a row of bead-shaped and vegetal motifs. Again, this is markedly different from the typical Central Javanese *kāla-makara* motif, in which the bodies are typically left unadorned.

With the above considerations in mind, the Dieng Plateau might prove that Indian sources were introduced and reinterpreted for a period of time extending beyond the early Central Javanese period and reaching into the entire Central Javanese period. The dating of the site has been based generally upon the architectural remains showing the earliest development of later Javanese *candi* architecture on the Kedu and Prambanan Plains. However, the sculptural sources from the region, as discussed above, and the architectural motifs, such as those of Candi Bima, do not support the idea that the site was occupied and used by locals only in the early phase of the Central Javanese period.[18] In addition to the fourteen statues discussed above, other sculptural examples from the Dieng Plateau, such as one Śiva Triśira (the three-headed Śiva), one Harihara (half-Śiva and half-Viṣṇu), and several Vaiṣṇavite sculptures, indicate that the Dieng Plateau's artistic activities coincided with those on the Prambanan Plain from the late eighth century to the first half of the ninth century.[19] Although I am still

---

[18] The art and architecture of the Dieng Plateau have mostly been used to show the early development of Central Javanese art and architecture prior to the construction of Borobudur (Chihara 1996: 101-12; Soekmono 1992: 67-95; Williams 1981: 31). Most recently, Degroot's studies of the distribution of Central Javanese temples suggest that several temples on the Dieng Plateau show traces of rebuilding, thus the Dieng Plateau might have been occupied until the tenth century CE (Degroot 2009: 161-62).

[19] Today, these statues are kept in Museum Dieng Kailāsa and the National Museum of Jakarta, but, unfortunately, they have not been systematically cataloged or published for further research. I believe that the latter examples can be traceable from the analysis of Van Kinsbergen's photographs taken in the 1860s and the list of his photographs published in 1914 (Kinsbergen 1914). In the list, he included a total of eighty-six photographs of the Dieng Plateau (nos. 89-175). Some of these sculptures

in the early stage of my research into this matter, I believe that, along with other major centers to the south of the Dieng Plateau such as the Kedu and Prambanan Plains, the Dieng Plateau served as a major artistic center in the creation of "new" artistic and iconographic features for a longer period of time than scholars typically acknowledge.

The idea of making Hindu deities with anthropomorphic *vāhana*s expanded from the Dieng Plateau to the Kedu and Prambanan Plains although this did not become a major practice in these regions. This lack of popularity is perhaps attributable to the growing trend of adding narrative relief panels to the exterior of the temples in much larger temple complexes, instead of small niches where this type of statue must have been enshrined. Yet it is still fascinating to see that this unique, eccentric feature was transmitted to the major centers in the south, and that these regions seemingly exchanged ideas during the Central Javanese period.

Historical Significance and Meaning

What then do we know about these idiosyncratic features in art and architecture from the Dieng Plateau? Regardless of the impact of their artistic innovations in other parts of Java, the artists on the Dieng Plateau must have been actively involved in the creation of "new" artistic and iconographic features just as in any other region in Central Java. Some of the architectural styles seen at Candi Bima and other temples did not make a huge impact in other parts of Central Java, but the eccentric Hindu iconography with an anthropomorphic *vāhana* demonstrates that at times Dieng artistic influence expanded beyond the region, reaching as far as the Kedu and the Prambanan Plains. In other words, the artists in the Dieng Plateau were specifically associated with the introduction and reinterpretation of Indian materials, which I believe were active, conscious reinterpretations, and not indicative of ignorance of the

---

were transported to the Batavia Museum, the present-day National Museum of Jakarta (inv. nos. 417, 191, 24, D58, 17a, and possibly more).

Hindu iconographic principles that had been conveyed from India.

Although the archaeological study of the Dieng Plateau has been limited, it has generally been assumed that small structures either in stone or wood were built in a relatively small area on the plateau, and that they must have accommodated worship by providing space for religious practices, mainly Śiva-related rituals. Several inscriptions describe the Dieng Plateau temples as being clustered together within enclosing walls and connected by stairways and paved paths. This has been supported by the inscription dated to 909 CE mentioning the Dieng Plateau as one of the sacred mountains of Java. It is described as a priestly city that could be reached by stairways hewn from lava blocks that led up from the plains of Bagelen and Penkalongan (Goor 1922: 21-25).[20] It seems that the site was forgotten for a long time, possibly since the thirteenth century when the last inscription was issued.[21] Many small-scale statues, including the Dieng museum statues discussed here, must have been part of the Śaivite rituals performed in the region.

The location of the Dieng Plateau on top of a mountainous area gives a vague impression of the site being isolated from the traffic generated to and from the well-known centers of Central Java. But a closer look at the geographic location of the Dieng Plateau tells us that it is, in fact, conveniently located for those who travelled between the coastal region in the north and inland Central Java. According to the inscriptions, up until the tenth century a number of communities were located along the route running north from Magelang and Wonosobo to the coast in Central Java, and many artistic and architectural remains dating to the ninth century have been reported from this route (Christie 1998: 362).

---

[20] In this book, the author explains that the site began to be reoccupied by locals beginning during approximately the 1830s, and this is the time when the temples began to be named after major characters from the *Bhārata-Yuddha*, the Javanese version of the Indian epic, *Mahābhārata*.

[21] The dated inscription (1210 CE) found on the Dieng Plateau, is known as "Dieng IV" and is included on Nakada's list (Nakada 1982: 116-17).

Interestingly, a Dutch scholar, Van der Meulen (1977), once argued that the name *Ho-ling*, one of the early Javanese states mentioned in Chinese sources, might indicate the Dieng Plateau. According to the *Qiu Tang Shu* and *Xin Tang Shu*, the old and revised versions of the Tang chronicle, *Ho-ling* was an independent state that included a mountain where the ruler frequently ascended; it belonged to a larger state, possibly a capital city located elsewhere (*She-po*), and it continually sent envoys to China from the mid-seventh century to the ninth century (Meulen 1977: 88-92). Van der Meulen also introduced two more textual records that include possible descriptions of the Dieng Plateau: one is a state (*dvīpa*) called *Yava* that appeared in an eighth-century Javanese inscription, and the other is a region called *Dihayng* (mountain) that is described as the cradle of the worship for Śiva and Gaṇeśa in Java, as mentioned in the East Javanese chronicle, the *Tantu Panggĕlaran* (Meulen 1977: 96-101).

Chinese chronicles portray these small Javanese states, including *Ho-ling*, as independently sending envoys to China without any dependence on another state and rarely banding together (ibid. 1977: 95). If this was the case in reality, unlike other early sites in Central Java, the Dieng Plateau must have served as a center that was politically and culturally independent from the rest of Central Java. The artistic and architectural diversity and distinctiveness of the Dieng Plateau support the idea of its having been an independent center throughout the Central Javanese period, and not just in its early phase. Thus, the Dieng materials, especially some of the sculptures discovered from the region, should be carefully re-dated, with the possibility that they may have been contemporary with some sculptures from the Kedu and Prambanan plains.

Several questions still remain, especially concerning the exact character of the Dieng Plateau. Was it simply one of many religious and political centers during the Central Javanese period, a place where a variety of Indian sources were actively reinterpreted? Or did it serve a special role, differentiating it from the rest of the sites in Central Java? One possible hypothesis is that the Dieng Plateau might have been associated with the worship of spirits or immortals. The suffix *po-ta* or *-wata* (the plausible translation of which might be "of the gods [spirits]") was frequently used in Javanese inscriptions and in Chinese sources bearing the site's name (Meulen 1977: 101-02). This suggests that the religious rituals that took place on the Dieng Plateau might have been associated with the worship of ancestors as divinities (Meulen 1977).

Although this particular theory of the Dieng Plateau as a place for worshiping ancestors or deified kings is still preliminary, I expect that studies of the Dieng Plateau as an independent, long-lasting religious center will help us change our views about the Central Javanese period. In other words, the development of Central Javanese art and architecture should not be read sequentially, from the Dieng Plateau and then to the Kedu and Prambanan Plains. Rather, we need to consider the possibility that these regional centers might have coexisted throughout the Central Javanese period.

References

Asher, Frederick M., 1980, *The Art of Eastern India: 300-800,* Delhi: Oxford University Press.

Banerjea, Jitendra Nath, 1956, *The Development of Hindu Iconography*, Calcutta: University of Calcutta.

Banerji, Rakhal Das, 1998 [first published 1933], *Eastern Indian School of Mediaeval Sculpture*, New Delhi: Archaeological Survey of India.

Baptiste, Pierre and Thierry Zéphir, 2005, *Trésors d'art du Vietnam: la sculpture du Champa, Ve-XVe siècles*, Paris: Réunion des musées nationaux.

Bautze-Picron, Claudine, 2002, "Flying from Heaven to Earth," *Asiatische kunst*, 32(2): 3-13.

Bhattacharya, Gouriswar, 1977, "Nandin and Vṛṣabha," in *Zeitschrift der Deutschen Morgenländischen Gesellschaft, Supplement III, 2: XIX. Deutscher Orientalistentag vom 28. September bis 4. Oktober 1975 in Freiburg im Breisgau,* ed. Herausgegeben von Wolfgang Voigt, pp. 1545-67, Wiesbaden: Franz Steiner Verlag.

Boisselier, Jean, 1951, "Garuḍa dans l'art khmèr," *Bulletin de l'Ecole française d'Extrême-Orient*, 44(1): 55-88.

Chihara, Daigoro, 1996, *Hindu-Buddhist Architecture in Southeast Asia*, tr. Rolf W. Giebel, Leiden: E.J. Brill.

Christie, Jan Wisseman, 1998, "Javanese Markets and the Asian Sea Trade Boom of the Tenth to Thirteenth Centuries A.D.," *Social History of the Orient*, 41(3): 344-81.

Degroot, Véronique, 2009, *Candi, Space and Landscape: A Study on the Distribution, Orientation and Spatial Organization of Central Javanese Temple Remains*, Leiden: Sidestone Press.

Girard-Geslan, Maude, Marijke J. Klokke, Albert Le Bonheur, Donald M. Stadtner, Valérie Zaleski, and Thierry Zéphir, 1998, *Art of Southeast Asia*, New York: Harry N. Abrams.

Goor, M.E. Lulius Van, 1922, *A short Guide to the Ruined Temples in the Prambanan Plain, the Diëng Plateau, and Gedong Sanga*, tr. from Dutch by H.S. Banner, Weltevreden: Landsdrukkerij.

Hall, Kenneth R., 2004, "Local and International Trade and Traders in the Straits of Melaka Region: 600–1500," *Journal of the Economic and Social History of the Orient*, 47(2): 213-60.

Jessup, Helen Ibbitson and Theierry Zéphir, 1997, *Sculpture of Angkor and Ancient Cambodia: Millennium of Glory*, Washington, D.C.: National Gallery of Art.

Kinsbergen, J. [Isidore] van, 1914, "Oudheden van Java, Fotografische Opnamen," *Oudheidkundig Verslag: 1914*, pp. 19-25.

Krishna, Nanditha, 1980, *The Art and Iconography of Vishnu-Narayana*, Bombay: Taraporevala.

Le Bonheur, Albert, 1998, "The Art of Champa," in *Art of Southeast Asia*, Girard-Geslan et al., pp. 251-307, New York: Harry N. Abrams.

Maitra, Akshay Kumar, 1920, "Garuda, the Carrier of Vishnu: In Bengal and Java," *Rupam*, 1: 2-7.

Marcus, Margaret F., 1967, "Sculptures from Bihar and Bengal," *The Bulletin of the Cleveland Museum of Art*, 54(8): 240-62.

Meulen, W. J. van der, 1977, "In Search of 'Ho-ling'," *Indonesia*, 23: 87-111.

Nakada, Kozo, 1982, *An Inventory of the Dated Inscriptions in Java*, Memoirs of the Research Department of the Toyo Bunko, no. 40, Tokyo: Toyo Bunko.

Pal, Pratapaditya, 2009, "Revisiting the 'Vṛṣa/Nandi' Issue," *Prajñādhara: Essays on Asian Art, History, Epigraphy and Culture in Honour of Gouriswar Bhattacharya*, ed. Gerd J.R. Mevissen and Arundhati Banerji, pp. 413-17, New Delhi: Kaveri Books.

Paul, Debjani, 1978, "Deity or Deified King?: Reflections on a Unique Vaiṣṇavite Sculpture from Java," *Artibus Asiae*, 40(4): 311-33.

Scheurleer, Pauline Lunsingh, 1991, "Isidore Van Kinsbergen Photographer of Javanese Antiquities," in *Toward Independence: A Century of Indonesia Photographed*, ed. Jane Levy Reed, pp. 37-39, San Francisco: The Friends of Photography.

——, 2009, "The Javanese Statue of Garuḍa Carrying Wiṣṇu and Candi Kiḍal," *Artibus Asiae*, 69(1): 189-218.

Sivaramamurti, C., 1977, *The Art of India*, New York: Harry N. Abrams.

Soekmono, R., 1992, "Indonesian Architecture of the Classical Period: A Brief Survey," in *The Sculpture of Indonesia*, ed. Jan Fontein, R. Soekmono, and Edi Edyawati, pp. 67-111, Washington, D.C.: National Gallery of Art.

Stern, Philippe, 1938, "Le style du Kulên (décor architectural et statuaire)," *Bulletin de l'École française d'Extrême-Orient*, 38(1): 111-50.

Theuns-de Boer, Gerda, 2002, "Java through the Eyes of Van Kinsbergen," *International Institute for Asian Studies Newsletter* (March), 27: 32.

Theuns-de Boer, Gerda and Saskia Asser, 2005, *Isidore van Kinsbergen (1821-1905): fotopionier en theatermaker in Nederlands-Indie = Photo Pioneer and Theatre Maker in the Dutch East Indies*, Zaltbommel: Uitgeverij Aprilis and Leiden: KITLV Press.

Tōkyō Kokuritsu Hakubutsukan, 1997, *Indoneshia kodai ōkoku no shihō/ Treasures of Ancient Indonesian kingdoms*, Tokyo: Tokyo National Museum.

Vogler, E.B., 1949, *De monsterkop uit het omlijstingsornament van tempeldoorgangen en-nissen in de Hindoe-Javaanse bouwkunst*, Leiden: Brill.

Williams, Joanna, 1981, "The Date of Barabuḍur in Relation to Other Central Javanese Monuments," in *Barabuḍur: History and Significance of a Buddhist Monument*, ed. Luis O. Gómez and Hiram W. Woodward, Jr., Berkeley Buddhist Studies Series, vol. 2, pp. 25-45, Berkeley: Distributed by Asian Humanities Press.

13

Making Merit by Making Buddhist Tablets

Inscribed Dedicatory Inscriptions on King Aniruddha's Clay Tablets

M.L. Pattaratorn Chirapravati

> ... the custom of inscribing tablets with the donor's name and aspiration does not seem to have been practiced in India, in the Chao Phraya valley (the so-called Dvāravatī culture) or the Malay Peninsula. ... It is from Pagan in Upper Burma that we have a wealth of sealings, inscribed and uninscribed.
>
> – Skilling 2008: 252, 254

In 2016, I visited an antique store in Singapore and saw a basket of terracotta tablets from Myanmar that were for sale (*fig.* 13.1). These new Buddhist tablets were made in a style similar to one type produced by the eleventh-century Burmese king Aniruddha (or Anawrahta). One of the tablets had an inscription on the back (*fig.* 13.2). Geok Yian Goh, a historian of Burmese Studies, translated this inscription for me as *suhtanpharphayar*. She explained that it can be read two ways depending on the system of transliteration: "A wish requested at the temple" or "A wish requested/carried [out], Lord Buddha." The word *phayar* can refer to both the Buddha and pagoda/temple. In either case, it is an invocation or expression addressed to Lord Buddha by the maker of the tablet.

During my visit to Bagan (Pagan) in the same year, I discovered similar tablets, with inscriptions on the back, at a shop near a temple that sold both antique and new tablets.[1] Unfortunately, I did not take pictures of them. Nevertheless, it is clear that tablet makers continue to inscribe traditional Burmese dedicatory inscriptions on the back of tablets. Why does this tradition still continue? Even though donative inscriptions were commonly made on Buddha images, mural paintings and manuscripts in India and China, they were not popular on tablets. Why did donative inscriptions on tablets become popular in the Pagan period? How did the practice begin, and what was its purpose? This article first focuses on the making of tablets in Myanmar by King Aniruddha (r. 1044-77 CE) of Pagan, and then traces the origin of his practice of inscribing names and dedicatory inscriptions on them.

Buddhist tablets are small Buddhist icons, usually made out of baked or unbaked clay using a press-mould technique, a process that has been used for more than 1,000 years to produce religious objects for merit-making. The stamping was repeated over and over as a method to gain merit and as a meditative devotional exercise (Pattaratorn Chirapravati 1994: 187-90; Lawson 1982: 57). The practice originated in India but gained its greatest popularity in Tibet and Southeast Asia. Unlike images of the Buddha that were produced by specialized craftsmen, tablets were made by monks and practitioners themselves. The practice of making Buddhist tablets was an important duty and was considered one of the best among many popular merit-making activities. In the seventh century, a Chinese monk who we know as Yijing (I-Tsing) wrote an account of his travels from China to India via Southeast Asia. In it he remarks:

> If a man makes an image even as small as a grain of barley, or builds a *caitya* as tiny as a jujube with a wheel sign and a spire as small as a needle on it, he will obtain special good causes as limitless as the seven seas, and his good rewards will last as long as four rebirths.
>
> — Li Rongxi 2000: 138

---

[1] In this article, I use Pagan for the name of the historic period but will use the current spelling of Bagan for the present city.

fig. 13.1: Buddhist tablet showing a seated Buddha with the hands in the earth-touching gesture, twentieth century CE, terracotta

fig. 13.2: Reverse side of Buddha tablet (*fig*. 13.1) with inscription, twentieth century CE, terracotta

fig. 13.3: Aniruddha tablets, eleventh century CE, terracotta

fig. 13.4: Aniruddha tablet, Khabin, Maung Di, eleventh century CE, terracotta

fig. 13.5: Inscription on the bottom of Aniruddha tablet, Khabin, Maung Di, eleventh century CE, terracotta

Buddhist tablets have been found in Nālandā that can be dated to around the time of Yijing's visit to India (seventh to early eighth century). Based on the archaeological remains of Buddhist tablets dated to this period, they appear to have been commonly produced by monks in Nālandā. Although at present Buddhist practitioners no longer stamp their own tablets as offerings, monks still make tablets at temples in Southeast Asia (e.g., Thailand and Myanmar) and they are often given or sold to adherents.

In his article "Buddhist Sealings in Thailand and Southeast Asia: Iconography, Function, and Ritual Context," Peter Skilling explains that the Sanskrit term, *sañcaka* (or sometimes *sacca*) refers to dedicatory tablets (2008: 250). This term appeared only on King Aniruddha's tablets, after which it disappeared from Burmese epigraphic records. Skilling proposes that the term "votive tablets," popularly used by scholars to refer to *sañcaka*s, should not be utilized because it is misleading. He prefers to call them "sealings" because he claims that their function and ritual context indicate that they were neither votive offerings nor souvenirs of important Buddhist sites. Skilling also points out that among the motives for making clay sealings and *sīmā* stones is the creation of merit (2008: 253). In this article, I refer to "sealings" as "Buddhist tablets" because they mainly feature Buddhist subjects and were primarily made in the form of a tablet with a square shape and arched top, although some tablets have a circular or oblong shape. They can be more than 2 ft in length, which is much larger than typical sealings. In addition, this tablet shape was commonly used for the shape of large stone inscriptions by other Buddhist kings of Myanmar (e.g., the Kalyāṇī *sīmā* inscriptions) as well as for *sīmā* stones, which define the area in which Buddhist ordination can be conducted.

The most common type of inscription found on these tablets is a Buddhist creed called the *ye dhamma* (Skt: *ye dharma*), which is written in one of various indigenous scripts that were based on Indian precedents (e.g., Nāgarī/Devanāgarī or Pallava script). This concise statement of the essence of the Buddha's teaching was immensely popular because it was believed to have secured the conversions of the Buddha's two leading disciples (Pattaratorn Chirapravati 1997: 16-17). The *ye dhamma* is commonly inscribed on the mold itself and appears underneath the Buddha's throne. The donative inscriptions that are the subject of this article, however, were inscribed individually on the reverse side or on the base of the clay tablet (the underside) before it was dried or fired (Guy 2002: 31). Dedicatory inscriptions on tablets seem to be limited to Southeast Asia, in particular to the Pagan period of Myanmar and the north-eastern region of Thailand (e.g., Si Thep in Phetchabun Province, and Maha Sarakham Province) (Pattaratorn Chirapravati 1994: 302-80; Mayuree Viraprasert 1989: 5-7).

The practice of stamping tablets in Myanmar began around the seventh century in the Pyu region in Śrī Kṣetra and in the Mon region in the south such as at Bago (Pegu) and Thaton. Even though there are tablets hand-inscribed in the Pyu language, unfortunately the language is only partially understood so the meaning of these inscriptions is not yet decipherable (Griffiths and Lammerts 2015: 1001). This tradition of hand-inscribing tablets thus pre-dates the Pagan period (ninth to thirteenth centuries). So far, the earliest readable inscribed tablets with donative inscriptions seem to have been made by the Pagan king Aniruddha (r. 1044-77), who produced many types in large numbers. Aniruddha's tablets have been discovered around Myanmar, in Nwatele, north of Tagaung, to Tagu, near Tenasserim, in the south (Luce 1969, vol. 1: 15-27). They range in size from four and three-quarters inches to 2 ft and 7 inches (approximately 12.07 x 78.75 cm). Several tablets bear distinctive donor inscriptions claiming that Aniruddha made the tablets with his own hands for the sake of "deliverance" (Luce 1969, vol. 2: 2, pls. 4-6, 9.e). Although the tablets were produced by a press-mold technique, the dedicatory inscriptions were inscribed individually on the front of the lower rim, on the reverse side, or on the base of the tablet. Aniruddha's tablet from Khabin reads:

> This Blessed One [i.e. the Buddha image on the tablet] was made

> by the Great King, the Glorious Aniruddha, with his own hands, for the sake of liberation. – Luce 1969, vol. 2: 2; author's tr.

Others read:

> By me, king Aniruddha, this mould of Sugata (Buddha) has been made; through this (good deed) may I obtain the path to Nirvāṇa, when Maitreya is (fully) enlightened .... .
>
> — Duroiselle 1927, 6.27: 162-63[2]

A common type among Aniruddha's Buddhist tablets depicts a seated Buddha in the earth-touching hand gesture under the *bodhi* tree, surrounded by small *stūpas* (*fig.* 13.3). Above the tree is the Mahābodhi Temple in Bodh-Gayā, symbolizing the site of the Enlightenment. The earliest of Aniruddha's tablets may be those at Maung Di Pagoda at Khabin (near Yangon), dated to 1050 CE (*fig.* 13.4) (Luce 1969, vol. 2: 2). Charles Duroiselle, a Pāli specialist who was the first to read and translate the inscriptions on these tablets, mentions that at the time of his writing (*c.*1920) more than twenty of them were still *in situ* encircling the two uppermost octagonal terraces (1915: 14-17). At 2 ft and 7 inches by 1 ft and 6 inches (approximately 78.75 x 45.72 cm), they are the largest known tablets made by Aniruddha. They are also the largest tablets known in Southeast Asia (Stadtner 2008: 24-25). A number of Aniruddha's terracotta tablets were also recovered from the relic chamber of the Shwehsandaw Pagoda at Bagan (Luce 1969, vol. 2-3: pl. 6.c). At least five types of tablets were produced that contain the king's name and his dedicatory inscription (Luce 1969, vol. 1: 15-17). Aniruddha's tablets are not inscribed in Burmese but rather in the Pāli and Sanskrit languages written in Old Mon script (*fig.* 13.5). G.H. Luce suggests that the earliest known Burmese language inscription (in Myanmar) is that of the Lekthayshay Pagoda, dated to 1058 CE

---

[2] This Nāgarī inscription in Sanskrit is below the lotus-seat. Charles Duroiselle reads it as follows: 1. *may-āniruddhade* — 2. *vena kṛtam* 3. *sugatasa(ñ)chchakaṁtena maitreya sambo* — 4. *dholabheyan* — *nirvṛttopadaṁ*.

(*Sakkaraj* 420) (Goh 2015: 74). Why did King Aniruddha choose to produce tablets and make donative inscriptions on them instead of using other prominent objects such as stone pillars or *sīmā* stones, and did he really inscribe and make the tablets himself as is claimed in the inscriptions?

As mentioned earlier, stamped tablets were made by people as a part of meditation and merit-making. It was also a common practice for monks to copy Buddhist texts onto palm leaves and paper manuscripts as an act of merit-making and meditation in both Southeast Asia and in Sri Lanka. In Aniruddha's case, he was not only reproducing the copy for merit-making (*ānisaṁsa*), but also creating a new form of offering — the donative inscription. Thus, stamping tablets and inscribing them seem to have fulfilled both the act of *ānisaṁsa* and meditation practice (Pattaratorn Chirapravati 2009: 172-88). The copying of images and texts and the making of specific Buddha images continue to be performed by monks as a part of merit-making in Cambodia, Laos, Myanmar, and Thailand to the present day.

Aniruddha was the first king of Pagan to travel to important Buddhist cities in search of Buddhist relics and texts. First, he conquered the Mon kingdom and took their Buddha relics to Bagan, where he had temples built to house them. Then he moved the relics from the Bawbaw-gyi Pagoda at Śrī Kṣetra to Bagan and replaced them with tablets displaying the fifty-Buddhas motif and with his name inscribed on the back (Luce 1969, vol. 1: 19). Aniruddha had the Pitakat-taik Temple built to house manuscripts of the *Jātaka Commentary* that he obtained from Thaton in 1060 CE (Luce 1969, vol. 1: 44, 285). He had the Shwehsandaw Pagoda built in 1060 CE to enshrine the hair relic given to him by the king of Bago (also referred to as Pegu) (Luce 1969, vol. 1: 27, 260). During the later years of his reign, Aniruddha also built three more temples: Myinkaba Zedi south of Bagan (1044 CE) and the West and East Hpetleik pagodas in Bagan (1070 CE).

As pointed out earlier, after invading Khabin, Aniruddha left his largest tablets on the upper terraces of the Maung Di Pagoda. Luce mentions that the king had two *stūpas* built: the Myinkaba Pagoda (*zedi*) in *c.*1044 and the Khabin Maung Di Pagoda in *c.*1050 (1969, vol. 1: 20; vol. 2: 69, pl. 79; vol. 3: pl. 79a-b). In his article "Demystifying Mists: A Case for the Mon," Donald M. Stadtner suggests that if the tablets were part of the original structure, then the Maung Di Pagoda should belong to the reign of Aniruddha. However, because the tablets do not seem to match the height of the terraces themselves, he suggests that Aniruddha placed his Buddhist tablets on a pre-existing structure (2008: 199-200). Stadtner also notes that fragments of identical tablets were recently found at Bagan (2005: 201).

In addition, Luce has pointed out that the Khabin region was known for its pottery. An earthenware pot with a recessed conical lid, decorated with a row of fig leaves stencilled below the neck, was discovered in Twante in 1920. A similar pot was recovered in a relic chamber of the Seinnyet Pagoda at Bagan. It was covered with tablets inscribed with Aniruddha's name. Luce speculates that Aniruddha had this pagoda built and the pottery was brought from Khabin/Twante (Luce 1969, vol. 1: 20). Thus the choice of using clay to produce large dedicatory tablets and the use of earthenware as parts of offerings and containers of Buddhist tablets may indicate that it was an easily available and prevalent material in this region at the time.

As mentioned, Aniruddha's tablets have also been found at places from Nwatele in the north to Tagu in the south of present-day Myanmar. Luce suggests that Aniruddha's main intention in scattering his plaques all over Burma was for religious purposes because the king wished to convert all the Burmese to Buddhism from animism (1969, vol. 1: 18). Aniruddha seems to have preferred that his name be written in either Pāli or Sanskrit. Goh explains that:

> The appropriation of Sanskrit and/or Pali Buddhist titles provided

> the context for how fellow Buddhist as well as non-Buddhist populations could perceive the king — a Buddhist monarch who could be seen simultaneously as divine (Aniruddhadeva).
>
> — 2015: 24

During his thirty-three years as the first king of a Pagan-based empire, Aniruddha was determined to acquire relics of the Buddha to be enshrined in his temples in Bagan and tried to obtain Tripiṭaka texts for establishing the Sinhalese lineage of Theravāda in Bagan. Goh (2015: 85) states that in the pursuit of this goal, Aniruddha led various expeditions to Thaton, Sri Lanka, and Tarup Gandhāra. The king compiled chronicles as part of his royal duty and as an act of purification (ibid. 2015: 79). He did not address himself as a universal monarch (*cakravartin*) however. In fact, this term was first used by a later king of Pagan who referred to Aniruddha as *cakravartin* on an inscription at the Lokananda Pagoda in Bagan dated to 1207 (ibid. 2015: 17). Goh, however, suggests that Aniruddha considered himself to be a universal monarch because he placed Pagan at the same level as Sri Lanka and Haripuñjaya in northern Thailand as the three leading centers of Buddhism at the time. She further states:

> He probably became aware of a greater Buddhist milieu within which he could make an impression. The distribution of votive tablets over a large swath of geographical space certainly demonstrates Anawrahta's determination to extend his presence throughout what he considered to be the boundaries of his polity.
>
> - 2015: 23-24

If this is the case, it seems that Aniruddha "killed two birds with one stone": he used his dedicatory inscriptions for both political purposes and merit-making.

Aniruddha was obviously not the first king to be a great supporter of Buddhism, but in whose steps did he follow? Among the early great supporters of Buddhism in South and Southeast Asia, King Aśoka of the Maurya dynasty (r. 279-32 BCE) and King Duṭṭhagāmaṇī of Sri Lanka (r. 161-37 BCE) were the two monarchs whose legends were most prominently circulated and whose names appear in numerous Southeast Asian chronicles as early supporters of Buddhism.

After the great Mauryan King Aśoka was converted to Buddhism, he is said to have acquired relics of the Buddha from the original (seven) *stūpas* and built 84,000 *stūpas* around India (Guruge 1993: 127-32). King Aśoka left his inscriptions, or edicts, of *dharma* (called *dharmalipi*), on rock slabs and erected stone pillars at major Buddhist sites in India, including Sārnāth, Saṅkisa, and Vaiśālī (ibid.: 648). To mark the fifteenth anniversary of *dharmavijaya* (meaning conquest by righteousness) as well as twenty-five years on the throne, three edicts of *dharma* (*dharmalipi*) were produced (ibid.: 236-37) and identical versions have been found on six pillars.[3] According to inscriptions of the fifth *dharmalipi* (Pillar Edict I–III), entitled "What I do for the Promotion of Dharma," King Aśoka mentioned that:

> For this purpose (*etāyeaṭhāye*) is this Dharma-document caused to be engraved by me: May they practise it in this manner (*hevaṁanupaṭipajaṁtu*). May it also last long (*cilaṁthitikā ca hotu*). Those who practise thus will do a good deed (*ye ca hevaṁsaṁpaṭipajīsati se sukataṁkacchatī*).
>
> – Guruge 1993: 238-40, 574-75

In the eighth *dharmalipi* (Pillar Edict VII), made during the twenty-eighth year of his reign, Aśoka clearly indicated that:

> This Dhamma-document should be engraved wherever there are stone pillars or rock slabs in order that it may last long. ... By me who was consecrated for twenty-seven years this Dharma-document made to be written. — Guruge 1993: 178, 580-83

The seventh *dharmalipi* (Pillar Edicts V–VI) made during the twenty-seventh year of Aśoka's reign, however, is the only record that

[3] There are eight *dharmalipis*: the first four were inscribed on rock slabs and the last four were inscribed on stone pillars.

clearly indicates that King Aśoka was the person who engraved these documents. It proclaims that:

> This Dharma-document was engraved by me who have [*sic*] been consecrated for twenty-six years. — Guruge 1993: 243-46, 578-79[4]

Although there is no available evidence that the inscriptions on Aśoka's columns were known in Bagan, the legends of King Aśoka were likely familiar in South and Southeast Asia in Aniruddha's time. Monks from Southeast Asia also went on pilgrimages to both India and Sri Lanka. There is ample evidence of contact between Myanmar and India as early as the eighth century though contacts must have begun far earlier. Written documents regarding the relationship between the kingdom of Pagan and the Pāla Empire in the regions of Bihar and Bengal in the eleventh and twelfth centuries can be found in two inscriptions from Bodh-Gayā. The first inscription was set up by King Kyanzittha (r. 1084–1112), who had been Aniruddha's general and followed closely the practice of stamping Buddhist tablets with inscriptions. The second inscription provides records of repairs to the Mahābodhi Temple carried out by a Burmese monk, Lord Thera Dhammarājaguru, with the help of a local ruler. The repairs commenced in late 1295 and were completed in 1298 CE (Barua 1981: 198-99). Even though the inscription post-dates Aniruddha, it is reasonable to suppose that the story of King Aśoka would have been known by him because King Aśoka's legends are included in the fifth-century Sinhalese chronicle, the *Mahāvaṁsa* (and later it was included in its extension, the thirteenth-century *Cūḷavaṁsa*), which credits Aśoka with sending Buddha relics and monks to spread Buddhism in Sri Lanka. Aśoka's significant role in disseminating Buddha relics and supporting the religion is also reverentially referred to in northern Thai chronicles (e.g., the

---

4 Guruge uses both the Sanskrit term *dharma* and the Pāli/Prākṛt term *dhamma* in this quote. As the original inscription is in an early form of Prākṛt (now identified as Middle Indo-Aryan), *dhamma* is the word that appears in the inscriptions.

sixteenth-century *Jinakālamālīpakaraṇaṁ*), which draw from Sri Lankan chronicles and local oral traditions and also attribute the presence of many relics in the region to Aśoka.

Who inscribed the donative inscriptions? Is it possible that Aniruddha wrote the inscriptions himself? In general, men learned how to read Pāli and Sanskrit during their monkhoods, but women did not have the same access so in general they could not read and write. Skilling's list of the contents of Pagan inscriptions clearly shows that several royal family members claimed that they made or inscribed tablets with their own hands (Skilling 2008: 257-59). For example, it is stated on Mahārāja Bajrābharaṇadeva's tablet that he made it with his own hands, and one of the two tablets by King Tribhuvanāditya claims that he himself "fired this image" (ibid.: 258). Similar phrases on Pagan tablets assert that they were inscribed by queens, monks, and high officials. The Buddhist scholar Daniel Veidlinger suggests that Aniruddha copied the Buddhist Tripiṭaka with his own hands and not through the intermediary of scribes (Veidlinger 2006: 35). Veidlinger cites the sixteenth-century Northern Thai chronicle *Jinakālamālīpakaraṇaṁ* and the eighteenth-century Burmese chronicle *Mahayazawingyi* in support of his arguments.

This evidence suggests that Aniruddha tried to style himself as a great Buddhist king in the spirit of King Aśoka and thus he may also have been inspired to produce dedicatory inscriptions "with his own hand." Neither Sri Lankan nor northern Thai kings left such dedicatory inscriptions in the manner of King Aśoka. Nonetheless, unlike the large, tall columns that King Aśoka had made, Aniruddha chose to make tablets and inscribe dedications on them personally. As mentioned earlier, tablets are much easier to make and can be produced by anyone with access to a mold and clay. The donative inscriptions were inscribed when the clay was still wet; hence it is clear that this required little labour and effort, and they could be pressed easily by the king himself. It seems that Aniruddha could have inscribed at least one of the tablets at each site where he had his temples built. In addition, during his military expeditions to other regions, Aniruddha left tablets that carried his name at the sites he conquered. In these cases, he was not only making tablets as an act of merit-making by a pious Buddhist, but also as a political act proclaiming his power over newly conquered land. Two of Aniruddha's generals also left tablets with donative inscriptions during their military expeditions (Luce 1969, vol. 1: 26-27).

After the Aniruddha period, similar tablets and donative inscriptions appeared on clay tablets that name other Pagan kings (e.g., Sawlu and Alaungsithu), queens (e.g., Trilokavataṁsakā and Ci'peh), monks (e.g., Abhirūpa and Raṭhapā), and high officials (Jesalya and Pintu) (Skilling 2008: 257-59). The inscriptions continued to be in Pāli and Sanskrit but, in addition to the old Mon script, Nāgarī script was also used (ibid.: 254). Skilling analyzed the royal tablets and surmised that the goal of making the tablets was "to produce merit, to share merit with others (both relations and all sentient being), and to realize liberation or Buddhahood" (ibid.: 255).

Another important Buddhist who pressed tablets instead of making other types of objects was Atīśa Dīpaṁkara Śrījñāna (982-1045), who was Aniruddha's contemporary. Atīśa was a Bengali monk who spent twelve years, *c.*1012-24 at Śrīvijaya in the present-day Malay Archipelago. In 1025 he became the abbot of Vikramaśilā, one of the two most important Buddhist centers in India. When he was at Śrīvijaya, Atīśa was known for making tablets in a cave as part of his daily meditation practices and merit-making. We know from the Chinese monks Xuanzang and Yijing, as well as from Atīśa, that in India and Tibet, after tablets or miniature *stūpas* were made, they were placed inside actual *stūpas*. The *ye dharma* inscriptions on them were typically written in Sanskrit. Atīśa continued to promote the making of tablets and miniature *stūpas* and wrote an important text, *The Ritual of Making Miniature Clay Stūpas of the Vehicle of Perfections* (*Pāramitāyāna*) in order to do so.[5] One type of Atīśa's tablets depicts fifty seated Buddhas, all the same size, with hands in the earth-touching gesture and seated in six rows with *stūpas* between their heads (Pattaratorn Chirapravati 1994: 187-90).[6] This particular type of tablet was also produced by Aniruddha; examples were recovered at the Shwehsandaw Pagoda, Minbu, and the Bawbaw-gyi Pagoda at Śrī Kṣetra (Luce 1969, vols. 2-3: pls. 12.a-e, 13.a-f). Aniruddha's fifty-Buddhas tablet is closely related, both iconographically and stylistically, to tablets found in limestone caves in the Thai Peninsula dated to around the eleventh century, as well as to some found in Tibet.

In addition, clay Buddhist tablets may have been chosen for merit-making by Aniruddha because he was on military campaigns in the Mon region, which is situated on alluvial plains where stone is scarce. Hence, the choice of medium could have been dictated by what was locally available. As mentioned earlier, Khabin, where the largest of Aniruddha's inscribed tablets were recovered, was famous for pottery. Thus, it seems reasonable that clay was chosen as the medium. Later, after his expeditions, Buddhist tablets continued to be made in Pagan both by Aniruddha himself and by his successors.

Although King Aniruddha invented neither the making of Buddhist tablets nor of donative inscriptions, he actively used tablets in acts of merit-making and was the first Burmese king to include donative inscriptions that proclaim devotion to Buddhism and the first to ritually stamp tablets with his own hands. He also stated clearly that his goal was to accrue merit and share the merit with others, and to realize liberation or Buddhahood. This unique practice continues in Myanmar from Aniruddha's time until the present.

---

[5] This text describes every step of how the miniature *stūpas* were made and what kind of *dhāraṇī* was recited during the ritual practice (Skilling 2008: 259-60).

[6] This particular type was baked and found at Buddhist sites in Vietnam, Indonesia, and the central and northeastern regions of Thailand. Similar types of Atīśa's tablets were recovered from two caves in the Malay Peninsula: Gua Korong Batang and Gua Berhala in Perlis.

Acknowledgements

I am grateful to Don Stadtner for photos, advice, and close reading of this article; to Geok Yian Goh and May O. Lwin for translating the inscription on the new Burmese tablet and for their collaboration on the symposium on the *Cultures of Myanmar: Art, History and Identity, and Archaeology* at Yale-NUS College (2017); to Amy McNair for permission to reproduce photographs originally published by *Artibus Asiae*; and to Drs. Robert DeCaroli, Paul Lavy, Richard E. Breedon, and Angela Chiu for editing this article.

References

Barua, Dipak K., 1981, *Buddha Gaya Temple: Its History*, Calcutta: Joyguru Printing Works.

Duroiselle, Charles, 1915, "Terra-cotta Plaques Found at Pegu," *Report of the Superintendent, Archaeological Survey, Burma, for the Year Ending 31st March 1915*, pp. 14-17, Rangoon: Office of the Superintendent.

——, 1926-27 [1990], *Excavations at Pagan, Annual Report of the Archaeology Survey of India, 1926-27*, Delhi: Swati Publications.

Goh, Geok Yian, 2015, *The Wheel-Turner and His House: Kingship in a Buddhist Ecumene*, De Kalb, Illinois: Northern Illinois University Press.

Griffiths, Arlo and D. Christian Lammerts, 2015, "Epigraphy: Southeast Asia," in *Brill's Encyclopedia of Buddhism*, vol. 1, ed. Jonathan A. Silk, Oskar von Hinüber, and Vincent Eltschinger, pp. 988-1009, Leiden: Brill.

Guruge, Ananda W.P., 1993, *Aśoka, the Righteous: A Definitive Biography*, Colombo: Central Cultural Fund, Ministry of Cultural Affairs, and Information.

Guy, John, 2002, "Offering up a Rare Jewel: Buddhist Merit Making and Votive Tablets in Early Burma," in *Burma: Art and Archaeology*, ed. Alexandra Green and T. Richard Blurton, pp. 23-33, Chicago: Art Media Resources.

I-Tsing (Yijing), see Takakusu 1982.

Lawson, Simon D., 1982 [unpublished], "A Catalogue of Indian Buddhist Clay Sealings in British Museums," Doctoral Dissertation, University of Oxford.

Li Rongxi, 2000, *Buddhist Monastic Traditions of Southern Asia: A Record of the Inner Law Sent Home from the South Seas, by Sramana Yijing*. Translated from the Chinese (*Taisho* Volume 54, Number 2125), Numata Center for Buddhist Translation and Research.

Luce, Gordon H., 1969, *Old Burma–Early Pagan*, 3 vols., *Artibus Asiae Supplementum*, vol. 25, Locust Valley, New York: J.J. Augustin.

Mayuree Viraprasert, 1989, "Terracotta Buddhist Votive Tablets Bearing Mon Inscriptions Found at Nadun, Mahasarakham, Northeastern Thailand," *The Siam Society Newsletter*, 5(1): 5-7.

Pattaratorn Chirapravati, M.L., 1994 [unpublished], "The Cult of Votive Tablets in Thailand (Seventh to Thirteenth Centuries)", Doctoral Dissertation, Cornell University, Ithaca.

——, 1997, *Votive Tablets in Thailand: Origin, Styles and Uses*, Kuala Lumpur: Oxford University Press.

——, 2009, "From Text to Image: Copying as Buddhist Practice in Late Fourteenth-Century Sukhothai," in *Buddhist Manuscript Cultures*, ed. Steve Berkwitz, Juliane Schober, and Claudia Brown, pp. 172-88, London: Routledge.

Skilling, Peter, 2008, "Buddhist Sealings in Thailand and Southeast Asia: Iconography, Function, and Ritual Context," in *Interpreting Southeast Asia's Past: Monument, Image and Text*, ed. E. Bacus, I. Glover, and P. Sharrock, pp. 248-62, Singapore: NUS Press.

Stadtner, Donald M., 2005, *Ancient Pagan: Buddhist Plain of Merit*, Bangkok: River Books.

——, 2008, "Demystifying Mists: A Case for the Mon," *Journal of the Siam Society*, 96: 193-215.

Takakusu, J. (tr.), 1982 [first published 1896], *A Record of the Buddhist Religion as Practised in India and the Malay Archipelago* AD *671–695*, 2nd Indian edition, New Delhi: Munshiram Manoharlal.

Veidlinger, Daniel, 2006, *Spreading the Dhamma: Writing, Orality, and the Textual Transmission in Buddhist Northern Thailand*, Honolulu: University of Hawai'i Press.

14

The Origins of the Emerald Buddha Icon (*Phra Kaew Morokot*)

Melody Rod-ari

THE Emerald Buddha or Phra Kaew Morokot is the most famous Buddha icon in Thailand (*fig.* 14.1). Its fame and religious potency are due, in part, to extensive narratives that describe it as being among the earliest images of the Buddha, and one that is directly linked to the *cakkavatti* (Skt: *cakravartin*) or Universal World Ruler. Such texts describe the Emerald Buddha's genesis as the result of divine intervention when the God Sakka (Skt. Śakra, i.e., Indra) and the celestial architect Vissukamma (Skt. Viśvakarman) came together to grant the wish of Nāgasena — the famed Buddhist monk whose discussion with King Milinda is recorded in the classical Buddhist text, the *Milindapañha* — who asked for an image of the Buddha to be made in order to increase the prosperity of Buddhism in the world. Contemplating what material from which a portrait of the Buddha should be made, Nāgasena decided that a sculpture made of silver or gold would solicit the greed and cruelty of others during eras of decline, and so decided that, because the Buddha represented one of the three gems (Skt: *triratna*) of the Buddhist faith, the image should be made from a gemstone. Hearing Nāgasena's thoughts from heaven, Indra — the king of all gods — secured the *cakkavatti's* wish-granting *amarakaṭa* (emerald crystal), for Vissukamma to sculpt into a portrait of the Buddha, thereby bringing the Emerald Buddha icon to life. Purportedly crafted in 44 CE, the icon came to be enshrined in the monastery of King Aśoka in Pāṭaliputra, India. From there the icon is said to have traveled throughout the South and Southeast Asian Buddhist world before eventually settling in the Kingdom of Lanna (modern-day northern Thailand) in the fifteenth century. It then made its way to Luang Prabang and Vientiane, in contemporary Laos, and finally to Bangkok, Thailand, where it has been enshrined since 1778 (Jayawickrama 1968; Notton 1931; Saeng Monwithun 1987).[1]

This essay will examine the Emerald Buddha's "life" from the mid-fifteenth century in Lanna, because it is from this period and locale that the earliest chronicles associated with the icon emerge and when details in its narrative can also be corroborated with historical events. While it is likely that an oral narrative associated with the Emerald Buddha circulated prior to the mid-fifteenth century, it was not until the writing of the *Ratanabimbavaṁsa*, sometime between 1436 and 1468, by the monk Brahmarājapaññā that we have a textual description of the icon (Chiu 2017: 22; Rod-ari 2010: 87; Skilling and Santi Pakdeekham 2004: 66).[2] Moreover, the Emerald Buddha's formal qualities suggest a fifteenth century date

---

1 Accounts and summaries of the Emerald Buddha from the *Ratanabimbavaṁsa* will be sourced from a Thai translation by Saeng Monwithun, which is based on an eighteenth-century translation of the text by Bhikku Phrommaratchapanya. Accounts and summaries from the *Amaragaṭabuddharūpanidāna* will be sourced from Camille Notton's translation, which is based on a Pāli/Yuan manuscript found in Chiang Mai; see Notton's *Chronicle of the Emerald Buddha* for more specific information. Accounts and summaries from the *Jinakālamālīpakaraṇam* will be taken from N.A. Jayawickrama's (Thera Ratanapañña) translation, which is based primarily on Aggamahāpaṇḍita Ambalangoda Polvatte Buddhadatta Mahāthera's edition published by the Pali Text Society in 1962. Jayawickrama also includes amendments and notations from Ayutthaya, Khmer, and Rattanakosin (Rama I-IV period) manuscripts.

2 Peter Skilling notes that the text's colophon suggests that the text was written in 1429. It is unclear if the *Ratanabimbavaṁsa* was completed in 1429 or if writing began in 1429. As noted in my dissertation, "Visualizing Merit: An Art Historical Study of the Emerald Buddha and Wat Phra Kaew", the text likely dates between 1436 and 1468 based on the historical events described in it (Rod-ari 2010).

fig. 14.1: Emerald Buddha (Phra Kaew Morokot), Wat Phra Kaew, Grand Palace, Bangkok, Thailand, fifteenth century CE, jadeite or nephrite

fig. 14.2: Phra Sihing, Buddhaisawan Chapel, National Museum, Bangkok, Thailand, mid–late fifteenth century CE, gilt bronze

fig. 14.3: Phra Suan Dok, Wat Suan Dok, Chiang Mai, Thailand, 1371-85 CE, gilt bronze

of production. To confirm the Emerald Buddha's date of genesis, this essay will bring together two strands of evidence that are not normally examined together: royal and Buddhist chronicles from the fourteenth–fifteenth centuries as well as Buddhist statuary from the fifteenth century. Taken together, these sources support the argument that both the Emerald Buddha's image and narrative were likely invented by a monk or group of monks in the first half of the fifteenth century in order to prevent the decline of Buddhism amid the 2,000-year anniversary of Buddhism (Chiu 2017: 42-43).[3] Their efforts were likely executed in concert with the expansion of King Tilok's (r. 1441-87) political and religious sovereignty in the region. Like Robert Lingat (1934: 33) and Frank E. Reynolds (1978: 177), I argue that the Emerald Buddha was crafted from a green stone that was worshiped regionally as a guardian deity.[4] It was likely modeled after the fourteenth-century Phra Sihing icon — the original now lost — that was enshrined in Wat Phra Singh in Chiang Mai (Griswold 1965: 182; Jayawickrama 1968: 182; Stratton 2004: 27).

The mytho-history associated with the Emerald Buddha is elaborated in texts such as the *Ratanabimbavaṁsa* (mid–late fifteenth century), the *Jinakālamālīpakaraṇam* (1516), and the *Amaragaṭabuddharūpanidāna* (second half of the sixteenth century). All three texts were originally written in Pāli in Lanna and are among the earliest extant narratives associated with the Emerald Buddha. The texts are a combination of mythological narratives that describe the genesis of the Emerald Buddha and its travels throughout the South and Southeast Asian Buddhist world and

---

[3] I would like to thank Angela Chiu for her extensive research on manuscript traditions and her recent work on the Buddha images in Lanna, both of which have informed this essay. I would also like to extend my gratitude to her for reading and editing a draft version of this essay. Any errors in the essay are solely my own.

[4] Robert Lingat suggests that the Emerald Buddha may be associated with the Angkorian King Sūryavarman I's jewel while Frank Reynolds notes that the Emerald Buddha is crafted from a highly revered jewel that was previously worshiped.

historical narratives that relate to certain political and religious events of fifteenth and sixteenth-century Lanna.[5] While the texts vary to a certain extent, all three include descriptions of the origins of the Emerald Buddha and its enshrinement in important Buddhist kingdoms. Beyond these early narratives, there exists an extensive bibliography associated with the Emerald Buddha (Rod-ari 2010: 1-10, 50-57). While most scholars agree on the icon's political and religious symbolism, there has been little consensus as to its date of artistic production.

The Politics of Lanna and the Emerald Buddha Icon in the Fifteenth Century

Although chronicles related to the Emerald Buddha would like us to believe that the story of the icon begins in 44 CE when it was purported to be fashioned from the *cakkavatti*'s wish-granting jewel, its origins date to the first half of the fifteenth century in Lanna during the reigns of King Sam Fang Kaen (r. 1401-41) and his son Tilok (r. 1441-87). The Lanna Kingdom (Kingdom of a Million Rice Fields) is situated in what is today Northern Thailand and some adjacent parts of present-day China, Laos, and Myanmar. Like many early kingdoms of Southeast Asia, the constant shifting of alliances resulted in ever-fluctuating political borders. The *mueang* (principalities) of Chiang Rai and Chiang Mai were important to Lanna and significant to the origins of the Emerald Buddha. The latter became the capital of Lanna in 1296 and served as the capital for both kings Sam Fang Kaen and Tilok.

King Sam Fang Kaen, having not supported the Buddhist *saṅgha,* but instead worshiping animist deities, is remembered in history as

[5] These three chronicles fall under the literary category of Buddhist history albeit in different formats: *vaṁsa* (dynastic elements), *tamnān* or *pakaraṇaṁ* (legends, epoch), and *nidāna* (legends). All three formats in Northern Tai literature typically narrate Buddhist history, the transmission of Buddhism from India and Sri Lanka to various Northern Tai principalities, and the discovery and enshrinement of the Buddha's relics.

a heretic. He is described as such in the royal chronicles of Chiang Mai and is specifically described in the *Jinakālamālīpakaraṇaṁ* as,

> He who was of little faith in the Dispensation [the Dhamma] but possessing [much] faith in external systems, without betaking himself to the virtuous, greatly honored the votaries of the demons.
>
> – Jayawickrama 1968: 128

There exist conflicting descriptions of Sam Fang Kaen's support of the Buddhist faith. While the above texts portray the king as a heretic, the *Sihiṅganidāna* describes him as a believer and supporter of Buddhism (Chiu 2017: 30). Phiset Chiachanphong (2002: 11-12) has suggested that Sam Fang Kaen supported a rival Buddhist order, the Flower Garden (Suan Dok), to which the author of the *Jinakālamālīpakaraṇaṁ* and the Emerald Buddha icon narratives did not belong.

The survival and prosperity of Buddhism has long been linked to royal patronage and, without the support of the monarch, the *saṅgha* needed to revive royal support. As described by Angela Chiu, a fierce rivalry arose between two monastic orders in Lanna in the fifteenth century, the Flower Garden (Suan Dok) and Redwood Grove (Pa Daeng) orders. Texts related to both orders reflect tension between them and a desire for religious authority and lay patronage in the region (Chiu 2017: 53-60). The authors associated with the Emerald Buddha chronicles were probably of the Redwood Grove order (ibid.: 39). It is quite possible that the Redwood Grove order was hoping for increased royal support from Sam Fang Kaen's son and successor Tilok. As will be discussed later in this essay, descriptions of Tilok's greater religious merit and political authority as compared to that of his father are clearly narrated in the Emerald Buddha chronicles. In addition to seeking royal patronage, Lanna Buddhist monks of the fifteenth century were anxiously commemorating the 2,000-year anniversary of Buddhism, which was fast approaching. This anniversary was believed to fall during the years 1456-57, and following a traditional belief that

Buddhism has a limited lifespan, devotees probably feared that the 2,000th year would be marked by a decline in monastic rules and observations (Chiu 2017: 42). This seems likely to have spurred the laity, both royal and non-royal, to support the *saṅgha* and the *dhamma* through the writing of texts, construction of temples, and crafting of icons. Such concerted efforts resulted in a fluorescence of art and architecture, marking the fifteenth and sixteenth centuries as a golden period for Buddhist art in Lanna.

In addition to material support for Buddhism, the laity also sponsored monks' travel abroad to Sri Lanka in order to retrieve texts and relics and to be re-ordained. One such example was an expedition of approximately twenty-five monks from Chiang Mai to Sri Lanka in 1423 (Cœdès 1926: 104-08; Jayawickrama 1968: 126-31; Le May 1963: 132).[6] By traveling to Sri Lanka, this group of monks and their patrons sought to restore what they believed to be the purest form of Theravāda Buddhism in Lanna by re-establishing the Sīhalabhikkhunikāya or Sinhalese order (Le May 1963: 132). Information regarding this mission is described in the *Jinakālamālīpakaraṇaṁ*, which explains that the monks stayed in Sri Lanka for four months before returning to Lanna via Ayutthaya, Sukhothai, and Sawankhalok in 1424-25 and eventually returned to Chiang Mai in 1430 (Jayawickrama 1968: 130-31). After a short sojourn in Chiang Mai, many of the monks dispersed to Lamphun, Lampang, Chiang Rai, and Chiang Saen while others remained to establish monasteries (Cœdès 1926: 104-08). One of these monasteries, the Redwood Grove Monastery in Chiang Mai, was the main residence of the author of the *Jinakālamālīpakaraṇaṁ* (Cœdès 1926: 104-08; Jayawickrama 1968: 132-33; Le May 1963: 132).[7] It is unclear if Brahmarājapaññā, the author of the *Ratanabimbavaṁsa,*

[6] According to Cœdès, the monks from Chiang Mai were also joined by eight monks from Cambodia.

[7] All of the monasteries associated with this particular group of monks were called Wat Rattavana.

had equally direct ties to this group of monks.[8] However, as Chiu argues, the author of the Emerald Buddha chronicle was probably a member of the Redwood Grove order (Chiu 2017: 39).

Upon their return to Lanna, some of these monks appear to have continued to struggle for monarchical support as is indicated in the chronicles by their critical treatment of Sam Fang Kaen. Therefore, it would have been in their best interests to devise a plan that would attract royal patronage in order to sustain their order, specifically, and the future of Buddhism more generally. This plan, I argue, materialized in the genesis of the Emerald Buddha's narrative and icon. While the *Ratanabimbavaṁsa, Jinakālamālīpakaraṇam,* and *Amaragaṭabuddharūpanidāna* do not mention such intentions, all three of the texts begin the Emerald Buddha's genesis with the monk Nāgasena's desire to have an image of the Buddha made in order to ensure the longevity of the *dhamma*. This aspiration parallels the monks' own concerns. Moreover, the chronicles repeatedly describe the Emerald Buddha as only availing itself to kings of great religious merit.

Sam Fang Kaen's lack of faith is described in all three texts, which clearly state that, although the Emerald Buddha was revealed during his reign, he did not come into possession of it. According to the texts, the Emerald Buddha was enshrined in Chiang Rai, the former capital of Lanna, and was originally covered in layers of plaster, when it was struck by lightning revealing its true form (Bowring 1857: 316-19; Jayawickrama 1968: 145). This is curious as nowhere prior in the chronicles is it ever explained that the Emerald Buddha's identity was concealed. In fact, the jewel icon is consistently praised and worshiped for its status as the *cakkavatti*'s wish-granting jewel. The revelation of the Emerald Buddha at this juncture in the narrative was likely a rhetorical device to manifest

[8] Some of the monks who traveled to Sri Lanka are named specifically; however, neither Brahmarājapaññā nor Ratanapaññā Thera are named. I am not taking into account the author of the *Amaragaṭabuddharūpanidāna* as it post-dates both the earlier texts.

Sam Fang Kaen's lack of merit as he had tried to have the icon moved to his capital of Chiang Mai with no success. Instead, the Emerald Buddha was successfully moved to the capital by his son and successor, Tilok, and enshrined at Wat Chedi Luang *c.*1468 or 1481 (Bowring 1857: 316-19; Wyatt and Aroonrut Wichienkeeo 1998: 102-03).[9] It is from this time that we have physical evidence of the Emerald Buddha in Lanna.

By all standard measures, Tilok was not destined for the throne. He was the sixth son of Sam Fang Kaen, however an ambitious minor palace official named Sam Dek Yoi helped to overthrow the king and enthrone Tilok in 1442 (Wyatt 1984: 66). Unlike his father, Tilok is remembered in the chronicles as a great Buddhist king and was rewarded with possession of the Emerald Buddha. During his reign, several Buddhist temples were built in addition to the convening of the Eighth Buddhist Council at Wat Chet Yot in Chiang Mai in 1477 (Chiu 2017: 42; Reynolds 1978: 186).[10] Tilok's possession of the Emerald Buddha is in keeping with the pattern described in the chronicles whereby only Buddhist kings who actively sponsored the *saṅgha* were able to enshrine the icon in their territories. As described in the chronicles, when such support waivered or the actions of the king were not in keeping with the *dhamma*, the Emerald Buddha departed to find a suitable new patron (Jayawickrama 1968; Notton 1931; Saeng Monwithun 1967).

The question that begs to be answered is: were the Emerald Buddha narrative and icon invented by Tilok or were they invented

---

[9] In a letter to Sir John Bowring, King Mongkut states that the Emerald Buddha was enshrined at Wat Chedi Luang by King Tilok in 1468. However, the main *stūpa* at the temple constructed under the patronage of Tilok was not begun until 1475 and was not finished until 1478-79. It is possible that the image was moved to Chiang Mai in 1468 but was not enshrined at Wat Chedi Luang until after its completion in 1481.

[10] Since the time of the Emerald Buddha's enshrinement in Thailand and Laos, the icon has always been placed near a complete copy of the Pāli canon.

by the monks of the Redwood Grove order? In the following pages, I will argue that Tilok's interest in expanding his political authority in the region resulted in the encouragement of monks to create narratives that would help him to manifest his sovereignty. Additionally, the production of such narratives also benefited monks who had their own religious and political agendas.

The lack of a centralized political structure in fifteenth century Lanna allowed local rulers to govern with a certain degree of autonomy from the king. In order to expand and simultaneously centralize his authority, Tilok used Buddhism as a means to unify disparate communities. It is quite possible that the transformation of the "green stone" from a local guardian deity into the Emerald Buddha during Tilok's reign was the result of such a projection of authority. As Dhida Saraya (1982: 103-05) has argued, Tilok's dispersal of icons and monastic land donations were tactics that the king used to project his authority over territories (see also Chiu 2017: 45). Furthermore, the chronicles associated with the Emerald Buddha, as well as other "traveling image chronicles" that likely emerged during Tilok's reign, relate stories of the icons helping to spread the Buddhist faith while at the same time centralizing the authority of their possessor and establishing their place of enshrinement as a Buddhist center (Rod-ari 2009: 55-61). In this way, the chronicles parallel Tilok's own agenda.

The Birth of an Icon

It is clear that the monk(s) who invented the Emerald Buddha narrative were knowledgeable about Buddhist and local history because references to earlier historical and Buddhist writings are included in the texts. Close examination of the *Ratanabimbavaṁsa, Jinakālamālīpakaraṇaṁ,* and *Amaragaṭabuddharūpanidāna* reveals that they reference earlier well-known texts such as the *Traiphum Phra Ruang* (*Three Worlds According to King Ruang*) and the *Sihiṅganidāna* (*Chronicle of the Sihing Buddha*).

The *Traiphum Phra Ruang* was written in 1345 by Prince Phya Lithai who later became King Ruang (r. 1347-68) of Sukhothai. The text is a cosmological treatise that deals with several issues; among them are the ordering of the Buddhist cosmos, karmic retribution and requisites for proper Buddhist kingship. Of particular interest to this essay is a section dedicated to the subject of the *cakkavatti*. The text explains that the marker of a *cakkavatti* in the world is the appearance of a gem *cakka* (wheel):

> The gem wheel is not made by an Indra, a Brahma, or a *devāta* who has great magical powers, but comes to be on its own. It comes to be because of the great merit of the Lord who is the great Chakravartin king. In any *kappa* (aeon) in which there is neither a Buddha nor a Pacceka Buddha, there is a great Chakravartin instead. In such a *kappa*, after the earth is consumed by fire, the gem wheel comes to be before anything else, and does so by the merit of the one who is going to become the Chakravartin king.
>
> — Reynolds and Reynolds 1982: 139

While scholars, such as Reynolds, have argued that the *amarakaṭa* (emerald jewel) from which the Emerald Buddha is crafted was likely the same gem *cakka* described in the *Traiphum Phra Ruang*, the Emerald Buddha chronicles make it clear that Indra was unable to secure the *cakkavatti's maṇījôti* (resplendent jewel) and was instead given the emerald jewel (Reynolds 1978: 181-83). Drawing this distinction, however, should not summarily dismiss the importance of the Emerald Buddha's material make-up and its association with the *cakkavatti*. Instead, one should think of the gem *cakka* as a manifestation of the *cakkavatti*'s political sovereignty and military prowess — visualized as a chariot wheel — whereas the *amarakaṭa* jewel, carved into the likeness of the Buddha, was a manifestation of the *cakkavatti*'s Buddhist sovereignty. Indeed, as the *Traiphum Phra Ruang* describes:

> The great Cakkavatti king knows merit and Dhamma, and teaches the people to know the Dhamma; it is as if the Lord Buddha had been born and was teaching the people to live according to the

Dhamma. — Reynolds and Reynolds 1982: 147-48

What this excerpt suggests is that the author(s) of the Emerald Buddha chronicles not only made references to this earlier royal text, but also sought ways in which to expand upon some of its main themes to their benefit.

As described in their respective texts, both the Emerald Buddha and the gem *cakka* only appear before a king who proves his great religious merit. It is quite plausible that the author(s) of the original Emerald Buddha narrative had read the *Traiphum Phra Ruang*, which, according to the Reynolds, had become an important text since the time of its writing (ibid.: 6). The careful distinction made between the *maṇījôti* and the *amarakaṭa* jewels in the Emerald Buddha chronicles could, therefore, have been for the express purpose of making clear the dependent relationship between political authority and religious authority.

In addition to the *Traiphum Phra Ruang*, another important narrative that informs the Emerald Buddha's chronicles is the *Sihiṅganidāna*, which describes the origins of the Phra Sihing image and events associated with it. The text was written around 1410 by the monk Bodhiramsī Mahāthera (Chiu 2017: 20; Penth 1994: 354; Stratton 2004: 91). Like the Emerald Buddha chronicles, the *Sihiṅganidāna* begins with the mythological circumstances under which the Phra Sihing image came into existence. The *Sihiṅganidāna* explains that the Phra Sihing image was sculpted in Sri Lanka 700 years after the Buddha's *parinibbāna* when three Buddhist kings asked a group of *arahants* (enlightened beings) if they had ever seen the Buddha when he was living — none had (Jayawickrama 1968: 120). At that moment, a *nāga* king who overheard their conversations, and who had seen the Buddha, transformed himself into the Great Teacher's likeness. After basking in the *nāga*-turned-Buddha's image, the three kings had a metal image cast based on witnesses' memory of the occasion. This description in the text posits that the Phra Sihing image is the most authentic image of the Buddha because it was based on his "portrait." Beyond describing the Phra Sihing's origins, the text also outlines the icon's travels from Sri Lanka to various kingdoms in modern-day Thailand (Sukhothai, Ayutthaya, Kamphaeng Phet, and Chiang Mai). According to the chronicle, 1,800 years after the Buddha's *parinibbāna*, the icon traveled to Sukhothai where it was enshrined by King Ruang — the author of the *Traiphum Phra Ruang* (Jayawickrama 1968: 121). During its enshrinement in Sukhothai, it brought great wealth and prestige to the king and to the city. Hearing of the Phra Sihing's powers and virtues, competing kings sought to acquire the icon as a palladium for their kingdoms. After the death of King Ruang, and through a series of cunning maneuvers and manipulations, two additional copies of the Phra Sihing were crafted in Kamphaeng Phet and Chiang Rai (Chiu 2017: 28-29). Today, three sculptures of the Phra Sihing circulate in Thailand and will be discussed shortly.

Hiram W. Woodward Jr. (1997: 502-03) has argued that the Emerald Buddha and Phra Sihing sculptures were intended to serve as a complimentary pair: the Emerald Buddha, crafted in *deva* heaven demonstrates its aerial qualities, and the Phra Sihing image, aided by the *nāga*, its watery aspects. Woodward also argues that the Emerald Buddha image may have been expressly invented to serve as a complement to the Phra Sihing image. He bases his argument on the fact that the *Sihiṅganidāna* was written in 1410, and that the earliest comparable text for the Emerald Buddha, the *Ratanabimbavaṁsa,* was written later. According to Woodward, "when the two accounts are compared, it becomes apparent that the author of the latter text modeled his account on the *Sihiṅganidāna*" (1997: 503). As I have previously suggested, the Emerald Buddha's formal characteristics were likely modeled after those of the Phra Sihing image, which, as the chronicles suggest, was a famous regional icon by the late fourteenth century. The remainder of this essay will focus on the Emerald Buddha's date of artistic production and argues that it was crafted in the first half of the fifteenth century.

The Making of an Icon

In order for an image of the Buddha to have religious efficacy, it must have some likeness or relationship to the Buddha himself. As noted by Stanley J. Tambiah,

> ... it is held that in order to inherit some fraction of the infinite virtue and power the Buddha possessed, an image must trace its linage back to one made in the 'authentic' likeness of the Master.
> – 1974: 6

In fifteenth-century Lanna, the most authentic likeness of the Buddha was the Phra Sihing image, which, according to its narrative, had been modeled after a "portrait" of the Buddha and was depicted seated in *vīrāsana* with its hands in *dhyāna-mudrā*. It is noteworthy that the *Sihiṅganidāna,* unlike other chronicles of its kind, is the only one that clearly states the iconography of the particular Buddha icon it is narrating (Chiu 2017: 154). To date, there are currently three extant images of the Phra Sihing claimed to be the original, which are located at the Buddhaisawan Chapel in the Bangkok National Museum, Wat Phra Singh in Chiang Mai, and the Office of Government and Justice in Nakhon Si Thammarat. Only one of these three, the image in Bangkok, has the iconography described in the *Sihiṅganidāna*. However, this sculpture is unlikely to be the original as it is probably a mid–late fifteenth-century sculpture (*fig.* 14.2).[11] As Carol Stratton has argued, the Bangkok icon demonstrates formal qualities, such as "extraordinary long and graceful fingers" of the same length, which were typical of Lanna and Post Classic Sukhothai images from the mid-fifteenth century onwards (2004: 274).

While the location/existence of the original Phra Sihing image is unknown, it is clear that the Emerald Buddha chronicles and icon responded to this earlier palladium. The Emerald Buddha

[11] The Phra Sihing images in Nakhon Si Thammarat and Chiang Mai are seated in *vajrāsana* and exhibit the *bhūmisparśa-mudrā*. This particular combination became popular during the reign of Tilok.

is depicted seated in *vīrāsana* with its hands in *dhyāna-mudrā*, suggesting that the Phra Sihing image could very well have been the archetype for the Emerald Buddha sculpture as is demonstrated by their identical postures. Moreover, if one revisits the chronicles, it is clear that the author(s) wanted to create a story for the Emerald Buddha that expanded its scope and power beyond existing "traveling image chronicles" such as the *Sihiṅganidāna*. For example, instead of being crafted on earth at the behest of royal laymen like the Phra Sihing, the Emerald Buddha was made in heaven at the behest of the monk Nāgasena (Jayawickrama 1968; Notton 1931; Saeng Monwithun 1967). Moreover, according to their respective chronicles, the Phra Sihing was associated with only Sinhalese and Tai kings, whereas the Emerald Buddha became a sought-after icon by Indian, Sinhalese, Khmer, Burmese, and Tai kings.

The earliest extant datable image that can be artistically linked to the Emerald Buddha is found at Wat Suan Dok (Flower Garden Monastery) in Chiang Mai. This temple was built in 1371 by the Lanna King Kü Na (r. 1367-85) (Stratton 2004: 184). The Buddha image at Wat Suan Dok, while not inscribed with a date, is believed to have been cast sometime between the temple's construction in 1371 and the death of the king in 1385 (*fig.* 14.3). Like the Emerald Buddha image, the Wat Suan Dok image is also seated in the *vīrāsana* posture with hands in *dhyāna-mudrā*. The articulation of the hands and feet of both Buddha images is strikingly similar in that they are depicted with puffy pads on the fingertips and toes. This exaggeration is not typically seen on Lanna images and suggests artistic influence from Sukhothai and Sinhalese examples dated to the Gampola period (1344–1409), which became popular in Lanna by the late fourteenth century and lingered until the end of the fifteenth century. Historical evidence for Sukhothai and Sinhalese artistic and religious influence in Lanna dates to the time of King Kü Na, who invited the monk Sumana from Sukhothai to establish the Sinhalese order in 1369 and who became the abbot of Wat Suan Dok until 1389 (Wyatt 1984: 65). It is likely that Sumana would have been aware of the Phra Sihing icon, which is believed to have been enshrined in Sukhothai during the reign of King Ruang (1298–1346/47) and later in Chiang Mai sometime during the reign of King Saen Muang Ma (r. 1385–1401). What this suggests is that the style of the Wat Suan Dok and Phra Sihing images may have been a major iconic and artistic type in the region during the late fourteenth century and thus could have spawned other "copies." The importance of copying is suggested by Alexander B. Griswold who writes:

> When the patron who commissioned an image was a rationalist, he wanted the comprehensible and undisturbing symbolism that was already familiar; and if he happened to be sensitive to beauty he chose a model that gave him aesthetic satisfaction as conveying more perfectly the Sage's [Buddha] qualities. On the other hand, when the patron wanted a talisman that would inherit some fraction of the Buddha's infinite power, he would seek to assure its legitimacy in the line of descent from one of the legendary authentic likeness; and so he would choose as a model some statue that had already proved itself by displaying unusual magical qualities. – 1961: 37

If the Emerald Buddha represents such a prevailing model, this would mean that a major iconic type in Lanna during the first half of the fifteenth century included a combination of Sinhalese and Lanna stylistic features. For example, Sinhalese influence can be seen in the Emerald Buddha's aforementioned articulated foot and finger pads, rounded "mango nut" chin, and the iconographical combination of *vīrāsana* and *dhyāna-mudrā*. Its Lanna qualities include ears splayed out from the face and pointed at both ends with slight recessions to indicate piercings. Pointed ears became a common feature of Lanna Buddha images from the fifteenth century onwards. Also situating the Emerald Buddha in the first half of the fifteenth century is its posture in *vīrāsana* and *dhyāna-mudrā*, which ceased to be major iconographic types by the second half of the fifteenth century under King Tilok, when it was replaced by the *vajrāsana* and *bhūmisparśa-mudrā* (earth touching) seated posture.[12] Lastly, the Emerald Buddha's long thin shawl is depicted lying almost at the center of its chest and ending at its lap, which was typical of early fifteenth-century Buddha sculptures in Lanna (Stratton 2004: 185). The treatment of the shawl is also similar to the Phra Sihing Buddha in Bangkok, which Stratton has argued was likely crafted in the middle of the fifteenth century.[13]

The mid-to-late fifteenth century date of the *Ratanabimbavaṁsa*, the earliest of the Emerald Buddha chronicles, coupled with the icon's formal stylistic qualities, as outlined by this essay, securely place the origins of the Emerald Buddha in the first half of the fifteenth century. It is a testament to the monk(s) who invented the Emerald Buddha chronicle that the icon and its story continue to be told in the twenty-first century. Since its invention, the Emerald Buddha has been a highly revered and sought-after icon by kings in Lanna and Laos. Today, the Emerald Buddha is the palladium of the Kingdom of Thailand and resides in the royal chapel, Wat Phra Kaew, at the Grand Palace in Bangkok where it is continually worshipped by the laity — both royal and non-royal. Its fame also extends beyond that of Buddhists to include visitors of all religious faiths who visit the Grand Palace, which is a major tourist destination in Bangkok. In this way, the monk(s) who invented the Emerald Buddha narrative fulfilled the desire, both of Nāgasena and themselves, to make a Buddha image in order to increase the prosperity of Buddhism in the world. Furthermore, the powerful associations between the Emerald Buddha and the presence of a *cakkavatti* in the world has ensured continued royal

---

[12] According to Alexander B. Griswold, the Phra Singh (Lion) Buddha image, characterized by the *vajrāsana* and *bhūmisparśa-mudrā*, was the main image type produced in Lanna during King Tilok's reign. The first Phra Singh image commissioned by the king was installed at the Temple of Seven Spires (Wat Chet Yot) sometime between 1455, when building began, and 1470, when building ended. See Griswold 1957: 38.

[13] Both the Phra Sihing images in Nakhon Si Thammarat and Chiang Mai have short shawls that end slightly above the Buddha icon's left pectoral.

patronage of both the image and the Buddhist *saṅgha* since the fifteenth century in Thailand and in Laos where the icon is known to have been enshrined.

Acknowledgments

Much of the research presented in this essay comes from my doctoral work and dissertation under the tutelage of Prof. Brown. It was his article, "The Miraculous Buddha Image: Portrait, God, or Object?," in which he discusses the symbolic and very real power of the Emerald Buddha, that inspired me to examine the history of the icon and how it came to be the most important Buddha image in Thailand. I wish to thank Prof. Brown for his patience, encouragement, and most of all for leading his students by example.

References

Bowring, John, 1857, *The King and People of Siam*, vols. I and II, London: John W. Parker and Son.

Brown, Robert L., 1998, "The Miraculous Buddha Image: Portrait, God, or Object?," in *Images, Miracles, and Authority in Asian Religious Traditions,* ed. Richard H. Davis, pp. 37-54, Boulder: Westview Press.

Chiu, Angela, 2017, *The Buddha in Lanna: Art, Lineage, Power, and Place in Northern Thailand,* Honolulu: University of Hawai'i Press.

Cœdès, George, 1915, "Note sur les ouvrages palis composés en pays thai," *Bulletin de l'École française d'Extreme-Orient,* 15(3): 39-46.

——, 1926, "Documents sur l'histoire politique et religieuse du Laos occidental," *Bulletin de l'École Française d'Extreme-Orient*, 25(1-2): 1-201.

The Chronicle of the Emerald Buddha, see Notton 1931.

Dhida Saraya, 1982 (unpublished), "The Development of the Northern Thai States from the Twelfth to the Fifteenth Centuries," Doctoral Dissertation, University of Sydney.

Griswold, Alexander B., 1957, "Dated Buddha Images in Northern Siam," *Artibus Asiae Supplementum*, 16: 1-99.

——, 1961, "The Architecture and Sculpture of Siam," in *The Arts of Thailand: A Handbook of the Architecture, Sculpture, and Painting of*

Thailand, ed. Theodore Bowie, pp. 25-166, Bloomington, Indiana: Indiana University Press.

——, 1965, "The Holy Land Transported: Replicas of the Mahabodhi Shrine in Siam and Elsewhere," in *Paranavitana Felicitation Volume*, ed. N.A. Jayawickrama, pp. 173-221, Colombo: Guasena.

——, 1966, "Imported Images and the Nature of Copying in the Art of Siam," *Artibus Asiae Supplementum*, 23, *Essays Offered to G.H. Luce by His Colleagues and Friends in Honor of His Seventy-fifth Birthday*, 2: 37-73.

Jayawickrama, N.A. (tr.), 1968, *The Sheaf of Garlands of the Epochs of the Conqueror: Being a Translation of Jinakālamālīpakaraṇaṁ of Ratanapañña Thera of Thailand*, London: Luzac and Company.

Le May, Reginald, 1963, *A Concise History of Buddhist Art in Siam*, Rutland: C.E. Tuttle Co.

Lingat, Robert, 1934, "Le Culte du Bouddha d'Emeraude," *Journal of the Siam Society*, 27: 9-38.

Mongkut, H.R.H., 1961, *Tamnan Phra Kaeow Morokot Chabap Sombu*, Phranakhōṇ (Bangkok): Bannākhān. [In Thai]

Notton, Camille (tr.), 1931, *The Chronicle of the Emerald Buddha*, Bangkok: Bangkok Times Press.

—— (tr.), 1933, *P'ra Buddha Sihinga*, Bangkok: Bangkok Times Press.

Penth, Hans, 1994, *Jinakālimāli Index: An Annotated Index to the Thailand Part of Ratanapanna's Chronicle*, Oxford: Pali Text Society.

Phiset Chiechanphong, 2002, *Ha Phra Ha Chao: Ruam Botkhhwam Thang Wichakan Kiaokup Khwammai Tahng Sangkhomlæ Watthanatham Khong Borannawatthulæ Borannasathan*, Bangkok: Matichon. [In Thai]

P'ra Buddha Sihinga, see Notton 1933.

Reynolds, Frank E., 1978, "The Holy Emerald Jewel: Some Aspects of Buddhist Symbolism and Political Legitimation in Thailand and Laos," in *Religion and Legitimation of Power in Thailand, Laos and Burma*, ed. Bardwell L. Smith, pp. 175-94, Chambersburg: Anima Books.

Reynolds, Frank E. and Mani B. Reynolds, 1982, *Three Worlds According to King Ruang: A Thai Buddhist Cosmology*, Berkeley Buddhist Series, no. 4, Berkeley: University of California Press.

Rod-ari, Melody, 2010 [unpublished], "Visualizing Merit: An Art Historical Study of the Emerald Buddha and Wat Phra Kaew", Doctoral Dissertation, University of California, Los Angeles.

——, 2009, "Thailand: The Symbolic Center of the Theravada Buddhist World," *Explorations: A Graduate Student Journal of Southeast Asian Studies*, 9: 55-64.

Saeng Monwithun (tr.), 1987, *Ratanaphimphawong: Tamnan Phra Kaew Morokot*, Bangkok: Krom Silapakorn. [In Thai]

Skilling, Peter and Santi Pakdeekham, 2004, *Pali and Vernacular Literature Transmitted in Central and Northern Siam*, Bangkok: Fragile Palm Leaves Foundation.

Stratton, Carol, 2004, *Buddhist Sculpture of Northern Thailand*, Chiang Mai: Silkworm Books.

Tambiah, S. J., 1974, "Famous Buddha Images and the Legitimation of Kings, the Case of the Sinhala Buddha in Thailand", *RES*, 4: 5-19.

Woodward, Hiram W., Jr., 1997, "The Emerald Buddha and Sihing Buddhas: Interpretations of Their Significance", in *Living in Accord with the Dhamma*, eds. Natasha Eilenberg, M.C. Subhadradis Diskul, and Robert L. Brown, pp. 335-42, Bangkok: Silpakorn University.

Wyatt, David K., 1984, *Thailand: A Short History*, New Haven: Yale University Press.

Wyatt, David K. and Aroonrut Wichienkeeo, 1998, *Chiang Mai Chronicles*, Chiang Mai: Silkworm Books.

15

Representing Heaven in Thai Painting

Rebecca S. Hall

Residents in Thailand, Laos, and Cambodia frequently talk about making merit for the purpose of going to heaven or in hope of sending deceased family members there. Because of this common goal, I have focused my research on representations of heaven across the visual arts in an attempt to reconcile whether Buddhist texts and visual imagery reinforce the widespread dominance of heaven in Southeast Asian religious thought. Until I spent significant time doing field research in Southeast Asia, I had not realized the dominance of heaven in merit-making and future birth goals because of its general absence in academic discussions of art and practice. Recent publications have worked to add local practices and beliefs into the larger scholarly dialogue (see, for example, Chiu 2017; Pattaratorn Chirapravati 2012; 2013; Collins 2016; Green 2015; McDaniel 2011). Yet, rather than applying practice and local belief into their studies, publications on the region's Buddhist art largely focus on the narratives, styles, and iconography of Buddhist sculpture and painting, or on placing these into cultural and historical contexts. This essay is an attempt to find reflections of local practices and beliefs in popular painted imagery and highlight connections between those images, the stories they illustrate, and the predominance of heaven in visions of kārmic rewards.

Buddhist cosmology offers an abundance of possibilities for rebirth in a complex system tied to karmic retribution. The Buddhist universe has thirty-one realms of existence, ranging from torturous hells to cerebral, formless heavens. The organization is vertically arranged, with the sub-human worlds, including hells and realms of hungry ghosts, at the bottom and increasingly formless and abstract worlds at the top. Because twenty-six of those realms are identifiable as "heavens," is it possible to make connections between the various heavenly realms and the "heaven" described in more general terms by contemporary Southeast Asian Buddhist laity? I argue that the predominance of specific iconography in painted images of heaven is evidence of local connections with Indra's heaven, to the exclusion of other heavenly realms. These connections tie together local concepts of rewards for a merit-filled life with longstanding Buddhist themes and iconography. This study of popular representations and the continued presence of Indra's Heaven in the arts at Buddhist monasteries of Thailand and surrounding countries helps achieve greater insight into the popular fixation on this particular heaven and its rewards.

Just as current scholarship has examined the local variations in narrative and textual traditions, the study of painted images needs to address local nuances and the way that images work to appeal to specific groups of people (Bowie 2017: 13-14). By blending the study of style and iconography with anthropological approaches, a great deal of insight can be gained.

Steven Collins has explored the significance of heaven as integral to the path from desire to renunciation and has highlighted the attention focused on Buddhist heavens in the premodern Pāli *imaginaire* (2006: 297). He warns that "it is easy to overlook the Buddhist heavens" and instead focus attention on *nibbāṇa* (Skt. *nirvāṇa*), but doing so distorts our understanding of the religion and its practice. Although Collins focuses his analysis on textual descriptions of the full cosmological hierarchy, his discussion serves as a guide for further evaluation of the infiltration of heaven into common Southeast Asian practice.

Any understanding of heavenly realms is intrinsically tied to the making of merit (*puñña*) and its eventual rewards. Merit can be made through proper actions, including wisdom, renunciation, and patience. However, generosity through donations (*dāna*) is often the main focus of merit-making because it is both achievable and central to the survival of the religion. It functions as a contract between monks and laity that is renewed on a regular basis (Findly 2003: 1). Everyone can make merit through proper actions, and the benefits of improved rebirth, especially rebirth in heaven, is available to all — rich or poor, urban or rural. The connection between merit and heaven appeals to nearly everyone and its repeated representation in texts and art solidifies its allure.

Although twenty-six heavenly worlds are believed to exist in the Buddhist universe, the one most commonly depicted in mainland Southeast Asia paintings is Indra's Heaven, known as Tāvatiṁsa in Pāli or Daowadeung in Thai. Because this heaven is presided over by Indra, the king of the gods, it is rife with royal and divine symbolism and has appealed to Buddhist kings since at least the reign of Aśoka (Strong 2004: 66-67). Discussions of Indra's Heaven often highlight these royal connections. They describe the heaven and the relics enshrined there as forming a specific relationship to the Buddhist concept of the ideal world ruler (*cakkavatti*), who is not only the embodiment of the *dhamma* but also rules by it (Swearer 2010: 73). But Indra's Heaven also has a widespread popular appeal that extends beyond kingship, at least in part because this heaven is an attainable aspiration, offers concrete comprehensive rewards, and exists within our realm of understanding.

As Nandana Chutiwongs states:

> The heaven of Indra is, in general, representative of the human concept of paradise, resplendent with the ultimate sublimation of the glory and the pleasures as can be conceived by man. — 2008: 38

Texts tell of the long lives and magnificent happiness achieved by those beings born in Tāvatiṁsa; its attainable rewards have led many among the laity to see it as an ideal goal. Specifically, the *Traiphum Phra Ruang* (*Three Worlds According to King Ruang*) is a key document for understanding Buddhist cosmology in a Thai context. This text was composed in 1345 by Phya Lithai (later King Lithai) when he was heir to the throne of the Sukhothai kingdom (Reynolds and Reynolds 1982: 5). It was recopied over many centuries, often to conform to the ideals of subsequent Thai kings, but it has held continued relevance in monks' sermons (Reynolds 1976: 204). This Thai language treatise on the realms of existence is a compilation of over thirty different Buddhist sources and has maintained popularity over the centuries, even serving as the content for the earliest known illustrated Thai manuscripts, dated to the seventeenth and eighteenth centuries (Ginsburg 1989: 13). Although the creation of illustrated *Traiphum* manuscripts waned in Thailand in the late eighteenth century, the depiction of the Buddhist cosmology continues to hold importance in *wat* murals, especially in Bangkok and the surrounding region of central Thailand. However, in neighboring countries such as Myanmar, cosmology manuscripts remained popular into the late nineteenth century (Green 2015: 42-69).

Understanding the complexity of the Buddhist universe as presented in cosmological manuscripts is foundational for a discussion of heaven. However, the heaven that has the most to offer laity is Tāvatiṁsa. Recognizing it through its attributes helps shed light on how and why this heaven in particular has gained dominance in the visions of Buddhists across the region.

Painted Images of Heaven

In paintings, heaven is made recognizable through repeated iconography with a range of overlapping elements. Visual emphasis in representations of Indra's Heaven parallel the descriptions in Buddhist texts, popular stories, and local narratives, and highlight many of the ideal aspects that contribute to that realm's widespread appeal. As the god-king presiding over Tāvatiṁsa, Indra (also known as Sakka) is essential to its representation. In Buddhism, Indra is associated with virtuous humans and he is a supporter of Buddhist ideals (Appleton 2016: 38). In Thai painting, he is usually depicted as a green-skinned, crowned figure no larger than average humans and celestial beings. Sometimes flying and sometimes seated, he interacts with figures who are either visiting his heaven or about to depart for rebirth on earth. Indra is also popular among many mainland Southeast Asian Buddhists because of his association with rain and fertility, his appearance in popular stories, his connection to the creation of powerful Buddha images, and his role in Jātakas and the Buddha's life story as a protector of Buddhism (Chiu 2017: 86; Reynolds 1978: 181-82).

Painted images of Indra's Heaven are overwhelmingly focused on its luxuries and the sacred and archetypal Cūḷāmaṇi *stūpa* (Thai: *chedi*). The nineteenth-century painted cloth example in *fig*. 15.1 is one such example. In the upper section of this painting the Buddha stands with his two disciples but, more important for the present discussion, at the bottom is a depiction of Indra's Heaven with the Cūḷāmaṇi *stūpa* as the central focus. Because the Cūḷāmaṇi *stūpa* is often described as holding two relics from the Buddha, it is sometimes depicted as being two separate *stūpas*, as can be seen here (note the white wall surrounding the *stūpas*). The Cūḷāmaṇi signifies Indra's Heaven as not simply a luscious and rich paradise, but also as an ideal reward for practicing Buddhists. The opportunity to continue to make merit at this *stūpa* is particularly important because the nature of heaven as a place for relaxation and riches does not provide many opportunities for merit-making activities. The accessibility of the Cūḷāmaṇi ensures that those beings who reside in heaven will be able to continue their progress towards perfection in their next birth.

Though described in the *Traiphum* as tall beyond comprehension, most paintings depict the *stūpa* as relatively small and resembling the shape of a *stūpa* typically seen in nineteenth-century Thailand — the features include the spire, bell, and base (Reynolds and Reynolds 1982: 232). The Cūḷāmaṇi is described in the *Traiphum* as a sight to behold, with a surface that has been covered with pure gold and seven types of gems and as being surrounded by numerous flags and parasols (ibid.: 232). Most paintings of the Cūḷāmaṇi illustrate it as a rich emerald jewel with a gold base and a spire covered with garlands of gold (*figs*. 15.1 and 15.2). The emerald coloration functions as both a connection to the green-skinned Indra and as a jewel that reflects the richness of heaven (Reynolds 1978: 181). Offerings of flowers, candles, or food may be depicted in front of the *stūpa*. Any variety of objects can flank the Cūḷāmaṇi: long poles topped with *hong* (*haṁsa*) or *nak* (*nāga*), banners, flags, lanterns, and an array of regalia. Each of these elements of decoration is placed around the *stūpa* to set it apart from the heavenly landscape and to honor it as a reminder of the Buddha.

In these scenes, devotional objects are essential because they indicate the visual and ritual focus of the *stūpa*. The objects beautify the Cūḷāmaṇi and proclaim the *stūpa* as a place of worship at the very heart of religious practice. The depictions often echo contemporary practice in Thailand. For example, a pair of banners is often depicted hanging next to the *stūpa*, one on either side. In *fig*. 15.1, banners are depicted, hanging from long poles on either side of the Cūḷāmaṇi *stūpa*. One also sees similar banners in northern Thailand, Laos, and Cambodia that are, appropriately enough, often donated for the purpose of aspiring to rebirth in heaven. Their depiction in the paintings links our earthly realm with Indra's Heaven, connecting merit-making in this life to a future practice of merit-making in the next heavenly realm.

Royal regalia is sometimes featured in representations of heaven alongside the Cūḷāmaṇi *stūpa*, as seen in this example from a nineteenth-century manuscript (*fig*. 15.3). In the image provided here, replications of the insignia, fans, umbrellas, and horsehair fly whisks that are typically associated with kingship are depicted on stands next to, and nearly as large as, the gilded *stūpa*. Like the crocodile and centipede banners discussed below, these forms of royal regalia replicate conventions used in *wat*s and at *stūpa*s in Thailand and surrounding areas. These facsimiles of royal regalia can be seen stationed at the sides of Buddha images or main altars and are produced in miniature specifically to be placed next to or inside of *stūpas* that house the Buddha's relics. This regalia functions as a visual reminder of the Buddha's unique status as a revered religious teacher equal to a universal monarch, something that was emphasized in the treatment of his remains, as described in the *Mahāparinibbāṇa Sutta* (Strong 2004: 115-23; Vajira and Story 2007: 83-84). The inclusion of royal regalia next to the Cūḷāmaṇi shows that the *stūpa* houses relics of the Buddha and creates another connection between heaven and human realms.

Offerings of flowers, garlands, candles, fruits and incense are usually painted in front of the Cūḷāmaṇi *stūpa*. The offering of objects like these is often discussed in texts that highlight merit-making and honoring the Buddha. Offering these sorts of objects at a *stūpa* is described in the *Mahāparinibbāṇa Sutta* as a means for showing that the Buddha had attained the status of *cakkavatti*. The *sutta* also states, "whoever shall bring to that place garlands or incense or sandalwood paste, to pay reverence, and whose mind becomes calm there — it will be to his well-being and happiness for a long time" (Vajira and Story 2007: 84). In the paintings, these flowers are brought by visiting *devas* (Thai: *thewada*), shown flying near the *stūpa* (*figs*. 15.1 and 15.2). They reflect merit-making actions commonly made by laity in Thailand.

Shimmering palaces with large windows and tall, painted rooftops often indicate the heavenly realm. These palaces help indicate depictions of Indra's Heaven, although they are typical of all the heavens of the Buddhist universe. Sometimes the palaces are pictured in the same area as the Cūḷāmaṇi *stūpa* but many times they stand on their own. The golden, gem-toned palaces are consistent with descriptions from the *Traiphum* that highlight carefree existence in heaven as a reward for proper actions in a previous life. In the text, heaven is described as a city filled with golden buildings covered with gems and with the melodious sounds of musical instruments and the scent of perfume filling the air:

> There is a golden wall covered with gems surrounding the city that has one thousand gates at various points; and there are peaks in the form of turrets made of gold and decorated with the seven kinds of gems. ... Outside of the city on the northeastern side, there is a large park; it has a gold wall surrounding it with gem turrets on top of each of its gates. In this park are one thousand gold castles decorated with the seven kinds of gems.
>
> – Reynolds and Reynolds 1982: 224-25

In both text and painting, walled enclosures are essential to the depiction of heaven. The walls surrounding heaven are most often depicted as white, though they may also be painted in gold or brick-red. Walls are a common device at *wat*s in Thailand for isolating sacred spaces from the profane world. They are often built around entire *wat* compounds and are often specifically positioned around the main *stūpa*. The walls demarcate the sacred in both Thai architecture and in paintings of heaven. The wall imagery in representations of heaven designates the area of heaven, and more specifically the space surrounding the Cūḷāmaṇi, separating it from the abyss or empty sky and clarifying its other-worldly nature.

Banners flanking Cūḷāmaṇi are represented in a variety of shapes and colors, often replicating quite closely the items of cloth and paper that hang at *wat*s across much of Southeast Asia. Banners are typically shown in paintings as long and narrow rectangles, but at times they are represented in other shapes. They hang on long poles, sometimes from the beak or neck of *hong* (Thai) or *haṁsa* (Pāli) birds, a convention that can still be seen at *wats* in Thailand, Myanmar, and Cambodia. A painted example can be seen in *fig.* 15.1, which features long, white banners hanging around the necks of green and gold *hong*. In addition to banners, or in lieu of them, triangular flags, or pennants of white or multi-colored material are also frequently depicted as decoration for the Cūḷāmaṇi. Furthermore and with surprising regularity, the banners shown flanking Cūḷāmaṇi are depicted in the shape of crocodiles or centipedes (*fig.* 15.4). Sometimes these crocodile and centipede banners are merely shaped to resemble the creatures; other times, like in the nineteenth-century example provided here, they are painted to look as if the real animals are hanging by the *stūpa*.

These two animals hold specific significance for merit-making activities in Thailand. A story associated with these animal motifs is related to the donation of monks' robes during *kathina*, the auspicious time of year that follows the Rains Retreat. The story explains that a centipede and a crocodile wanted to participate in the donation, but because they were animals they were not allowed to join. Banners were made with their image so that the crocodile and centipede could be a part of the festivities. These banners are carried in the merit-making procession and then placed at the front of the *wat* (Hall 2008: 75; Woodward 2010: 48).

These animals wanted to honor the Buddha, and their representations remind viewers of the importance of participating in merit-making activities to whatever extent is possible in one's current existence. The painted images and their specific details, from the size and shape of the Cūḷāmaṇi to the objects surrounding it, point to clear connections between Thai contemporary practices and painted depictions of heaven. The Cūḷāmaṇi and its surrounding area become the heavenly version of the local *wat*, as reflected in the regional use of the crocodile and the centipede. This visual link emphasizes the reality of heaven, provides a connection to the lives of common people, and demonstrates that the rewards of merit can be enjoyed by all.

Popular Buddhist Narratives and Indra's Heaven

Painted images of Indra's Heaven are most often featured in illustrations of — or visual imagery related to — popular stories recited by monks and laity. In addition to its description in the *Traiphum*, Indra's Heaven, complete with the Cūḷāmaṇi, appears in several different popular narratives. When these stories are depicted in paintings, artists use the opportunity to portray heaven in all of its grandeur. Indra's Heaven is most often seen in the

Nimi Jātaka; at the beginning of the *Vessantara Jātaka* before Queen Phusati is sent to rebirth on earth; in the Buddha's life story when he returns to earth after preaching to his mother; and as part of the story of Phra Malai (*figs.* 15.2 and 15.3). The most frequently seen representations in current collections of nineteenth and twentieth centuries Thai paintings are those that illustrate or accompany the Phra Malai narrative, either as a standalone text or as the introduction to a rendition of the *Vessantara Jātaka*.

The *Vessantara Jātaka*, referred to in Thai most often as "the Great Life," is a story that tells of the great generosity of the *bodhisattva* in his penultimate birth, as Prince Vessantara, before his incarnation as Siddhārtha Gautama. Beyond its place in the Pāli canon, the *Vessantara Jātaka* has had widespread appeal for both kings and common people in Southeast Asia (Jory 2017: 13). In Thai contexts especially, the *Vessantara Jātaka* is associated with the survival of Buddhism and the hope of seeing Metteyya (Skt: Maitreya), the future Buddha, after he arrives on earth (Bowie 2017: 17). In the past, the *Vessantara Jātaka* was recited across Theravāda Southeast Asia for entertainment, to earn merit and because of its association with the promise of rebirth during Metteyya's arrival. This specific connection is explicitly made in the Phra Malai narrative which is usually read before the recitation of the *Vessantara Jātaka* in Thailand, linking the two stories together and providing another layer of meaning in the envisioning of heavenly realms.

Phra Malai has been a popular story in Thailand for many centuries. It is represented in a variety of painted media and formats. The exact origins of the story are unknown, but it bears relationships to many texts from Sri Lanka, including the *Cūlagalla-vatthu*, a story that, like Phra Malai, involves travel to Tāvatiṁsa Heaven and a lesson about the rewards of making merit (Brereton 1995: 25-42; Collins 1993: 1-17). The Phra Malai story was written in manuscripts and painted in various formats across Southeast Asia, including Laos and to a lesser extent Myanmar and Cambodia, but its most pronounced and longest lasting influence has been in Thailand. The popularity of Phra Malai extends beyond cultural and class-based boundaries; textual versions of the story have been written in both court and local languages (Brereton 1995). The Phra Malai narrative emphasizes the significance of merit-making and its rewards. It gives many Southeast Asian Buddhists reason to be optimistic about future births and provides insight into what good intentions and proper merit-making activities can achieve.

In the story a monk named Phra Malai has great powers as a result of his accumulation of merit through actions and meditation, and he is able to travel to different realms. First, he travels to hell, and learns of the suffering of the beings there. Then he returns to earth and implores the relatives of the hell-beings to make merit on their behalf. They do, and as a result the beings are reborn in heaven. He uses his powers again, this time to travel to Indra's Heaven (Brereton 1995).

While at Cūḷāmaṇi, Phra Malai meets Indra and converses with him. From Indra, Phra Malai learns that the *deva*s in heaven are there as a result of meritorious actions in their previous lives. Their donations may have varied depending on their social status and access to wealth, but each shared purity of heart, a desire for beauty in their donated materials, and an adherence to the five precepts. Phra Malai then meets Metteyya, who is accompanied by an infinite number of *deva*s. Metteyya's beauty is described as magnificent, "like the moon casting a luminous glow through a cloud" (Brereton 1995: 204). After Metteyya pays his respects to the Cūḷāmaṇi *stūpa*, he begins a discussion with Phra Malai. This discussion includes a description of the many different ways to make merit in the human realm and the benefits of being alive on earth when Metteyya is reborn there. Metteyya instructs Phra Malai that people should listen to the complete recitation of the *Vessantara Jātaka* if they wish to be reborn during Metteyya's time on earth. Not only will there be great riches, peace, and happiness, but all will gain enlightenment. Phra Malai is then given the task of spreading this knowledge back home.

The message of Phra Malai is clear, vivid, relatable, and accessible. It confirms what Buddhist laity have been taught through other stories and texts — specifically it reinforces the consequences of actions, both good and bad, and the idealized nature of heaven in the complex cosmology of the Buddhist universe. Making merit through generosity and respect for others is of central importance while living in the human realm, but the ability to continue to gain merit by paying respects at the Cūḷāmaṇi *stūpa* also has great significance, and it is an important way to make merit during one's life in the heavenly realms and thereby prevent a negative rebirth. Throughout Phra Malai's visit to Indra's Heaven, celestial beings and even Metteyya himself make offerings at the *stūpa*. Not only does one avoid the tortures of hell by acting properly, or, escape hell after death because others act correctly and transfer merit on one's behalf, but one can also gain luxuries and have daily opportunities to make merit as a result of living in heaven.

Phra Malai paintings teem with images of heaven, hell, and the human realm (Ginsburg 1989: 73). These representations help viewers visualize the consequences of both good and bad actions, thus making the system of karmic effects far more concrete. Hell scenes are creative and rely on a great deal of compelling imagery to capture the attention and imagination of viewers. They provoke a visceral reaction intended to influence people to avoid such consequences. Humans being boiled in a cauldron over a large fire, nude men and women climbing up thorn trees, and skeletal forms with animal heads are often featured in the hell realms that Phra Malai visits. Standalone depictions of hell as part of the Buddhist cosmology have increased in popularity in the last few decades of the twentieth century and continue to be common in the twenty-first century, with special attention given to theme parks that provide visitors with large three-dimensional depictions of the suffering of hell-beings and the gruesome physical nature of hungry ghosts (Anderson 2012: 9-12; McDaniel 2017: 107-11). Heaven, on the other hand, is a peaceful and cerebral setting, represented visually by borrowing from objects and settings familiar to people living at the times the paintings were made (ranging from the nineteenth to the twenty-first centuries). This creates an easily understandable ideal. Heaven becomes a seemingly tangible reality, one that allows the individual to escape their own mundane world for the possibility of living in a better one. In other words, images of hell are popular for feeding the imagination and as didactic reminders not to do bad things, but images of heaven have longstanding appeal and are in fact replicated through laity's regular meritorious actions at the *wat*.

Examining textual descriptions of Phra Malai's experience in Indra's Heaven as found in manuscripts can help to explain the reasoning behind specific details that are commonly reproduced in painted representations of heaven. In the royal translation of Phra Malai (called the *Phra Malai Kham Luang*), the Cūḷāmaṇi is significant less for the appearance of the *stūpa* and its surroundings and more for its function as a place for reverence and merit-making. While the grand *stūpa* is described as "sapphire-studded," Indra explains to Phra Malai that he built the Cūḷāmaṇi "to provide the *deva*s a means of worship" (Brereton 1995: 193-94). Overwhelmingly the text focuses on the various *deva*s and their retinues as they visit the Cūḷāmaṇi, the actions that brought them merit from their previous lives, and the offerings they bring. This can be seen, for example, in a conversation between Indra and Phra Malai as they wait for Metteyya at the Cūḷāmaṇi:

> As they sat continuing their discussion, a powerful *deva* came to pay obeisance accompanied by his entire retinue totalling a hundred. Phra Malai, in noticing his arrival, immediately asked Indra, "Is that Phra Metteya who has come?"
>
> Indra answered, "No, it is not."
>
> Then Phra Malai said, "Who is that *deva*?"
>
> Indra replied "I don't know his name."

> Phra Malai inquired about the *deva*'s deeds in his previous life, asking, "How did he make merit?"
>
> Indra replied, "This *deva* was an extremely poor man. He wandered about constantly, cutting grass and selling it to make a living. One day he gave his sole portion of rice to a crow so that it would not suffer. When he died, he went to heaven and enjoyed good fortune with a retinue of a hundred, all because of the fruit of the merit that he created." – Brereton 1995: 196

Despite being set in Indra's Heaven, the Phra Malai text focuses on the importance of actions and their consequences. It contains few descriptions of the physical features of heaven that could be used to inspire artists in their visual representations for the setting of the *deva*. Certainly, far less attention is given to describing the heavenly setting than is given to descriptions of hell in the Phra Malai texts (Brereton 2017: 4). But many painted scenes of the story depict heaven with details inspired by the local practices outlined above. Perhaps this emphasis in the visual materials is evidence of the substantial interest in heaven by individuals or localities.

Heaven is a place that is rich with luxuries yet simultaneously rooted in the accumulation of merit. The *Traiphum*, for instance, explains that *deva* residents of heaven live in palaces, have beautiful complexions and figures, and eat celestial food. The air of Indra's Heaven is scented with sandalwood perfume and flowers. In contrast to the *Phra Malai Kham Luang*, the description of the Cūḷāmaṇi in the *Traiphum* is fulsome and stresses its opulence: the *stūpa* is tall beyond our comprehension (80,000 *wa* or 160,000 m) and enclosed by a wall of gold. Cloth flags, victory flags, and long-handled parasols surround the *stūpa*, which shine with gold and seven kinds of gems (Reynolds and Reynolds 1982: 232). This is the popular image of the Cūḷāmaṇi as it was depicted in Phra Malai paintings in the nineteenth century and the image that has continued in paintings into the twenty-first century.

Evidence of the ongoing relevance of painted images of heaven comes from a section of a wall mural in Xishuangbanna

fig. 15.1: *Phra Bot* painting, Thailand, *c*.1880–1900

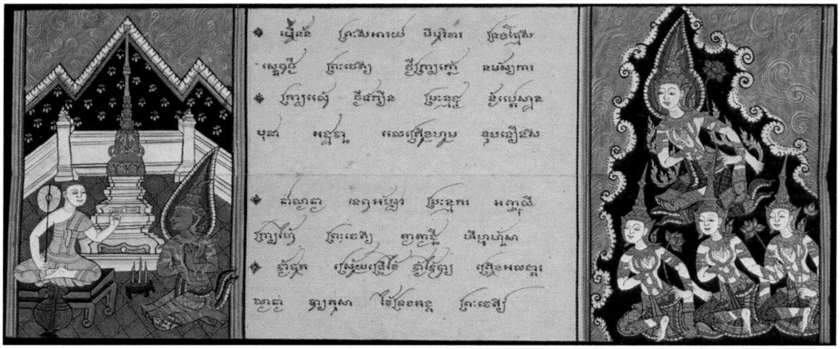

fig. 15.2: Folio from a Thai painted manuscript showing an assembly of *thewada* with Phra Malai and Indra at the Cūḷāmaṇi *stūpa*, Thai manuscript with text in Cambodian Mul script, late nineteenth century

fig. 15.3: Folio from a Thai painted manuscript showing Phra Malai at the Cūḷāmaṇi *stūpa* with royal regalia, 1833

fig. 15.4: Painted altar with image of Cūḷāmaṇi *stūpa* flanked by crocodile banners, Thailand, nineteenth century

fig. 15.5: Painted mural featuring Indra's Heaven and the Cūḷāmaṇi *stūpa*

(called Sipsong Panna or "twelve thousand rice fields" in Thai), a predominantly Tai region of Yunnan in the People's Republic of China that shares strong cultural and historical connections with Northern Thailand and Laos (*fig.* 15.5). Buddhist practices in this region bear great similarities to Thailand, Laos, and the Shan states, and in recent years religious and cultural exchanges have been renewed with vigor (see Casas 2011; Kang Nanshan 2009). The photograph was taken in late 2005 and the mural was probably painted within a year or two of that date. Unpretentious in execution, color, and technique, the scene appears to be a depiction of Phra Malai in Indra's Heaven. Utilizing the Cūḷāmaṇi flanked by banners, this scene is borrowing both from the earlier Thai paintings as well as from popular local imagery in the area, where banner production is still common and many banners often hang near *stūpas*.

Comparing the nineteenth-century images of heaven with the contemporary example, the iconography has clearly maintained its popular appeal; this standardized image of Indra's Heaven is a durable one that has held up over time and across broad distances. Its sustained popularity can be credited to two basic factors: first, the direct relationship between the iconography of heaven and objects used in contemporary Buddhist practice and, second, the continuous, accessible appeal of rebirth in heaven. Because the rewards of heaven are both irresistible and attainable through merit-making and proper actions, it makes sense that art and life surrounding these notions would mimic each other. Laity know the rewards of merit-making, and gentle reminders of the luxuries that await are common. Beautiful riches and a carefree life are indeed attractive outcomes to nearly everyone.

The accessibility of heaven is made believable through stories like that of Phra Malai. The narrative gives people a sense of control over their next life and a chance to look forward to luxuries they might not have in their current existence. The familiarity of images from the manuscripts, other painted art forms, and objects employed in real life allows people to easily visualize heaven, to believe in a better rebirth in heaven, and thus to continue in their meritorious actions. The way these images maintain heaven's glory and luxury while simultaneously resonating with everyday practice at the *wat* cannot be understated. The rewards of merit-making are remote but attainable and paintings help to bridge the distance. These depictions show viewers a distant, alluring realm and present them with something attainable by linking it to their everyday experience. Heaven has become a focus because of its accessibility, made identifiable through painted imagery. This connects to, and verifies, local practices in which Buddhist devotees replicate Indra's Heaven through their merit-making activities, further cementing its familiarity and its many parallels to the earthly realm.

References

Anderson, Benedict, 2012, *The Fate of Rural Hell: Asceticism and Desire in Buddhist Thailand*, London and New York: Seagull Books.

Appleton, Naomi, 2016, *Shared Characters in Jain, Buddhist and Hindu Narrative: Gods, Kings and Other Heroes*, New York: Routledge.

Boisselier, Jean, 1976, *Thai Painting*, Tokyo, New York, and San Francisco: Kodansha International.

Bowie, Katherine A., 2017, *Of Beggars and Buddhas: The Politics of Humor in the Vessantara Jataka in Thailand*, Madison: University of Wisconsin Press.

Brereton, Bonnie P., 1995, *Thai Tellings of Phra Malai: Texts and Rituals Concerning a Popular Buddhist Saint*, Tempe, AZ: Arizona State University Program for Southeast Asian Studies.

——, 2017, "Phra Malai Texts–Telling Them Apart: Preface or Performance," *Journal of Mekong Studies*, 13(3): 1-18.

Casas, Roger, 2011, *Wat Luang Muang Lue: Buddhist Revival and Transformation in Sipsong Panna*, RCSD Working Paper, no. 4, Chiang Mai: Regional Center for Social Science and Sustainable Development, Chiang Mai University.

Chiu, Angela S., 2017, *The Buddha in Lanna: Art, Lineage, Power, and Place in Northern Thailand*, Honolulu: University of Hawai'i Press.

Collins, Steven, 1993, "Braḥ Māleyyadevattheravatthu," *Journal of the Pali Text Society*, 18: 1-17.

——, 2006, *Nirvana and Other Buddhist Felicities: Utopias of the Pali Imaginaire*, Cambridge: Cambridge University Press.

—— (ed.), 2016, *Readings of the Vessantara Jātaka*, New York: Columbia University Press.

Findly, Ellison Banks, 2003, *Dāna: Giving and Getting in Pali Buddhism*, Delhi: Motilal Banarsidass.

Ginsburg, Henry, 1989, *Thai Manuscript Painting*, Honolulu: University of Hawai'i Press.

Green, Alexandra, 2015, "Space and Place in a Burmese Cosmology Manuscript at the British Museum," in *Mulberry Leaves to Silk Scrolls: New Approaches to the Study of Asian Manuscript Traditions*, ed. Justin McDaniel and Lynn Ransom, The Lawrence J. Schoenberg Studies in Manuscript Culture, vol. 1, pp. 42-69, Philadelphia: The University of Pennsylvania Libraries.

Hall, Rebecca, 2008 [unpublished], "Of Merit and Ancestors: Buddhist Banners of Thailand and Laos", Doctoral Dissertation, University of California, Los Angeles.

Jory, Patrick, 2017, *Thailand's Theory of Monarchy: The Vessantara Jātaka and the Idea of the Perfect Man*, Albany, NY: State University of New York Press.

Kang Nanshan, 2009, *Theravada Buddhism in Sipsong Panna: Past and Contemporary Trends*, RCSD Working Paper, no. 12, Chiang Mai: Regional Center for Social Science and Sustainable Development, Chiang Mai University.

Keyes, Charles F., 1975, "Buddhist Pilgrimage Centers and the Twelve-Year Cycle: Northern Thai Moral Orders in Space and Time," *History of Religions*, 15(1): 71-89.

Mahaparinibbana Sutta, see Vajira and Story 2007.

McDaniel, Justin, 2011, *The Lovelorn Ghost and the Magical Monk: Practicing Buddhism in Modern Thailand*, New York: Columbia University Press.

——, 2017, *Architects of Buddhist Leisure: Socially Disengaged Buddhism in Asia's Museums, Monuments, and Amusement Parks*, Honolulu: University of Hawai'i Press.

Nandana Chutiwongs, 2008, "A Relic Shrine in Paradise," in *Roland Silva Felicitation Volume*, ed. Nandana Chutiwongs and Nimal De Silva, pp. 37-47, Columbo: Postgraduate Institute of Archaeology.

Pattaratorn Chirapravati, M.L., 2012, "Corpses and Cloth: Illustrations of the *Paṁsukūla* Ceremony in Thai Manuscripts," in *Buddhist Funeral Cultures of Southeast Asia and China*, ed. Paul Williams and Patrice Ladwig, pp. 79-98, Cambridge: Cambridge University Press.

——, 2013, "Funeral Scenes in the Rāmāyaṇa Mural Painting at the Emerald Buddha Temple," in *Materializing Southeast Asia's Past: Selected Papers from the 12th International Conference of the European Association of Southeast Asian Archaeologists*, ed. Marijke J. Klokke and Veronique Degroot, pp. 221-32, Singapore: National University of Singapore Press.

Reynolds, Craig J., 1976, "Buddhist Cosmography in Thai History, with Special Reference to Nineteenth-Century Culture Change," *The Journal of Asian Studies*, 35(2): 203-20.

Reynolds, Frank E., 1978, "The Holy Emerald Jewel: Some Aspects of Buddhist Symbolism and Political Legitimation in Thailand and Laos," in *Religion and Legitimation of Power in Thailand Laos, and Burma*, ed. Bardwell Smith, pp. 175-93, Chambersburg, PA: ANIMA Books.

Reynolds, Frank E. and Mani B. Reynolds, 1982, *Three Worlds According to King Ruang: A Thai Buddhist Cosmology*, Berkeley: Center for South and Southeast Asian Studies, University of California.

Strong, John S., 2004, *Relics of the Buddha*, Princeton, NJ: Princeton University Press.

Swearer, Donald K., 2010, *The Buddhist World of Southeast Asia*, Albany, NY: SUNY Press.

Vajira, Sister and Francis Story (trs.), 2007, *Last Days of the Buddha: The Mahaparinibbana Sutta*, Kandy: Buddhist Publication Society.

Woodward, Hiram, 2010, "Phra Malai Manuscript," in *Pilgrimage and Buddhist Art*, ed. Adriana Proser, pp. 48-49, New York: Asia Society Museum in association with Yale University Press.

Contributors*

Robert DeCaroli is Professor of South Asian Art History at George Mason University. He is the author of two books: *Haunting the Buddha: Indian Popular Religions and the Formation of Buddhism* (2004) and *Image Problems: The Origin and Development of the Buddha's Image in Early South Asia* (2015). He is also the author of numerous articles, book chapters, and catalog essays. He recently co-curated *Encountering the Buddha: Art and Practice across Asia* at the Sackler Gallery of the Smithsonian Institution (2017-22).

Nicolas Morrissey is Associate Professor of Asian Art History in the Lamar Dodd School of Art at the University of Georgia, where he also currently serves as Director of the Center for Asian Studies. His research focuses on the visual and material culture of Buddhism in early medieval South Asia. In 2018 he curated the exhibition *Images of Awakening* at the Georgia Museum of Art, which featured a diverse collection of little-known Buddhist stucco sculptures from Afghanistan and Pakistan.

Mary Storm completed her Ph.D. in South Asian Art History in 1999. She taught Indian and Southeast Asian Art History at Jawaharlal Nehru University, New Delhi, from 2002 to 2005. From 2005 to 2017 she was Academic Director of Himalayan Arts and Architecture, and National Identity and the Arts, under the aegis of School for International Training (SIT) Study Abroad. She is the author of *Head and Heart: Valour and Self-Sacrifice in the Art of India* (2013). She now lives in Habaraduwa, Sri Lanka.

---

* In chapter order.

Kurt A. Behrendt, Associate Curator of South Asian Art, has been at the Metropolitan Museum of Art since 2006. He has curated eight exhibitions including *Buddhism along the Silk Road* (2012), *Cosmic Buddhas in the Himalayas* (2017), and *Sita and Rama* (2019-20). He has published widely on the Buddhist art of the Indian subcontinent, most recently a survey of the Met's holdings entitled *How to Read Buddhist Art* (2020). His 1997 Ph.D. from UCLA focused on the Buddhist Architecture of Gandhāra.

Debashish Banerji is the Haridas Chaudhuri Professor of Indian Philosophies and Cultures and the Doshi Professor of Asian Art at the California Institute of Integral Studies. He is also the program chair in the East–West Psychology department. Banerji has curated several exhibitions, edited a book on poet Rabindranath Tagore (2015), co-edited one on *Critical Posthumanism and Planetary Futures* (2016), and authored two books: *The Alternate Nation of Abanindranath Tagore* (2010) and *Seven Quartets of Becoming: A Transformational Yoga Psychology Based on the Diaries of Sri Aurobindo* (2012).

Nalini Rao is Associate Professor of World Art at Soka University of America, California. Her publications include *Royal Imagery and Networks of Power at Vijayanagara: A Study of Kingship in South India* (2010), *Sangama: Confluence of Art and Culture during the Vijayanagara Period* (2006), and *Sindhu–Sarasvati Civilization: New Perspectives* (2014). She is the Chair of Dr. S.R. Rao Memorial Foundation for Indian Archaeology, Art, and Culture.

Santhi Kavuri-Bauer is Professor of South Asian and Islamic Art History at San Francisco State University. She is the author of *Monumental Matters: The Power, Subjectivity and Space of India's Mughal Architecture* (2011), as well as articles on the subject of Islamic architecture and South Asian diasporic art. She also curated *Picturing Parallax: Photography and Video from the South Asian Diaspora* (2011) and co-curated *Mashrabiya: The Art of Looking Back* (2017) for the Fine Arts Gallery at San Francisco State University.

Stephen Markel (Ph.D., University of Michigan) is the Senior Research Curator of South and Southeast Asian Art at the Los Angeles County Museum of Art (LACMA). A specialist in South Asian decorative arts of the sixteenth–nineteenth centuries, his numerous publications on this extraordinary material include the forthcoming online volume, *Mughal and Early Modern Metalware from South Asia at LACMA: An Online Scholarly Catalogue*. He was the President of the American Council for Southern Asian Art from 2011 to 2014.

Tushara Bindu Gude is the Associate Curator in the South and Southeast Asian Art Department at the Los Angeles County Museum of Art (LACMA). She has organized several exhibitions and contributed to various publications and exhibition catalogs. She was co-curator of both *India's Fabled City: The Art of Courtly Lucknow* (2010-11) and *The Jeweled Isle: Art from Sri Lanka* (2018-19). Her forthcoming projects include *Realm of the Dharma: Buddhist Art across Asia,* an international traveling exhibition drawn from LACMA's collections.

Saleema Waraich is an Associate Professor in the Department of Art History at Skidmore College. Her research engages with a variety of issues involving the early modern, colonial, and national eras in South Asia, including the relationships between discourse, representation, and cultural memory; the ways in which different forms and strategies of visual representation shape our collective and personal memories; and the politics of architectural preservation, conservation practices, and urban development.

Paul A. Lavy is Associate Professor of South/Southeast Asian Art History at the University of Hawai'i at Mānoa. His research and publications are focused on the history and development of the *circa* fifth–eighth-century Hindu–Buddhist artistic traditions of pre-Angkorian Khmer civilization, Thailand, and the Mekong Delta of Vietnam, as well as their relationships with the art of South Asia. He is currently writing a book on early Southeast Asian sculpture entitled *The Crowned Gods of Early Southeast Asia*.

Bokyung Kim is Adjunct Assistant Professor in the Department of Art and Art History at the University of Mississippi, Oxford. She received her Ph.D. in art history from UCLA with a dissertation on Central Javanese art. Her current research emphasizes the early interactions between Java (Indonesia) and mainland Southeast Asia.

M.L. Pattaratorn Chirapravati is Professor of Asian Art History and Curatorial Studies at California State University, Sacramento. She specializes in the art of mainland Southeast Asia with particular interests in the political uses of religious icons and the interpretation of religious practices from artworks. Her publications include the books *Votive Tablets in Thailand: Origin, Styles and Uses* (1987) and *Divination au royaume de Siam: le corps, la guerre, le destin* (2011), as well as numerous articles on Buddhist art.

Melody Rod-ari is Assistant Professor at Loyola Marymount University where she teaches courses on the history of Asian Art and Museum Studies. She has also curated permanent installations and exhibitions for the Norton Simon Museum and the University of Southern California, Pacific Asia Museum. Her research and publications are focused on the Buddhist art of Thailand, and on the history of collection and display of South and Southeast Asian art in American and European museums.

Rebecca S. Hall is Assistant Curator at the University of Southern California Pacific Asia Museum. Previously she was Postdoctoral Curatorial Fellow in Asian Art at The Walters Art Museum and Visiting Assistant Professor at Virginia Commonwealth University. Recent articles focusing on funeral arts in the Chiang Mai region of northern Thailand were published in the *Journal of Southeast Asian Studies* and *Ars Orientalis*. Her research interests include the visual expressions of belief related to Buddhist cosmology and the relationship between art and Buddhist practice.

Index